The Sea on our Left

With best wishes

from Shally Hunt

Shally Hunt

SUMMERSDALE

Summersdale Publishers
46 West Street
Chichester
West Sussex
PO19 1RP
United Kingdom

A CIP catalogue record for this book is available from the British Library.

Printed and bound in Great Britain.

ISBN 1 873475 96 9

Acknowledgements

Richard and Shally would like to thank all those Rotarians, friends and contacts who gave us hospitality on our walk round Britain in 1995. They all went the extra mile for us; without their enthusiasm and encouragement we could not have got through the low moments.

Many thanks to my energetic father who gave us invaluable back-up in Wales, Scotland and Lincolnshire and raised £3,000 for our charities. Also to Richard's family who helped make the walk possible in so many ways. Our daughters, Katie and Jo, gave us total support from the outset, kept the home fires burning and met us along the way. Jo has done the line drawings for this book. If they were proud of us, we were also proud of them.

We owe the year off to Richard's dental partner Nick Woodgate, who weathered the storm of locums and baby booms. Also my hospital Trust, who allowed me a year's career break.

Our thanks to all our friends, patients and colleagues who have been so generous and supportive.

Three Rotary friends deserve special mention, Frank Leach, John Hill and Daniel Boatwright. Frank, whose faultless organisation ensured we had Rotary hospitality whenever this was required, John, who kept us in touch with the real world and organised a hero's welcome for our return. Daniel not only let us use his hotel as a 24-hour phone base, but also gave us the most luxurious night of the trip in his comfortable Boatwright Calverley Hotel when we returned to Tunbridge Wells.

Our thanks to those who travelled (often hundreds of miles) to walk with us and share a little of the experience.

Finally, my personal thanks to Richard, Chris McCooey, Mervyn Davies, and Rosemary Lance for helping me 'keep the faith' while writing this book.

At the time of writing, our walk has raised £18,000 for Hospice in the Weald and Friends of the Earth.

The Sea on our Left

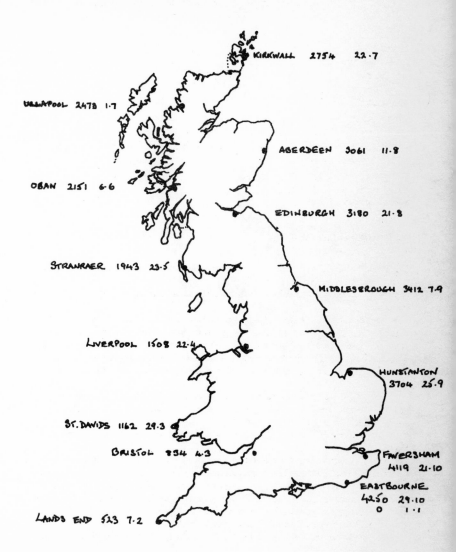

KIRKWALL   2754   22.7

ULLAPOOL 2473 1.7

ABERDEEN   3061   11.8

OBAN   2151   6.6

EDINBURGH 3180 21.8

STRANRAER 1943 23.5

MIDDLESEROUGH 3412 7.9

LIVERPOOL 1508 22.4

HUNSTANTON
3704 25.9

ST. DAVIDS 1162 29.3

BRISTOL 834 4.3

FAVERSHAM
4119 21.10

EASTBOURNE
4250 29.10
0   1.1

LANDS END 523 7.2

Introduction

'I'd like to walk all of it,' Richard said.

'All of what?' I asked, curious.

'The whole coastal path, from Poole to Minehead. We're so familiar with this stretch, I'd like to see the rest.'

I reflected on this suggestion, hypnotised by the deeply scored granite cliffs.

I heard my voice say,

'Why stop there? Why don't we walk *all* the way round.'

'Round what?'

'Round Britain,' the voice said quietly. 'What a challenge that would be!'

It was May 1993. Richard and I were walking a familiar stretch of the coastal path in West Penwith, the real 'toes' of Cornwall. Richard was silent. He is often silent, while I vocalise my thoughts almost before they are thoughts at all. Just as there is 'a time to speak and a time to be silent', so there is 'a time to live and a time to die'. What better way to 'live' than to do something totally different, something challenging that would mean lifting ourselves out of our mainstream ordinary lives, with a chance to get to know our own *kingdom by the sea* better.

Richard had worked in the same dental practice in Tunbridge Wells for thirty years, and I had been a Chartered Physiotherapist in the same hospital for nearly as long. We were both in our early fifties, still fit enough to contemplate such a project. Our two daughters were 26 and 24, both financially independent. Last year we finished paying the mortgage. My hospital might give me a career break, Richard could get a locum, and we could walk off into the sunset. These thoughts flew through my head as we walked along those hypnotic cliffs.

The silence on my left finally broke. Richard must have been doing mileages in his head for he replied slowly. 'It would take nearly a year. I'll have to ask Nick'. Nick was Richard's dental partner who feared Richard might be abandoning ship for good. When he learned it was only a year, permission was granted. A possibility became a probability.

Why walk?

Walking carrying everything with you is tough but rewarding. The foot-slogger can 'reach the parts' that no other transport system can. In the fresh air, closer to Nature, dormant senses are gradually reawakened and s/he becomes less of a clumsy intruder. Walking is environmentally friendly and economical, for as yet the chancellor hasn't thought of toll paths. Parking a pair of feet is certainly no problem! The walker who carries a large rucksack is something of a curiosity. Total strangers come up to chat and enthuse. Doors open. Things happen. People are able to confide in the foot traveller because he is accessible and transient, while the walker, can be an objective observer who gets a good flavour of the places seen and people visited. Regional changes are gradual, therefore more easily absorbed. Long-distance walking gives the traveller a chance to compare and contrast with time to ruminate. All these things are luxuries in our high-speed, high-tech. world.

Maps were a must. Richard worked out that we would need nearly one hundred Ordnance Survey Land Ranger Series. A few of our non-walking friends found this puzzling.

'Don't you just keep the sea on your left?' They asked innocently.

Richard loves maps and books and was a happy man when they arrived. Every spare moment for the next few months found him busy with calculators and a strange instrument that looked like a fob watch, which he wheeled round the maps with a grin on his face.

While all this was happening, I was shut in the dining room completing an Open University course, with little time to think of anything except work, assignments and exams. On our return, Richard had no desire to relive the walk, his route-planning had primed him before we left. On the other hand, I needed a retrospective. Writing about the odyssey has been my necessary debrief.

Early in 1994 our estimated date of departure was January 1st 1995. Starting at Eastbourne, Richard planned to walk clockwise round the coast, as near the sea as possible, averaging 15 miles per day. He estimated the walk should take ten months, or 302 days. Before we left, Richard had already walked the estimated distance of 4,300 miles across his maps. On the walk itself, he would often have a sense of déjà vu, having mentally crossed bridges, boarded ferries and rounded peninsulas. He carried about six maps at a time and exchanged them at pre-arranged staging posts.

Meanwhile I dived into the library to find any books I could about the coast of Britain. The only walker I could find who had written about it was John Merrill, who had circumnavigated every millimetre in 1978 and achieved a well-deserved entry into the Guinness Book of Records for his pains (which included a stress fracture in one foot).

Richard and I had only managed four days on Offa's Dyke and three days on the Weald Way. Richard could also boast a ten day tour of Mont Blanc. Hardly an impressive record but we refused to be put off.

In the summer of 1994 we heard of 24 year-old Spud and her dog Tess. Katherine Talbot Ponsonby, alias Spud, had just finished a similar round Britain walk for the charity Shelter. Although young and strong, she was not a professional walker. Later that year we read that Robert Steel, a septuagenarian, would be doing the same circuit as part of the National Trust Centenary celebrations. As far as we knew, no middle aged couples had attempted it.

In November 1993, my mother died. Thanks to the committed care of community nurses she was able to stay at home. My father and I were with her at the end, and, although I have spent twenty seven years in a hospital environment, nothing could have prepared me for this difficult time. Without the dedicated professional care of three nurses we could not have coped.

Back in Tunbridge Wells, money was being raised to build a much-needed residential hospice. Suddenly our Round Britain Walk seemed to have more purpose, we would walk for the charities, Hospice-in-the-Weald and Friends of the Earth. Richard and I both feel that, in a commercial world, our fragile environment is suffering. Walking round our coasts would give us a unique opportunity to see how nature was coping with the human onslaught.

The next thing was the kit, another unknown area. We were tipped off to use a catalogue from a mail order firm who specialise in outdoor pursuits gear. This became our guru, and we studied the mysteries of the three-layer system. Their creed sounded promising, 'designed to keep the body at a constant, comfortable and safe temperature throughout the day.' More worrying was 'no single garment can protect against wind, moisture and extremes of temperature . . . so layered clothing is recommended.' We then spent large sums of money layering ourselves up to the eyeballs. Like Jack Spratt and his wife, I feel the cold and Richard feels the heat, so, as our base layer garments promised to both 'wick away moisture from sweating and provide the initial thermal layer'. They were worth every penny.

Richard bought a 50 litre capacity rucksack with a 20 litre extension, (both a blessing and a curse), and mine was 50 litres. Our first mistake was to fill them to the brim. After all we should be away for ten months, and there was no knowing what we might need. As five months of the walk was to be spent camping, we purchased a lightweight two-man tent, too small to do anything but lie down or pray in. However, our equipment bible assured us it was strong and weatherproof. We should just have to hope that marital relations would be as stable as the tent.

Having worked out the parameters of the walk, Richard's calculator was busy reckoning the cost of bed and breakfasts during the winter months. We were collecting friends and contacts round the coast, but this left a shortfall of sixty nights when we would have to pay for bed, breakfast and an evening meal. Just as we were wondering what we could pawn, the Rotary Club network was activated and stepped into the breach. Richard has been a Rotarian for the past twelve years. By the time we left, we only needed a handful of bed and breakfasts before we started camping after Blackpool at the end of April. Without this help and support we could never have done the walk. Apart from the hospitality, we made many new friends. This was an enriching experience and a facet of the walk we had not considered. In the end, we were looked after by sixty-one Rotarians, and ninety-five friends and contacts. We used eight Youth Hostels and only twenty-eight bed and breakfasts. The remaining one hundred nights we used our own little tent, which gave us great satisfaction.

During the walk, we left our 'real' world behind. Although not strictly 'vagrants of no fixed abode', we were often anti-social by the norms of our usual lifestyle, definitely not squeaky clean. When we rested along the way, we either sat on the ground, or in shelters which varied from a church porch to a golfer's hut. This experience of squatting, often reliant on the kindness of others to give us food and shelter, was a salutary one. We were never 'moved on', but I think this was only because we never sat anywhere long enough.

Travelling light is the very best. In spite of our few possessions, we didn't want for anything, which just goes to show what you can do without. Richard's most treasured possessions were his maps and itinerary. His luxuries: an occasional newspaper, sketch pad and a few cigars. For me it was my camera, tape recorder and exercise books in which I wrote my diary. I used my tape recorder constantly, recording our impressions, data, noises and even dialects.

This little black box became my confessional, and in the early days often caused friction between us. While camping, we each had one paperback, which we only just managed to read in three months. When we eventually returned home, I couldn't cope with all our boxes of possessions which had been stored in the basement; only gradually has the house been restored to its familiar clutter.

Why the coast?

This was a question asked us by Frank Bough in a radio interview before we left. *The sea washes all Man's ills away* was said by the ancient Greek philosopher Euripedes. It is ironic that this 'cleansing' water includes vast quantities of effluent, detritus and toxic waste. Economic fortunes rise and fall as Man exploits his natural resources. Yet the sea is still man's last wilderness and Britain's coastline is varied and beautiful. Richard and I crave space in our over-crowded little island. The sea's space is hypnotic and powerful; a paradox and an enigma; friendly and hostile. The rhythmical sound of the sea became a pulse which we missed when inland. Up on the cliffs we felt an empathy with these ancient rocks, a feeling of continuity, a humbling ability to appreciate that we are just a tiny part of an immense ecosystem. It was a secular pilgrimage. Travelling on foot, we saw the results of Man's disproportionate impact on this fragile environment; we also saw how rapidly Nature heals scars and redresses balances. Spiritual amphibians threading our way along the margins, on cliffs, beaches, sea walls and promenades, we felt an integral part of our 'Kingdom by the sea.'

Last, but not least, there were the people. Round the edges, traditions stick. G.K Chesterton said, *The whole object of travel is not to set foot on foreign land. It is at last to set foot on one's own country as a foreign land.* Walking is a good pace both to see and to meet the locals. We met 'foreigners' from Cornwall, Wales, Scotland, Northumberland and Norfolk. To a degree, every area has its own customs and specialities. Everyone, without exception, gave us something of themselves, whether that something was overnight hospitality, charity money, a freebie, or even just a smile. We were vagrants of no fixed abode; a middle-class middle-aged couple travelling hopefully.

So it was, with a lot of help from family and friends, we were able to cut ourselves loose from the self-imposed net of our everyday lives and enjoy a taste of structured freedom. Our own land, if not the world, was at our feet.

Chapter One

Queer are the ways of a man I know:
He comes and stands
In a careworn craze,
And looks at the sands
And the seaward haze
With moveless hands
And face and gaze,
Then turns to go . . .
And what does he see when he gazes so?
Thomas Hardy

Bright winter sunshine melts the frost on close-cropped grass, alight with blazing gorse. Blue waves rock the whitewashed cliffs of Durlstone Head. A dry stone wall, propped by muddy sheep, is under repair. An unheeding fox lopes quietly across the path, lost in a pall of smoke from the burning furze. Distant tapping from the Purbeck Quarries is drowned by the louder clunk of graded stones, carefully placed on the growing wall. The soulful mew of a lone gull cuts across the crackling fire. Two middle-aged back packers, far from the madding crowd, survey the ageless scene in their own peripheral time-warp. On the edge; together, yet apart.

* * *

Our grandfather clock chimed twelve strident notes to the bare room. It was midnight; 1995 had just begun. Most of our belongings were stored in the basement. The house waited expectantly for its new occupants. Richard and I snatched a few hours rest rising at 6 a.m. Staggering under our bulging rucksacks, we stepped out into the cold pre-dawn of New Year's Day, quietly closing the door on our home for a year.

We left Eastbourne pier in a daze, cheered, hugged, kissed and snapped by family and friends. Climbing the steep hill onto Beachy Head like sleep-walkers, we were too numb to notice the weight of our over-filled rucksacks. At the top we gazed down the sheer wall of chalk to the toy lighthouse far below; a stick of candy in a hypnotic sparkling sea. A young man in shorts and T-shirt ran passed us.

'Don't do it. Don't do it! Life's too good!' He panted cheerfully as he ran by.

Our eyes met. Life was good. Our marathon walk round the coasts of Britain had really begun.

'Come on'. Richard took my hand and pulled me gently away from the cliff.

'We've only got 4,300 miles to go!'

'You mean 4,298. Just a ten month stroll,' I replied, grinning.

That was the best of the day. The sun melted the hard frost and we slipped and slithered across the chalk waves of the Seven Sister's cliffs. Friends met us at Cuckmere and watched my ataxic progress with concern.

'Shally. What you need is a stick,' Margaret said, with firm cheerfulness.

Before I had time to say anything, she disappeared into the Country Park shop and emerged triumphantly waving a light walking stick. A mile further, and I felt blisters ripening on both heels. My morale nose-dived. By mid-afternoon we had lost the sun and I had run through an assortment of plasters. At Newhaven, squally black clouds threw sleet at us making the muddy cliffs treacherously slippery. It was nearly dark as we picked our way gingerly towards the raw neon lights of a wet Peacehaven. We were two hours late and our host for the night had long since given up his vigil at the Meridian. There was nothing for it but to walk the extra miles to his house.

It was an inauspicious start. Richard had miscalculated the mileage, which had grown from 16 (our daily average) to 23 miles. He was pouring over his Ordnance Survey maps frowning.

'I had originally planned to start from Beachy Head not Eastbourne pier,' he prevaricated.

'I'll forgive you but I'm not sure if my heels will. Mary's homeopathic book said blisters need 'circulating air and rest!' I replied, washing all my ills away in a life-saving bath.

While our bodies rested, our minds raced. The walk had taken eighteen months of preparation, and Richard had been working in his dental practice right up to the last minute. Cutting ourselves loose from what the Evening Standard described as our 'gentle middle-class life style' hadn't been easy. Six weeks before we left, our carefully planned marathon walk looked as though it would abort. Richard had no locum for his practice, we had no tenant for our house, and even our ageing tabby cat was in danger of joining the homeless. At the eleventh hour, everything fell neatly into place; we were committed to spending the next ten months walking clockwise round the coast of Britain.

Everyone wanted to know our reasons for leaving home to walk for 302 days in all weathers, carrying all our needs in heavy backpacks, avoiding roads wherever possible, and camping for five of the ten months. A sabbatical year they could appreciate, but:

'Why not go somewhere warm and comfortable?'

'What will you do about your underwear?'

'How could you go with your husband? If I went with mine we'd kill each other!'

These were typical questions. Others who understood and envied us included an elderly lady who had seen the article about us in the local paper and rang me up - 'I've always wanted to do that she said. You are escaping for us all!'

Our two daughters had been supportive.

'Go for it!' They encouraged. 'We'll look after Granny. Wish we could come too.'

Jo and her boyfriend, Tim, had driven us down to Eastbourne that New Year's morning while most youngsters were nursing their hangovers. My 82 year old father was planning to meet up with us in Wales and Scotland and give us back-up support from the luxury of his mobile home. Rotary clubs around the coast had been asked to give us hospitality. We couldn't fall at the first fence. I tossed and turned in the comfortable bed . . . until suddenly I was back on Beachy Head, absailing off the cliff with a marathon runner . . .

I often had cause to remember our host's words that second morning.

'Just remember Shally, walk through the pain.'

With the Seven Sisters behind us, the south coast flattened into an uninspiring plod of endless promenades, manicured beaches, chippies and car parks, poopscoops and lamp posts.

Brighton was different. Dwarfed by the high cliffs, we found ourselves staring at the Marina, opened in 1978.

'No soul' said Richard. 'Cut-and-paste arrogance for city sailors. I bet lots of these boats never move further than the buoys.'

A frustrated sailor himself, Richard could sneer.

The brick high-rise apartments soared above the cut-out yacht basin. A dinky Legoland oasis for weekend yachties; broad acres of car parking and supermarkets.

My heels were happy with the Marina as long as they could continue to be non weight-bearing on the low wall beside the supermarket.

Brighton's front, with its still functioning pier, gleamed in the winter sunshine. We enjoyed a hot chocolate on the promenade watching the world go by. Everyone was out and about in holiday mood, walking off the excesses of Christmas, clutching dogs, bikes, skateboards, grannies and small children. Lunch was cuppa soup and a sandwich on the concrete steps above Shoreham harbour, watching a boat loading up with a cargo of aggregate. It was the first of many lunches squatting, by road or path.

On day three, at Littlehampton, I reached my nadir. Each step was a nightmare. My pack seemed to be full of aggregate, my blisters oozed and screamed. We'd only just started, so how on earth was I going to get to Land's End, never mind John O'Groats?

'Let's stop here and take a break.' Richard had one eye on a café which had a special offer on doughnuts and hot chocolate, and one on my limping frame.[1]

'I should take your boots off and wear your trainers for a while,' he suggested.

I adjourned to the privacy of the loo and gingerly removed my socks. My heels were like the insides of two jam tarts and I had my first twinge of real despair. I sat miserably on the shabby seat and tried some lateral thinking: perhaps I could bike and meet Richard every evening, although with my non-existent sense of direction I could foresee problems. Perhaps I should never have had the arrogance to think that I could walk 4,300 miles. Perhaps it had all been a dreadful mistake. I dressed my heels, thankfully hiding them away in my socks, raked a comb through my hair and looked at a worried face in the cracked mirror. We pulled a face at each other and a voice in my head told me blisters weren't going to stop me walking.

I voiced my doubts to Richard between mouthfuls of doughnut. After a short pause he said.

'It's either both or neither of us. I'm not going on without you.'

'Good on ya,' I thought, gulping down the hot chocolate, more determined than ever not to let the side down.

On reflection, I think this was a turning point. Although the dread of not finishing never left me, Richard's words were what I needed to hear.

I changed my boots for trainers and we detoured to Boots for more dressings. For all this bravado, I'd had enough by the time we reached Bognor, and empathised with George Vth, who, while convalescing here in 1928, was heard to mutter the immortal words 'Bugger Bognor'.

We owe much to our hosts that night. Jo and Hugh were walk-saving if not life-saving. While I drank a welcome cuppa, my feet were treated to a mustard bath, a novel and rather Dickensian experience. We then threw out 35 lbs of excess luggage from our packs. We had learnt the hard way, that when you carry everything on your back, there is only room for the essentials.

After miles of brick, tarmac and promenades, it was good to reach Pagham Harbour and enjoy the bird-life of this tidal marshland. At the the southern end of the harbour we passed the hamlet of Church Norton, where the tiny chapel of St. Wifred looks out over the lonely saltings. Wilfred, we learned, was a 7th century missionary who preached Christianity to the South Saxons, a heathen lot who lived on Selsey (Seal Island). The origin of the name Sussex, is derived from these South Saxon peoples.

In our first taste of strong winds and pouring rain we discovered the joys of squeezing the water out of wet gloves every half hour, and realised that there is no such thing as watertight clothing. Bosham's only shelter for wet walkers was the church, and we didn't quite have the nerve to eat our sarnies within such hallowed walls. The porch, traditionally for paupers, had no seats. We plodded on along the road trying to ignore the rumbles from our empty stomachs until we eventually found a draughty bus shelter. We sat thankfully on the damp wooden seats. A steady jet of rain blew in through a hole in the glass, and water oozed through gaps in the woodwork. A drip splashed onto the tinfoil of our sandwiches.

'Just look at these!' I exclaimed. 'They're smoked salmon and they must be an inch thick.'

They had been made by friends of ours who ran a pub, and were delicious.

As we munched we read the 'wall paper':
Philip is cool. Kelly is a wanker. Willie for Sharon. Kids rule OK.

Our host that night was a retired surgeon and keen sailor. The garden of his elegant house was lapped by the River Ems. A pair of ducks waddled happily on the sodden lawns. We felt like a pair of sails as we dripped pools of water onto the kitchen floor.

'Don't worry!' Sheila said cheerfully, as she hung us out to dry round the Aga. 'We're used to this.' Divested of our dirty wet carapace, we felt able to proceed to our ablutions where a bewildering array of soaps and shampoos waited for us, along with bathrobes, kleenex tissues and hairdryers. We wafted downstairs leaving a wake of perfumed bubbles, ate a huge meal and placed our weary bodies under a down duvet. I dreamt of ducks eating smoked salmon while copulating in a bus shelter.

Breakfast was memorable. The long mahogany table, ringed with Hepplewhite chairs, was laid with gleaming silver and gold-rimmed china. Sparkling cut glass awaited our fruit juice, boiled eggs sat upright in silver egg cups and a crisp linen napkin lay serenely by each place. Much refreshed after this regal repast, we eased our stiff bodies into our stiff dry walker's gear and set off at a crackling pace for Portsmouth.

My feet swung happily on the ferry to Ryde on the Isle of Wight. A planned island-hop avoiding the tarmac of Portsmouth and Southampton. Like so many others before us, we felt this island was a place to escape the hectic pace of the south east. Tennyson settled at Farringford House, Freshwater, which rapidly became an artistic melting pot. Hestor Thackeray Fuller wrote, *'Is there no-one who is commonplace here? Is everybody either a poet, or a genius or a painter or peculiar in some way?'*

We knew which category we belonged to.

Sitting on rotten hay bales watching container ships passing along the Solent, Richard reminisced.

'On holiday here as a child, I remember seeing the Queen Elizabeth and the Queen Mary, dressed overall with sirens blaring making their way down the Solent from Southampton.'

'Doesn't that make you feel old?' I teased.

I took the ensuing silence to be affirmative. A few miles further on Richard asked if he could take a photo of me.

'Smile.' Click. 'Now look behind you.'

The house I had posed in front of was called *Far Enough*.

Our one night on the island was spent at Northwood near Cowes, very topical at that moment as three prisoners had just escaped from Parkhurst prison and were still at large after three days. The prison was just down the road from our overnight stay, and was bristling with T.V. cameras and reporters.

The following day our route took us past the little village of Newtown, a sort of 13th century Milton Keynes, purpose-built by the Bishop of Winchester. As an incentive to move there, the serfs were relieved of their feudal duties. Now the place was so quiet and peaceful that a brilliant gold crest (Britain's smallest bird) perched only feet away from us, quite unafraid.

Leaving this sleepy island from the Georgian town of Yarmouth, my scruffy husband was accosted by a hopeful policeman,

'Avin' a nice walk?', he asked eyeing Richard carefully up and down, and then glancing at me,

'Together are you sir?'

The prisoners were still at large, and it is curious how guilty the innocent can feel when interrogated, however politely. We hopped on the ferry and made our escape to Lymington, avoiding a dreary urban plod through Southampton.

West of Christchurch, the scenery became more open. Sand replaced shingle on the beach; hibernating beach huts stood in neat rows; large cedar trees along the pathway gave a whiff of the English Riviera along miles of manicured promenades.

Physically, our bodies were already falling into a routine. We set off about 9 a.m. with springy steps and light hearts. My body would demand a break for elevenses, and was very ready to stop for lunch. By mid-afternoon fatigue set in and my feet, legs and back would threaten a 'sit-in' rather than a 'walk-out'. I tried to ignore them, but the winging persisted. At this stage of the day there were three wonderful things to look forward to on arrival, removing our boots, soaking in a hot bath, and tea, usually in that order. The expectation of these simple pleasures would prevent my body going on strike. Richard tired less easily, but anxious to arrive, he would speed up as I slowed down in the afternoons; the gap between us widened.

Walking along the pleasant esplanade at Bournemouth we noted the neatly raked sand and plethora of signs relating to dogs. Our late 20th century dog culture was much in evidence; to own a dog seems a pre-requisite to living on the south coast. At times there seemed to be more dogs than people and more poop scoops than lamp posts. Our walk around Britain's coasts bought home to us the need for people to own a pet, usually dogs, a need that was greatest on the south coast where the retired population is particularly high. Time and again we patted and admired overfed, under-exercised, over-indulged dogs, picked our way around the vast quantities of crap, ubiquitous on paths and pavements, or hastened our steps as would-be walker-eating species would bark, growl and slaver as we passed their territory. The burgeoning numbers of authoritarian notices regarding dog prohibitions seem themselves a pollutant.

It was a relief to arrive at the chain ferry at Sandbanks. Waiting on a small bench, drinking bovril, we gazed longingly across the short stretch of water at the mouth of Poole Harbour, to the heathlands of Studland and the gently rising silhouettes of the Purbeck hills. As we chugged and slewed towards the Isle of Purbeck with the wind in our hair and the waves slurping the decks, we felt a mounting excitement. Nine days into the walk, and every chug of the ferry took us further away from the tarmac and cement, parked cars and litter bins, towards the start of the 550-mile South West Coastal Path from Poole to Minehead. We were crossing our Rubicon.

In their infinite wisdom, the guide books have decided that everyone should walk anti-clockwise round Britain, so we had to read the books from back to front Chinese-style. I say we, but I should make it clear that Richard did all the map reading. I kept well out of it, for one thing I have no sense of direction, and am always told that if I so much as hold a map, it is upside down. I felt to interfere would court disaster. It says a lot for Richard's back-to-front map reading that we rarely got lost, - *I think he called it mislaying the path!*

'Well met! You're on time.' My father looked proud and pleased when he met us in Swanage. We bundled ourselves wearily into his car, and drove inland to Corfe Castle while logistics for our first rest day were briskly outlined.

'We've got The Echo coming to interview you tomorrow morning, a friend has lent us her video for you to see a retrospective of your Meridian interview, we're going to drinks tomorrow evening and I've arranged a send-off for you in the Square at 8 a.m. when you leave.'

I felt as breathless as my father sounded. Between these engagements, we spent a long time trying to decide what was really essential to carry with us.

'How many pairs of socks and trousers are you taking?' I asked Richard anxiously, bemused by the ten-month supply of everything-we-might-need littering the bedroom.

'Ummm. I'm thinking. As few as possible.'

In the end we decided to take three of most garments, one and two spares. My medicine chest shrank from a chemist's shop to just plasters and paracetamol. Our ever-growing pile of 'superfluous to requirements' grew rapidly. Out went the Evening Primrose, vitamins, hand-warmers, foot cream, second pairs of evening trousers, soap, paper backs, trainers and talcum powder. Shampoo was carefully decanted into a film canister. When we finally repacked, the rucksacks had room to breath.

Swanage was looking its best in the bright sunshine of an early winter's morning. A few working boats were pulled up on the cobbles by the lifeboat station. The chalk stacks of Old Harry and his pinnacled Wives grinned at us across the bay. After a day's rest and a change of boots, my blisters were history.

We set off into Durlston Country Park in high spirits. Sea, cliffs and a welcome absence of poopscoops, beach huts and bungalows made us feel wonderfully liberated.

Chapter Two

*The great inviolate place had an
ancient permanence which the sea
cannot claim. Who can say of a
particular sea that it is old?
Distilled by the sun, kneaded by the moon,
it is renewed in a year, in a day, or in an hour.*
Thomas Hardy

This next stretch of Dorset coast has been described by the travel writer Eric Newby as one of the most beautiful in Europe. The cliffs at Durlston Country Park are renowned for sea-bird colonies, one feature of the varied wildlife of this area. It was too early in the season for breeding birds, but that morning we saw a fox, a field mouse, wrens, stonechats and partridges. We also felt we had moved back a century when we saw several men busy building a dry-stone wall, and others burning the furze bushes. If you turned a blind eye to the National Trust landrover, it was an idyllic scene straight out of one of Hardy's novels. When we asked the wall-builders how much more they had to do, their reply was,

'All of it, it's not a job it's a life sentence.' This set me wondering where the nearest prison was.

There were no sandy beaches here, only chiselled cliffs exposing stony ledges and shallow caves at low tide. Places had evocative names like Dancing Ledge, Winspit and Seacombe. Our path took us through disused quarries where once the precious Purbeck Marble was shipped to Swanage and further afield. Now the stone is taken by road through Corfe Castle, by juggernauts who rattle the ancient bones of this somnolent village.

Our little path now began to rise and fall, and we climbed steeply up to the viewpoint of St. Alban's Head with its tiny Norman chapel, perched 350 feet above sea level. St. Aldhelm, born in the 7th century, was a Saxon Bishop. Apart from being a place of worship, the chunky little building served as a seamark, and was one of the earliest lighthouses, originally tended by monks. It wasn't hard to imagine a robed and tonsured figure, seated at the little window, with his solitary candle, praying, writing or reading. This spluttering seventh century flame was the precurser of the powerful beams of contemporary lights, equivalent to millions of candlepower. We found many similar Celtic chapels all round the coast providing an unwitting guide; if not to 'lighten the Gentiles', possibly to save their souls.

Perched up on the cliffs we had uninterrupted views of the coast in both directions. With such wide horizons we could look back with satisfaction at what we had achieved, and forward with anticipation. At times, looking either way could be depressing.

Looking back, we could see the hazy outline of the Isle of Wight and the solid limestone cliffs of Purbeck, and forward to Weymouth Bay and the long arm of Portland Bill. The sombre black cliffs of Kimmeridge have left a rich legacy of fossils and oil. The bituminous shale here, known as 'Kimmeridge coal', was once used as a fuel for industry. In the last century an unsuccessful attempt was made to light the gas lamps of Paris with Kimmeridge shale. The Parisians turned up their noses at the sulphurous smell, while the more robust 'Dorzet' locals used it to heat their houses right up to the end of the nineteenth century. A gently nodding 'donkey' showed that contemporary bounty hunters were still busy extracting oil from the area.

The sun was sinking as we approached Clavell's folly. This brick edifice was more temple than tower, with a circle of Corinthian columbs decorating the lower story. Built in 1820 by the Reverend John Clavell of Smedmore, it stands on the headland above Kimmeridge, a perfect spot for the aristocratic Rev. to star-gaze through his telescope. It made an attractive, if rather eerie, land and sea mark. As we were to discover, men of the church in days of yore had both the wear-with-all and the time to indulge their eccentricities.

As we reached the jetty a few surf boarders were braving the cold water. The old village of Kimmeridge threads neatly up the valley, not a reed out of place on the thatched roofs, or a ruffled feather in the hens scratching round the pond. As we climbed up out of village in the gloaming, we could see warships silhouetted in the fading light on Portland Bill.

I wrote in my diary that night:- *No pain from blisters or feet today. Wonderful! I feel really alive after a week of unreality.*

We set off from East Lulworth in bright cold weather, past the camp of the Royal Army Tank Corps. The army have a high profile on this outstandingly beautiful stretch of coast and the deserted village of Tyneham lies within their firing zone. This feudal little back-water, with its own manor house owned by the Bond family, was sequestrated by the army in 1943, and the inhabitants have never been able to return to their homes. When the army are not firing, the public can walk through this empty village, and wonder down the mile-long track to the wide sweep of Worbarrow Bay. The romantic ruins have had their faces scrubbed and have been given a short back and sides. The trees and undergrowth have been cleared, new gravel paths gleam yellow, the little church is now a museum, and there are some very excellent latrines.

Exploding shells thudded on the ranges and red flags were flying strongly in the stiff breeze. There was no way we could use the coast path along the steep chalk 'waves' from Kimmeridge to Lulworth. As we gave the ranges a wide berth, I remembered an unofficial visit to Tynham when I was a teenager, and took great delight in telling my law-abiding husband of our exploits.

'A group of us drove over to Tynham one summer night. We ducked under the barbed wire fence, ignoring warning signs of unexploded shells, and struggled through the nettles and brambles to find the old manor house. The stone ruins were tucked into trees, deep in the little valley. A full moon cast ghostly shadows across the worn flagstones. An owl hooted. My companions had disappeared, and I was on my own with Tynham's ghosts. I shivered and retreated. When a disturbed blackbird squawked in the undergrowth, I took to my heels and didn't stop until my stinging scratched legs were safely back on the road.'

'You haven't changed,' was the reply.

Once through the neat thatched village of West Lulworth, we took the cliff-top path through the massed steel of static caravans, above the graceful arch of Portland limestone known as Durdle Dor. Those fluent in Saxon will know that 'durdle' means through. From the undulating cliff tops, a blue sea creamed the cinnamon shingle far below. On the grassy tops, we were surprised to find a line of stone alcoves each housing a sculpture of giant shells and fossils. They looked so right in their indiginous landscape, echoing the space of sky and sea and smooth, convoluted cliffs.

Weymouth Bay was alive with boats. We sat on a beach below Osmington Mills, with a couple of pied wagtails, munching sandwiches in warm sunshine. The Royal Navy had thoughtfully provided entertainment for us; a fleet auxillary and a frigate, in combined operations between their aircraft and a lifeboat. Good sound effects came from a Harrier jet which buzzed us like an angry mosquito all afternoon. We could see the Georgian houses on the front clearly through the binoculars. The town's red brick suburbs sprawled over the green sward, behind an uninviting grey marsh. In the dimming light, Portland Bill looked like a huge castle patrolled by warships.

Weymouth is like a beautiful woman wrapped in a tatty coat. Once on the front the buildings are a mixture of Victorian and Georgian architecture. Richard pointed out the figure of a horseman carved in chalk, riding high on the hill behind Weymouth.

'Who do you think it is?' He asked.

I'd had the Duke of York on the brain from humming the little ditty up the hills, but it was, of course, George III. The King visited the town in 1789, establishing it as a fashionable resort, and was the first monarch to use the bathing machine. We passed some very smart Victorian terraced beach houses along the front, with what looked like garages beneath their glazed upper stories. We fancied bathing machines might have been housed in them. After all, if sea bathing was therapeutic for the monarch, it must be good for everyone.

In the eighteen century, a certain Dr. Granville wrote:

'*The sea-bathing is perfect at Weymouth . . . the timid lady may indulge in the great luxury of open sea-bathing, with the additional comfort of perfect security, and of sea-water pure, clean and transparent; in fact, genuine, unpolluted sea-water.*' Not a statement we felt, that anyone would dare make today!

We had been loaned a flat in a substantial Victorian terrace overlooking the bay. Relaxing in comfortable chairs, we watched the calm waters blush beneath the setting sun. St. Alban's Head head glowed faintly in the distance, while warships, fishing boats and a cross channel ferry moved quietly over a wide sweep of pink glass.

Richard was gazing at an RNLI tea towel of Great Britain, pinned to the wall.

'Just think, we've walked six inches of this already.'

It was one of those moments when looking back was satisfying, but looking forward was depressing.

Our bodies had begun to accept the fact that they would be subjected to eight hours hard labour every day. Initial muscle stiffness was easing, although our feet complained bitterly when we first put weight on them in the morning.

'You should see yourself,' I laughed, as Richard crept off towards the bathroom doubled up and looking as though he was walking on nails. Then it was my turn to look geriatric.

'It's just as well none of our sponsors can see us now.'

In fact, it took months for the soles of our feet to toughen up enough not to give us the early morning hobbles.

After bathing in our 20th century machine, we set off to explore the architectural delights of Weymouth. The town exuded genteel elegance. Regency terraces, the elaborate blue and red clock tower, (in honour of Queen Victoria's Jubilee) and seats along the promenade with iron fretwork covers so delicate they might have been parasols. The old harbour and quay were ablaze with welcoming lights from the many pubs and restaurants. A small fishing fleet adorned centre stage.

This was the first meal we'd had to buy since leaving home. Watching the pennies, we chose a modest fish and chip bar. A bronzed youth was in charge, rippling muscles on show under a tiny singlet. I glanced anxiously at the tank, where some manky looking goldfish gazed mournfully at us. Our battered cod tasted alright, but a few hours later my stomach decided they must have been goldfish and forcefully rejected them.

We took a long time to extract ourselves from the murky suburbs of Weymouth and then ran into mud. Not just any mud, but real 'Dorzet' clay that turned our footwear into ten league boots and made the miles seem very long. My stomach was still unhappy, and mentally I would set my sights on the next stile where I could sit for a few seconds, the next official break where we could rest for a few minutes, and above all our destination, and eight blissful hours in the horizontal position.

Behind Chesil Beach lies a eerie lagoon of water called The Fleet. Virtually tideless at the east end, it creats a unique natural habitat, where we saw many water birds including merganzer and pintail ducks. Merganzers have an untidy swept-back crest, which gives them a cheeky unkempt look, in marked contrast to the neat pencil-lines of their dapper companions. The beach is a walker's nightmare. Billions of pebbles, (obviously graded by E.U. regs), get larger from east to west, making mountains of up to forty feet in places. The limp grey lagoon was deserted and strangely silent. A few working boats were pulled up on the mud, as lifeless as the lagoon. As we climbed the hill, we looked down on the ten mile shingle strip, the graveyard of many ships over the years. The lonely cry of flying swans enhanced the haunting atmosphere.

Richard, as always, strode ahead, fearful that we might be late for our rendez-vous. From now on, the afternoons would follow the same pattern. I would fall behind, while Richard's tireless legs blazed the trail. As he was sole navigator and keeper of contact addresses, it was in my best interests to keep him in sight, even if that was on the horizon. As the walk went on, Richard's retreating back became a major problem as I often had no idea how much further we had to go. I felt an extendable dog lead would be a good investment.

West Bexington was a dreary place in the winter gloaming, miles of steeply shelving shingle and a huge car park. There was no sign of my friend Liz who was hosting us for two nights. We sat on a rickety trestle table at a deserted pub by the roadside.

After ten minutes of waiting we were both feeling cold and weary. Our warm wet bodies turned cold and clammy. Hips and knees stuck fast at ninety degrees. I was just fantasisng about cups of tea and hot baths, when a car roared down the hill and a smiling Liz climbed out. We spent an entertaining evening with her, consuming quantities of delicious local pheasant and good claret. After this we fell into bed and slept the deep sleep of the physically tired and well fed, waking wonderfully relaxed, an enviable sensation which I'm sure would cost a junkie dear. This 'feel-good' factor on waking, seemed to us one of the many bonuses of our physical exertions during the day, and also indicated an enviable lack of stress.

I met Liz at the Banff Springs Hotel in Canada when we were globe-trotting in our late teens. In later years, she and her mother would put Richard and me up for a weekend every year when Richard played Fives for the Jesters at Sherbourne. Liz was blue-blooded and green-fingered, with immaculately manicured red nails and an infectious deep-throated laugh. She ran on cigarettes and amber nectar. In Canada I remember her being the only one of our group who could hold her booze. When we stayed in her little manor house those February weekends, she would be out and about in green wellies and barbour showing us her collection of silver and golden pheasants, unusual bantams and orphan lambs. One such weekend, she said.

'One of my lambs is looking grotty Richard. Do you think you could deal with it?' she asked, laughing apologetically.

As the only man in the house, he could hardly refuse to put the little creature out of its misery, but at Sunday lunch I saw him looking pensive as he helped himself to the mint sauce, and accepted another glass of wine with alacrity.

After the foot-crippling pebbles of Chesil Beach, we bounced along the green springy Axminster carpet lying across the undulating and rapidly eroding cliffs. West Bay still has a little fishing fleet, but it is hard to believe that, in its 19th century hey day, it was visited by as many as five hundred ships a year.

Above Seatown, we could see across the great sweep of Lyme Bay to the chalk cliffs of Beer Head. Golden Cap, the highest point on the coast of Southern England, was our next obstacle. At the base of the cliffs, hundreds of tiny waves made regular indentations on the fine shingle, like the hem of a long lace curtain. We watched hang-gliders launching themselves from Golden Cap, floating silently in the thermals like great colourful birds. Then, below us, we spotted the Anchor Inn at Seatown.

'Do you see what I see? After 200 miles we need a celebratory pint!'

Richard then charged down the cliff path and we reached the pub breathless and elated. Dedicated as we were to the serious business of walking, we nevertheless decided that every hundred miles must be celebrated with the local brew; although I have to admit that this resolve weakened during the ten months, especially if we just happened to be passing a pub at lunch time.

This pub had an open fire, but a young couple in cycle shorts sat entwined in front of it, generating their own heat but leaving the rest of the room cold. We downed a pint of 'Tally-Ho' each and watched our fellow customers with interest.

'What do you think of that clock?' Richard asked, indicating the one behind the bar.

'It's wrong,' I replied briefly.

'No it's not,' he assured me, 'It's a mirror image.'

I puzzled over this for a while, and then quite expected a white rabbit to appear muttering 'No time! No time!' or the lady in the maroon outfit to break her silence with a peremptory 'Off with her head!' We were in 'Wonderland', behind a clock, with time the same, but different.

We galloped up Golden Cap, pausing at the top to admire both the view and one of the few backpackers we met on the entire trip, a young man with rastafarian locks, a big smile and a didgeree doo.

Here was a figure who could easily have stepped out of the pages of a Hardy novel.

At this two-week mark, Richard and I were feeling really confident for the first time since we set off. The walking was easy, the weather was kind, the blisters were healing and our coast was beautiful. From the top of Golden Cap, we could see a sweep of coast from Portland Bill in the east, to Start Point in the west. The erosion on these cliffs has dragged the scrubby trees and bracken downwards, leaving stark areas of sandstone like naked flesh. From this vantage point we could see the famous undercliff near Lyme Regis, where a large chunk of land has subsided from ground floor to basement, taking its rich covering of trees and ferns with it.

As we climbed the Black Venn hill, owned by the National Trust, the coastal path was completely eroded, and we had to detour across the golf course. In 1965 the National Trust launched 'Enterprise Neptune'; its policy was to acquire as much of the unspoiled coastline as possible, and 1995 happened to be the National Trust centenary year.

On our way round the coast we came to appreciate the value of 'Enterprise Neptune' and were impressed by all 600 miles of this well signed and beautifully kept coastal path, stewarded by the Countryside Commission. Their neatly carved acorns on every signpost and stile, cheered us on our way, while the National Trust oakleaf logo, informed us exactly where we were along the path. Excellent guides, for those like me, who have trouble finding the way.

We must have hauled ourselves over literally hundreds of stiles along this stretch, and it was helpful that they were always in good repair. In some places dogs were also catered for, with a little wooden guillotine gates, taylor-made for two pairs of paws. For those with one pair of feet, there was only one complaint. The path was often so narrow that both feet could not be placed parallel on it. On very rocky areas, this meant a hop-along-Cassidy manouvre, with one foot on the rocks or brambles, and one on the path. Along the bare cliff-tops, the ribboning path was visible for miles. On some of the steepest hills, wooden steps were cunningly placed to prevent erosion. The height and spacing of these steps was never right, and our knees woke up and complained bitterly.

The old houses of Lyme Regis snuggle below the high cliffs which backdrop the bay. Once an important port, the town now suffers from a plethora of traffic, teashops and tourists. Touched, but untouched, by the twentieth century, it makes the perfect setting for a play. As we approached the fourteenth century Cobb, I quite expected to see the cloaked figure of Meryl Streep gazing soulfully across the bay looking for her French Lieutenant.

The Axmouth-Lyme undercliff is now a National Nature Reserve. This eight mile stretch is one of the best examples of land-slipping in the British Isles, a constant process. I found the walk through the dense undergrowth reminiscent of a Gothic horror story. The ivy-clad trees, trailing vegetation and knarled roots reminded me of Arthur Rackham's illustrations in Grimms Fairy Tales. The eerie sound of the undertow from an invisible sea added to the claustrophobic atmosphere, and I was glad I had my English Lieutenant with me.

Warned that the walk from Lyme to Sidmouth was very tough, we were pleased to cover the fifteen miles in well under the recommended time and cross the River Axe into Devon. We soon discovered that the walker in Devon works hard for his rewards. We toiled endlessly up hill and down dale. 'The Grand Old Duke of York' helped me march up them with bursting lungs, and the downs just gave me time to recover before the next assault. The wind had been rising all afternoon, and the weather was on the change.

Our hosts for the night were Rotarians, who lived in a quite perfect Queen Ann house near Otterton. We had a stately bedroom with long sash windows which looked over broad acres. In our guest bathroom, we worshipped at the shrine of a ball-and-claw bath-tub, raised on a carpeted dais and surrounded by botanical icons. In the morning we woke to the screech of peacocks and roar of gale force winds.

We battled up Peak Hill. As the full force of the wind met us at the top, both rucksack covers blew off. I rescued Richard's, but there was no-one behind me to stop mine sailing off to France.

Ladrum Bay's sandstone stacks were attacked by a frenzied sea. Inland, static caravans spewed indiscriminately all over this attractive bay. In Devon, these metal boxes littered the coastline. Oblong larvae with lidless eyes gazing seawards, ugly and lifeless, waiting for the turn of the key to metamorphose for a season.

Strong winds are exhilarating but tiring, and I was lagging well behind by the time we reached Exmouth. Here we hopped on a train to spend a night in Topsham, before walking to Dawlish. We started on the towpath of the Countess Weir Canal.

'Is this the scenic route?' I asked Richard innocently.

'Murphy's Law. Today's Tuesday, the one day there aren't any ferries from Topsham.'

We were already having trouble with days of the week. A sort of, 'we've-stopped-the-world and-got-off,' amnesia was setting in. The days blurred together, the names of those we had been staying with, and those we were about to see, blew over the cliff. Remembering where we were only two or three nights ago, was an effort. Our cerebral computers were in a TODAY default mode.

It was wet and windy and conditions deteriorated as the day wore on. However, we saw several pairs of avocets, and many other waders. Brought into focus, a whole new world came to me through the binoculars. Nondescript brown birds, on land or water, became colourful and distinctive, whether the brilliantly demarcated colours of the many varieties of ducks, or the subtler tones of waders such as curlews and sandpipers. I watched the streamlined avocets with their thin black upturned bills, long lead-coloured legs, and neat black stripes on head and wings with the thrill of discovery. By this time I could tell a redshank from a lapwing and a shelduck from an oyster catcher. Well . . . almost.

As the walk progressed I never lost the excitement of bird watching through binoculars. Behind the glasses, even the humble linnet, caught in the right light, would be surprisingly colourful with red on head and chest. Watching a hawk in flight, was memorable. With effortless controlled power, the pointed arched wings gently beat the air as the bird hovers above its prey. A split-second swoop earthwards for the kill; and a triumphant upward retreat of vivid linear grace.

Reluctantly I handed Richard the magic glasses.

'You'd better take them. If I keep looking through them, it'll take us a year and ten months to complete the walk.'

Atrocious weather was an excuse, if not a reason, to dry off and warm up in another Anchor Inn at Cockwood by the Exe estuary. The local brew slid easily down eager throats leaving a delicious foaming wake. Our damp trousers steamed as we hugged the little coal fire. It was hard to move out into the elements.

By the time we reached the cliffs above Dawlish Warren the wind was gusting so strongly and the waves were so high, we were unable to walk in along the sea wall, but had to use the road instead, quite literally clinging to lamposts during strong gusts, just to remain upright.

Chapter Three

Winds stampeding the cliffs
Floundering black,
The wind flung a magpie away and a black
Back gull bent like an iron bar, slowly . . .
. . .the brunt wind . . . dented the balls of my eyes.
Ted Hughes

Narenta was the name of the substantial Victorian terraced house on the outskirts of Dawlish where Richard had spent many happy family holidays as a child. Apart from one fleeting visit ten years ago, he had not been back. The house has been divided into four spacious flats.

'This is where I used to play football with my cousins,' Richard said as we turned into Barton Crescent, a wide road just opposite the 13th century church of St. Gregory's. 'There wasn't any traffic then.' As we approached the front door with its brass-bound step, he inhaled deeply.

'Is that where you smelt brasso and wallflowers?' I asked.

'Mmmm. Memories . . .'

We cooked a meal and enjoyed a really relaxing evening in one of the flats which is kept for family and friends. It was a relief to be on our own, reading, writing and even watching television . Richard's childhood memories of holidays with sisters, cousins, aunts, uncles and granny were coming back thick and fast.

'Dawlish was a parochial place in those days,' he said, choosing his words carefully.

'My great aunt was the quintessential Nora Batty. She seldom left the town. One memorable occasion she was on a coach trip and the driver asked the passengers if they would like to stop at Hey Tor. Before anyone had a chance to say yes, a loud voice from the rear shouted,

'Drive on driver. Uz 'as seed it all before!'

Richard warmed to his subject and told me about Great Aunt Alice. She was, he told me, a large lady with carpet slippers, wrap-around pinny, flannel vest and petticoat at half mast. She would lean on the gate watching the world go by, vocalising her thoughts with the volume up. Whenever there was a wedding at the church opposite, every gate down the terrace would be lent on. One Saturday afternoon, she emerged with a colander of potato peelings to put in the pig bin. There was a wedding in the church. The bride and groom were safely inside, but the vicar was a little late. As Auntie Alice opened the gate, complete with colander and curlers, the vicar appeared puffing up the hill on his push bike. Whirling the colander above her head like a discus, my great aunt accosted the vicar and proceeded to air her ideas on marriage.

'This 'uz just the starrt. 'Ers alright now.' Her head and the potato peeling shook in unison. 'You just wait, things 'ull be very divverent. I've seed it 'appen.'

The vicar wobbled off his bike and retreated into the vestry.

Slowly the stories came out as he re-lived the summers of his childhood. He remembered bird-watching on Dawlish Warren with his father, feeding the hens with his great uncle, the huge breakfasts his granny used to cook in a great black iron pan, the lady upstairs who loved jig-saw puzzles.

Our rest day was spent wandering round the town in sunshine and showers. Richard reckoned that apart from a lot of in-filling of houses and a modern rather jazzy front, Dawlish hadn't changed much. The Lawn, a small park through which a fast-flowing stream called The Brook runs over a series of mini-weirs, was just the same as he remembered it, black swans and all. The railway came to Dawlish in 1846 as part of Brunel's innovative Atmospheric System and is an integral part of the beach, lapped by the sea at high tide.

Looking west the Parson and Clerk sculptured cliffs were silhouetted against an ominously stormy sky.

We left in what seemed like a mini-hurricane. Smuggler's Lane led us down to the sea wall which linked up with the coast path. Just as Dawlish has tried to resist our entry, it even more forcefully resisted our exit. The full force of the wind funnelled up the tiny high banked lane with such force that it pushed me into the ditch, and even Richard was barely able to stand upright.

'This is ridiculous,' I shouted into the wind from the shelter of my ditch.

The sea boiled with grey-green malevolence. I half expected to see the The Flying Dutchman appear.

'The sea wall is impassable - it's underwater!' Richard yelled from the bottom of the lane.

Regretfully we turned our backs on this exhilarating scene, and crawled back up the steep lane to the road.

Then it began to rain; not ordinary rain, but sheets of wet stuff propelled by the strong winds. We battled on. I was walking, for the first and last time, almost on Richard's heels, hoping his body would give me a little shelter. I noted wryly a large sign by the roadside advertising 'THE ENGLISH RIVIERA', complete with palm tree and blue sky. Several cars stopped and offered us lifts but we took a perverted satisfaction in declining.

Finally we dropped down into a battered-looking Teignmouth and fell into a smoky cafe. The waitress glared at us as we stood pouring water onto her worn carpet, peeling off our outer garments and spreading ourselves over several chairs and tables. Apart from a sour-faced man chain-smoking between mouthfuls of bacon and egg, we were the only customers. Coffee was grudgingly served and we stayed in the comparative comfort of this little refuge listening to the old shop signs creaking loudly as they tossed to and fro in the wind.

'Where you going to my dears?' the waitress finally enquired, curiosity getting the better of her. 'Fawcasts terrible, you'll be blown right orf Shalden bridge. I'd take bus f'I were you.'

Thanks and no thanks, I thought, as we struggled back into our wet gear, and braced ourselves for the elements.

Alfred Lord Tennyson described Torquay as 'the loveliest sea village in England' and I wondered what he would make of it now. The place certainly has style, even the bus shelters had a curvaceous Grecian look. Large architect-designed homes lurked behind sub-tropical vegetation with panoramic views over the bay. Brixham, at the west end, blends into Paignton which merges into Torquay. It certainly looks the largest, if not the loveliest 'sea village in England'.

As often happens, when the end is in sight, fatigue hits, and I had the added discomfort of a small stone in my boot. At this moment we met a couple of retired 'real' walkers.

'You must have had a bad time this morning,' one observed.

'Where are you from? How far are you going?' said the other. 'You're limping,' he added looking sympathetically at me.

Politely, we answered their queries and listened to their stories. There didn't seem to be anywhere they hadn't been. Precious minutes passed as we walked the world with them.

'I'm afraid we must get on. We've got a rendez-vous to keep,' I said in desperation, looking at my watch.

We had arranged to meet our Rotarian host at The Grand Hotel, which we understood to be on the east side of the bay. After a pressurised couple of end-of-day miles, we eventually arrived at the Hotel Imperial and saw 'The Grand' laughing at us a good mile across the bay. I had made the arrangements with Irene our hostess, whose sense of direction must have been on a par with mine. Richard was not amused.

'What exactly did you say?' he demanded.

'What was the hotel called? Which side of the bay was it? What time did you arrange for us to meet?'

'I can do without the Inquisition, thanks. I'll phone and tell them where we are.'

Luckily our host, Philip, had a mobile phone. He raced across from his vigil at The Grand Hotel and swept us back to his home on the Cockington side of the town.

A warm light shone on the immaculate pile carpet. The scent of furniture polish drifted out. As we looked in, Irene looked out. Her eyes focused on two tired, smelly walkers, with mud that hid the leather on their boots and crept up their over trousers to the knee. Her face froze into a smile. To her everlasting credit, there was only a moment of hesitation. We rapidly removed our boots and over-trousers and in no time at all were sitting in her warm kitchen eating a large cream tea.

'Just time to bath and change,' she said firmly, 'before our guests arrive for dinner. Philip will show you your rooms and how the power shower works.'

This was our first formal dinner party, and my 'posh frock' consisted of a pair of stretch sports trousers, a designer 'wicking' top and sport sandals. Richard was in similar gear. We tidied and cleaned as best we could, and emerged, a little purer, in time for drinks and dinner with the Rotary President, Secretary and their other halves. I lost count of how many courses of rich and delicious food Irene had prepared, then we had photo-calls and exchange of Rotary banners. It was after midnight before we fell into bed, with nineteen hard miles to Kingswear the next day. Wind, rain and thunder kept us awake much of the night.

The worst of the weather had passed during the night, and we only had two short-lived hail storms. These were so sharp, the only thing to do was to batten down the hatches and stand like cattle with our backs to the weather.

The next stretch of the Devon Coast Path was lit by brilliant sunshine between the squalls. We puffed up hill and down dale above a curdling sea. The coast path here was a purist. It descends rapidly to every tiny cove and ascends equally rapidly to every single cliff top, each higher than the last. Yet nobody ever talks about the south Devon path being hard. Eveyone had warned us of the severity of the north Devon path, but the stretch from Teignmouth to Plymouth is unrelentingly tough and made harder by the ubiquitous mud which often meant two-steps-forward-and-one-back.

In spite of this, the beauty of the scenery in the dramatic stormy winter light kept the fatigue at bay. We were to find again and again that when in varied and beautiful scenery, we could manage the hardest walking. The feel-good factor got the upper hand, and the aches and pains were pushed into the sub-conscious.

We rounded the headland, glad of the shelter the estuary afforded. Below us lay the gently curving River Dart, with the historic little town of Dartmouth snuggled in front of us on the opposite bank. Shafts of evening sun lit the 15th century castle, built to deter Breton raiders. For the moment we had left the wind and weather out on the cliff tops, and we revelled a sense of sanctuary, a boat coming in after a storm.

Brookhill Cottage was right on our path, an interesting house built on the side of the hill, with views of the mouth of the River Dart and the cliffs beyond. We rang the bell. After a pause we heard deep barking and footsteps. They seemed a long while approaching.

We stood wearily on many a doorstep over the next few months, and it was always a moment of apprehension, both for us, and no doubt our hosts, who were welcoming total strangers. Although I was brought up with dogs, I was bitten by a German Shepherd two years ago, and since then am ashamed to admit that a fierce barking increases my heart rate, a fear immediatly sensed by the dog in question. Walkers with packs are regarded with deep suspicion by most dogs, and we were barked, snarled and slavered at by every watch dog round the coast.

I glanced anxiously at Richard. The door opened slowly and Jennifer emerged restraining an enormous doberman who looked distinctly hungry.

'Paul's at an anti-veal calf export demonstration in Plymouth,' she explained over tea.

'A strange occupation for a retired eye surgeon,' Richard commented later as we enjoyed a hot shower.

'Thank goodness that doberman's bark was worse than his bite,' I said, happily.

Supper was a good hearty plate of spaghetti bolognaise without the meat.

In spite of the filthy weather we splashed round Dartmouth, a jumble of tiny streets and crooked houses. I pushed my anorak hood to one side in order to see the great bulwark of Naval College on its hill above the town. My brother did time there, so I bought him a card of the college and zipped it carefully inside my map pocket intending to write it later. Emptying my pockets long afterwards, I found some damp coloured wood pulp. The Royal Naval College had disintegrated.

As we passed the jetty on our way out, a ferryman was putting out a sign which read: NO MORE FERRIES DUE TO BAD WEATHER.

Once more we could hardly stand. We had to crouch behind stone walls or hang onto fence posts during the strong gusts. Like toddlers, it required all our concentration to keep on our feet. While the wind tugged at our tiny frames, the mud played games, sucking and sliding our well-tempered boots into its slippery softness.

Back on the road things were easier, especially after a beer and a pasty in Stoke Fleming. The only customers in the pub were two black labradors and a large tabby cat. The dogs lay stretched out on the bare floor in front of the hissing coals of a warm fire. The cat was curled up on the red dralon cushion of a wooden arm chair. I removed first my wet Gortex and then the cat, who quickly re-instated himself on my lap, a fluffy ball of warm contentment which was catching. A hot pasty and chips washed down with real ale felt like the best meal we had ever eaten. Refreshed in body and spirit we set off in a moderated wind and glimpses of pale sunshine.

'I remember this from Crusader Camp days. We spent a week here one summer,' Richard said, as we looked down onto the golden shingle beach of Blackpool Sands.

'Lucky you.'

'It's also immortalised as the spot where I was told I had swallowed a dictionary.'

Years ago Richard had told me this story. He was asked a question by a local lass twice his age, and being intellectually precocious at the tender age of twelve, he had answered her fairly comprehensively. She stood, open-mouthed and then uttered those immortal words. I have teased Richard about them ever since. Once on the official coast path, there seemed no end to Richard's knowledge. It took me a while to realise that he was usually cribbing from trail guides which he devoured avidly every night while I was scribbling into my diary. After this I was a little less impressed.

Puffing up the muddy cliff path and trying not to slip too far back, we were nearly knocked over by a line of fit-looking runners with tiny shorts and bright red legs. The leader hailed us cheerily with,

'Stop the world, I want to get off.'

At the speed with which he flew down the slippery path, I thought he might well do just that.

'It's alright for them,' I grumbled, 'they're not carrying anything.'

Our rucksacks were becoming heavier than ever in the rain. At times our path was like a lake, and neither the mud nor the rain let up. However, even in these poor conditions, the dramatic cliffs headlands and bays lured us on. At Gammon Head a large wreck was clearly visible, lashed by the waves in its watery grave. Richard, nose in trail guide, pointed out that this stretch was very pig-orientated - Gammon Head is followed by Pig's Nose and Ham Stone.

That seemed a good moment to give our flagging energy levels a boost especially as the weather had cleared. Leaving his professional hat at home, Richard was happy for us both to devour Mars Bars as required. We then rounded the point and strode on to Mill Bay and East Portlemouth in weak sunshine where we fell thankfully into the little ferry which took us to Salcombe.

Ferries were becoming a very significant part of our walk. Without them, we had to trudge up rivers and esturies to the first bridge, frustrating miles which only took us within spitting distance of where we started. We were often the only passengers and the ferryman was usually friendly. My feet savoured every moment of those short journeys.

We slept like tops, and set off in sunshine and high spirits to Aveton Gifford or 'Orton Giffurd' as they say in these parts. Devonian names are very descriptive. On our way up from

Salcombe we had passed a Splatcove Point followed by a Stink Cove, and now we were on a path from Bolt Head to Bolt Tail.

After a quieter day, the wind had livened up again, and the spume at Soar Mill Cove looked as though a washing machine had gone berserk with an overdose of Persil. From the Iron Age Earthworks at Bolt Tail we had a bird's-eye view of Burgh Island, Thurleston and Bigbury-on-Sea at the mouth of the River Avon. Just below us lay the snug little fishing villages of Inner and Outer Hope, once famous for smugglers. We had a cosy lunch in a hut on Thurleston golf course with the wind screeching and rattling round the corrugated iron.

Few ferries run during the winter months, and Bantham Jetty on the River Avon was deserted with only a few rowing boats pulled up onto the shore.

A man in waders, looking like a disorientated heron, was trying to cross but changed his mind.

Up this esturary we came across the first mangle-worzells I had ever seen. Giant elongated turnips with a tassle of huge green leaves.

'What are they?' I asked the dictionary.

'Worzell Gummage,' it replied.

Having bolted from head to tail we arrived at our destination an hour ahead of schedule, one of the few times this happened. It was a relief not to have the usual rush for the last few miles, especially as my 'wind down' time was from 3 p.m. onwards. Richard would disappear onto the horizon, stop and wait, and then immediately set off again as I hove to.

'Phew, don't I get a stop, too?'

'We'll be late,' would be the reply.

However, 'Oreton Giffurd' had no tea shops to warm up and refuel in so we had to make do with the church porch. We were getting used to feeling like vagrants, grateful for shelter of any kind.

We arrived at the River Avon only to find a high tide had flooded our path. Our attempts to ford it only gave us wet feet.

'It'll have to be a road day. Damn these wretched rivers, I knew this stretch would be a problem.' Richard sounded like a man with a boot full of water.

'Schlurrrp.' The boot came out of the mud, and we headed for the road and a village called Holberton, where we were booked in for our first bed and breakfast.

The day was overcast and threatening rain as we again puffed up steep cliffs to be rewarded with the unwelcome view of Burgh

Island, with Bolt Tail looking near enough to touch. When making detours up rivers and estuaries, we missed the pulsating roar of the sea far below. Without the robust wind, our detours inland were strangely silent and we felt almost claustrophobic without coastal views. The sea was a high-spirited turbulent companion whose company we missed.

A late start and hard going meant we would have a job to arrive before dark. It started to rain. The road rose and fell with monotonous regularity. Daylight was fading, and Richard took a short cut across the Mildmay's Estate. The path was boggy and waterlogged . We picked our way up stoney paths, through dark woods and under a disused ivy clad bridge. An owl hooted mournfully. I hurried my steps to keep Richard's dusky back in view. We emerged on the road just half a mile from The Mildmay Colours Inn.

Once inside, we collapsed onto the bed leaving a shameful trail of mud behind us, too tired at that moment to care. The advantage of B & B's was that we could just relax, emerging to eat and drink before resuming the supine position.

'Phew!' I sighed, spread-eagled on more than my share of a small double bed. 'I'm not sure I can make it to supper. Even the shower seems a long way today.' Richard produced a cup of tea, and eventually we made it to the bar for something stronger.

We had been walking for 25 days, and I think I felt more physically exhausted that evening than on any previous day, although it had been a mere 14 miles. A typical male, Richard would never admit this, but I had noticed him standing leaning his pack on walls and gates more often than usual that day. Our bodies were having a steep fitness curve, and we were beginning to shed weight. As time went on, we still puffed and blew up the hills, but our recovery time became shorter and shorter. That night I wrote in my diary:

'Welcome filling meal. Curious listening to others' conversations about the real world. Early night.'

In view of the exhaustion factor, we had a lie in, while Richard planned a less arduous day. It was pouring with rain, and the next entry in my diary came from The Dolphin Inn, perched above the River Yealm at Newton Ferrers. From our warm dry vantage point, we looked down on the protective arms of this steep-sided valley, embracing the many pleasure craft sitting gently on the quiet river, and acting like a funnel, amplifying every sound. Across the river, the toy houses of Noss Mayo clung to the steep, densely wooded slopes, defying gravity as they hung above the river.

The tiny street of Newton Ferrers was lined with small cottages, nestling along the river bank with names like Vine, Virginia and Jasmine. Each had a tiny neat garden and their own mooring by the boat-filled river. The shiny brass-lit interiors looked warm and welcoming. It reminded me of *The Wind in the Willows*.

Back on the road we passed a William and Mary mansion called Puslynch. Here, we made good use of a bench, thoughtfully placed by the fast flowing Yealm. A large notice read 'Quiet please'. We enjoyed a short break sitting quietly ankle-deep in snowdrops, (a pleasant change from mud), and were amused to hear the woods echoing to the sound of guns as his lordship enjoyed a noisy shoot.

Plymouth surprised us. We approached from Wenham Bay and walked past H.M.S. Gunnery School where Her Majesty's soldiers were playing with their noisy and expensive toys. Our trail guide gave sensible advice here: '*It is unwise to picnic or hang about in front of the guns!*'

Taking their advice we picnicked in the shelter of Jennycliff Bay in a rare sunny interval. The stormy skies gave drama to the great panorama of Plymouth Sound as shafts of sun illuminated Rame Head and Mount Edgecombe to the west, and the modern skyscrapers of the rebuilt city itself, with their commanding position looking over the Sound.

To me Plymouth is synonomous with lighthouses. An 'enlightened' Archbishop of Canterbury in the 13th century founded a Guild of Seamen (Godly disposed men), who were to 'build and light proper beacons for the guidance of mariners'. This Guild eventually became known as Trinity House and today controls almost 100 lighthouses around the coast of England and Wales. Scotland, as ever, has to be different, and its lighthouses are run by the Northern Lighthouse Board created in 1786. I remembered the solitary monk and his one candle at St. Aldhem's Head, as I read that the lighthouse beam is still measured in candlepower. Now, the most powerful light is St. Catherine's Point, on the Isle of Wight. Here, the diesel-driven generators produce a beam equivalent to five and a quarter million candle power and can be seen at a distance of twenty six miles.

Early wooden lighthouses were square or octangonal in shape. They inevitably either fell down or caught fire. One of the early

Eddystone lighthouses, fourteen miles off Plymouth, caught fire while men were still working on it. Molten lead poured from the burning structure into the foamy brine, where the struggling survivors swallowed water from these now toxic waves. A gruesome story relates, how one poor man was rescued, only to die in agony four days later in Plymouth. A post-mortem found a caste of his stomach in lead.

It took a London clock-maker, John Smeaton, to design an enduring solid fireproof structure of interlocking granite blocks in 1759. This one lasted one hundred and twenty years and gave out a light from 24 candles that could be seen at a distance of five miles. Cracks in the rock on which it stood, rather than in the granite of the lighthouse, necessitated a replacement.

We sat alone in the little boat waiting to cross the Tamar, leaving England on a seven-minute voyage to our first 'foreign land'. Cornwall, in the Cornish language is Kernow, meaning 'the strangers of Corneu' an indication of the perceived remoteness of the district.

Although it was after 9 a.m. the street lights shone wetly on cobbles and paving stones. Rain streamed from a leaden sky onto the old naval buildings, the marina, Drake Island, Mount Edgecombe and Rame Head; a taste of things to come. However, we were in no mood to let the weather dampen our pioneering spirit, as we chugged across the Tamar to Cremyl. Our walk was well under way, and we were about to enter a county that was no foreign land to us.

Chapter Four

The rain hacks my head to the bone, the hawk hangs
The diamond point of will that polestars
The sea drowner's endurance.
Ted Hughes

The rain didn't let up all day and low cloud obliterated any views, so we stuck to the road which was several inches deep in rust-coloured water. Our boots and our morale were both put to the test. On one stretch of cliff path, the stiles became surreal bridges, crossing torrents of brown water. Without shelter in the rain, eating was an ordeal. Any smug warm flesh lurking under the base layer of clothes, turned cold and clammy, exacerbated by invasive rivulets of rain water which trickle down back and chest. Lifting a soggy sandwich to the mouth meant more water trickled ineluctably up the forearm. Dark patches of damp on our sleeves and trousers, stuck fast to cooling limbs. Water streamed off our hair and faces, tempers frayed, and all our bodies wanted to do was to arrive. Drinking tepid cuppa soup in the pouring rain, leaning against a tree-trunk whose winter branches gave as much shelter as a waterfall, was reminiscent of a Victoria Wood sketch.

In a little place called Downderry my 'fuel tank' was empty. There was no sign of shelter, and, in desperation, I sat myself down in an inviting porch. 'Perfect,' I said, 'there's even room for two.' I leaned my back against the door post, with two wet appendages stretched in front of me, leaving a trail of water and mud. A banana, washed down with cold water, tasted remarkably good. Richard wasn't so sure about loitering in someone's porch, but he swallowed his scruples and crouched beside me, streaming water. Before we left, he insisted on a photo; in deference to the camera, I combed my sodden mop of hair, and smiled wetly. We were learning something about being vagrants.

At Seaton we left the road and took the steep dramatic cliff path to Looe. It was a hard wet scramble and by the time we dropped down into the town, our legs were set in aspic, and our high tech. clothes were wicking well. Remembering Torquay,

Richard rang our Rotary hosts, while I retired to the Ladies to resuscitate my white fingers under the hand drier.

We stood by the quay, moody and silent, water streaming off our Gortex. Our bodies cooled rapidly and we stiffened up in minutes. After what seemed an eternity, but was probably only ten minutes, a large Jaguar swept up to the quay. John jumped out, and proffered a friendly hand. He was smartly dressed in well-tailored casuals and shirt sleeves. We sank damply into the leather upholstery of the warm car and slid smoothly away. It was then I became aware of a strong 'odeur de walkers' and rapidly wound down my window.

We needn't have worried. In no time we were immersed in hot water with tea on the side, while our clothes were also being given a wash and blow dry. No dinner parties tonight, just a really good meal and an early bed.

Battling against the usual head wind leaving Looe, we passed a Scottish gentleman walking east. 'Och! He exclaimed with a smug grin 'you're going th' rrong wey!'

We hoped that once we had turned right at Land's End we should have the wind as a help not a hindrance.

On our way to Polperro we passed a war memorial on which were inscribed the patriotic words:- *True love by life / True love by death is tried / Live thou for England / We for England died.*

Up on these very English cliffs, this jingoism bought a lump to the throat. That day marked the fiftieth anniversary of the Allies entry into Auschwitz concentration camp at the end of the Second World War.

'Whoops!' Richard was way ahead. I had to hurry to catch up.

The little fishing port of Polperro looked like a picture post card on that January day. The asymmetrical little cottages crammed together round the inner harbour, sheltered below the wooded slopes of the steep hills. Watchful gulls perched on the stone roofs; ducks and swans had made their base in open boats on the water. Apart from one or two 'old salts' there was no-one around. From our vantage point on the cliffs it was the very best place to see it.

No hassle with parking, no ugly outskirts, just a gull's-eye view of an old fishing village.

Just at that moment I wouldn't have swapped my feet for a car. Our destination was Fowey, and the easier going and better weather meant we didn't hurry. As we were pausing yet again, enjoying the views just beyond Lantic Bay, Richard looked at his watch.

'We'd better get a move on,' he said, 'we've still got quite a way to go.' With that he shot off, and I did my best to keep up. Never at my speediest in the afternoon, I only just managed to keep him in sight as I more or less ran down the steep streets of Polruan. I couldn't understand why there was such a rush until I saw a small ferry just departing across the river to Fowey.

'Why didn't you tell me?' I puffed angrily. 'I had no idea we had a ferry to catch.'

'I thought you knew,' Richard replied. 'Fortunately there'll be another one in a few minutes. I don't think we shall be too late.' My head sulked and my feet smiled, until the next ferry arrived.

The river was a strange mixture of large ocean-going ships loading china clay, and small craft bobbing up and down in the natural harbour. The narrow streets of Fowey, lined with tightly-packed old houses, tumble down the steep hill to the stout quays.

'Are you the walkers?' The jovial ferryman enquired as we climbed into the modest clinker-built boat. 'There's a lady bin 'cross once looking for you both. Says she'll ring tonight.' Cornish bush telegraph was working well.

China clay continues to be mined in north Cornwall, as witnessed by the strange white mountains of spoil round St. Austell. At Par, we found ourselves walking through the settling beds, pipes, and smoking chimneys of this still viable industry. Our boots echoed on iron bridges above great steel vats of milky liquid, past empty buildings and belching chimneys. Silent and empty, this remote-controlled factory sits uneasily on such a beautiful coastal path, leaving the walker with a strange smell in his nostrils and a fine white covering of powder on his clothes.

The Mariner's Mark at Gribbin Head, built by Trinity House in 1832, stood like a giant stick of red and white candy to signpost the eastern tip of St. Austell Bay. The 84 foot Daymark helps the sailor to distinguish The Gribbon from others south Cornish headlands. For us, it was depressingly visible for days.

'Let's stop here,' Richard suggested, eyeing the pub in Charlestown. It was lunch time, but as it wasn't raining, I felt we should be strong-minded. There was a convenient seat outside the pub, but it was hard to sit in the cold and eat our meagre fare with warmth and beer only yards away. Feeling virtuous wasn't half as good as enjoying a pint in the warm, I decided. As we ate our soggy sandwiches on the cheerless bench, we watched a couple of youths jumping off the stone jetty into the icy grey water below with blood-curdling screams, blue faces and chattering teeth.

'Beware of the ducks!' read a large sign in the old harbour of Pentewan. In winter, there were certainly more ducks than people. Only a row of elegant Georgian houses and the gates and rusty winches of the old dock, reminds the visitor that once this had been a bustling port, sending building materials and its own sand to the china clay works at St. Austell. Paradoxically the dock, built in 1820 by a local landowner, silted up shortly after the First World War, choked by the silt washed down from the clay works it was built to serve.

We were beginning to appreciate that the men responsible for the wave of industry which attacked the coast in the 19th century, were hoisted by their own petard. Now these little places were industrial relics, embalmed for, and worshipped by, the tourist.

'Quack, quack,' agreed Jemima and her friends as they waddled across the road.

Richard pointed to the memorial of a 19th century sea captain from Pentewan, who had four sons. They in their turn also became sea captains. Within only two generations they had lost seven children at sea. These were dangerous coasts.

As we climbed up onto the cliffs again, we had a good view of the famous fishing port of Mevagissy. In its hey day, pilchards came in vast numbers every August, ceasing abruptly at the turn of the century. Many of these were cured, and exported to Italy, Portugal and other Catholic countries as far back as 1555. This little ditty shows how much Lent was appreciated by the local fishermen:-

Here's health to the Pope / And may he repent, / And lengthen by six months / The term of his Lent.

'I've heard of Bombay Duck, but how about Mevagissey Duck? It's what the Navy nicknamed the cured pilchers,' I told Richard proudly, spotting a plaque before he did. It was hard to visualise these tranquil little coves as they must have been a hundred years ago, alive with people, boats, noise and stench.

As we reached the top of the cliff again, I groaned as I spotted the square red and white chimney on Gribben Head leering at us.

'It's further than it looks,' Richard reassured me. 'We can still see it because the coast is so indented here.'

The concertinering cliffs were a challenge, even for our now fitter bodies. Dodman Point is described as 'a major landmark' on this stretch of coast. We could see across Veryan's Bay to Nare Head, and just make out St. Anthony's Head in the far distance. I felt as pleased as Cortez when he was viewing the Pacific. Others had thought likewise, for a great granite cross, erected by a local clergyman in 1896 read, *In the firm hope of the Second Coming of our Lord Jesus Christ and for the encouragement of those who strive to serve him.* It was a reminder of a more devout age and the extreme dangers for those 'in peril on the sea'. Dodman Point had been the graveyard of many ships which missed Falmouth in the days before radar.

We didn't get much encouragement as we studied the coast ahead. It was going to be tough and we still had a long way to go. No more dawdling, we had to push it to reach Portloe by 5 p.m. We pelted past Caerhays Castle, built by John Nash in 1808 (no time today for research or plaque spotting). Richard pointed out the double doors on a little row of cottages at Portholland.

'To keep the sea out,' he panted, before assuming his usual vanguard position.

Sitting on a seat above St. Just in Roseland, we watched daffodil and broccoli harvesting. There was no doubt about being in a 'foreign land'. In the 5th century, after the Romans left, Cornwall shared a language with Brittany and Wales. *Aye by Tre, Pol and Pen, Ye shall know Cornishmen,* Polperro, Pendower, Tregonhawke. Place names like Breage, Castle-an-Dinas, Woon Gumpas and Nancledra describe rivers, hills, rocks, cliffs and other landscape features and made us feel more than five hundred miles from home.

It is a land of little-known saints, St. Just, St. Levan, St. Enodoc. St. Pyran is the patron saint of Cornwall. His name slips into villages like Perran-porth, and Perran-uthnoe. The county boasts its own black flag with a silver cross, representing tin coming out of the rock. Having made a pilgrimage to Cornwall every year since we married, we felt on home ground.

The gale-force winds had whipped Carrick Roads into a frenzy of white horses, throwing the moored pleasure craft into a see-sawing dance. As the only hopeful passengers waiting for the little ferry to take us to Falmouth, we were relieved to see the sturdy little craft yawing and writhing towards us. On board it was difficult to stand up as the boat bucked and swayed its way past St. Mawes castle, the phut-phut of the engine occasionally missing a beat as we battled across the racing water. Never a good sailor, I was too frightened to feel ill. In a fit of bravado, I attempted a photograph, wedging my back against the doors to maintain my equilibrium. The print was badly out of focus.

The Georgian and Victorian streets of Falmouth were hibernating on a bleak January afternoon. A few fishing boats and yachts decorated the sheltered waters that must once have been filled with the famous mail ships called 'Falmouth Packets'. We sat in a draughty bus shelter watching tugs skillfully manoevre a huge cargo boat in fading light. History-on-the-plaque informed us that a Regency incinerator, used to burn confiscated tobacco, was known as the King's Pipe. We also learned that those members of the aristocratic Killigrew family not involved in pub brawls, had been Govenors of Pendennis Castle.

We left Falmouth in teeming rain for another detour up the Helford River to Gweek (best known for its seal sanctuary). There were no winter ferries from Helford Passage, where in summer we could have saved ourselves a good few miles. The path ran across steep-sided fields which were extremely slippery. Suddenly there was a cry ahead.

'Wheeee!' Richard was doing a Torville and Dean manoeuvre which took him 'Splat!' firmly into a bramble-covered fence. The weight of the pack pinned him down securely, he was as helpless as a fly on its back. Once I realised that only his pride was dented, I made my own way gingerly down the steep slope and laughed at his posterior and two protruding legs.

'You look like Pooh Bear stuck in Rabbit's house. Definitely too much pasta last night!'

'OK. Quit the cackle,' he smiled. 'I need a hand.'

'You might even need two,' I replied, helping to pull him off the fence. Morale was restored, and we lunched on a convenient seat under the Monteray Pines of a large house that could have been Manderlay. With no wind and no sea sound, we were struck by the quiet.

Just as we were approaching Helford Passage, a black Labrador joined us. No sign of an owner, and, although I told him about our 4,300 mile walkies, he was not immediately deterred. However, after several miles of mulling this over, he sloped off quietly, deciding descretion was the better part of valour.

Once in Helford Passage, we sat by the river where the ferry would have run in the summer. From here to Gweek would be on roads, and the sloping terrain and mud had started another blister on my heel. I wasn't really in the mood for conversations with strangers, but an elderly inquisitive lady, in hand-knitted jumper and Oxfam skirt, darted towards us. Her eyes twinkled mischievously as she gave her views on tourists.

'T'other volks round 'ere can' wait for end of season be rid of 'em.' She glanced over her shoulder and lowered her voice.

'Load of niffs they be. I'm Corrnish. Born and bred in Boscastle. I'm workin' claas an no ashamed of it. Why should'nt 'ard-workin volks come 'ere and enjoy all this too?'

She went on to tell us that she had been employed in the big house, under whose gracious pines we had lunched, and had been left her cottage 'down wi' the gentry' when the lady on the house 'passed on'. She didn't quite fit with the smug middle class ethos of the little place. Her parting shot to us was,

'Buy yerselves a pair o' roller skates at the next jumble sale my deers!'

The Lizard Peninsula is famous for its soft climate and hard Serpentine rock. The Lizard itself is the southernmost point on the British mainland, and boasts the first lighthouse in Cornwall, built by John Killigrew of Falmouth in 1619. His philanthropy was not appreciated by the locals who vigorously opposed the project. *'They have been so long used to reap profit by the calamity of the ruin of shipping that they claim it as hereditary,'* Sir John noted sadly. Now the 5 million candlepower beam can be seen from a distance of 21 miles, and the wreckers are out of business.

'We should be at the cottage in only four more days,' I said, excitedly.

The thought of having completed this first testing 'leg' was a good morale booster. Mentally I had sectioned our walk into managable stretches, and felt that if I reached Land's End, I should be able to complete the rest. Richard had no doubts in his ability to complete the 4,300 miles, but feared he might have to carry either me, or my pack or both. We felt physically very fit, eating and sleeping well, and arriving on time in good shape every evening.

'We've still got some long days before we get to St. Just,' Richard replied, ever-cautious, but then he had studied the map. We both felt very confident at that moment.

Pride is something to be wary of especially on a long walk when you never know what's round the corner. With only twelve miles to Cadgwith, we didn't hurry. It was grey and misty. The former quarrying village of Porthoustock, with its grim deserted quarry buildings, looked menacing. It is here that divers, marine necromancers, come from all over to explore the many boats which have sunk to a watery grave beneath the treacherous Manacle Reef. Richard and I had a difference of opinion about the word 'manacle'. I was sure it meant handcuff or fetter, but Richard, (having swallowed a dictionary), thought it had a Cornish origin. He was right of course. Manacles derives from the Cornish words 'men eglos' which means 'stone church'. This was both apposite and sinister. More than four hundred victims of shipwrecks on this reef are buried in the churchyard at St. Keverne.

'This place is spooky,' I said which prompted Richard to recall the haunting tales of Sir Arthur Quiller Couch, known as 'Q', himself a Cornishman who lived at Fowey. I shivered. 'Let's go.'

From Godrievie I took a photo of the deadly black rocks from the cove, itself black and deserted. It was almost a relief to find some life at Dean Quarry, humming with the roar of lorries moving tons of cliff and neatly graded aggregate for roads all round Britain. The natural cliffs were being hollowed out into strange artificial shapes, while 'new' cliffs of spoil looked ill at ease in a strange juxtaposition of natural forms.

After an unhurried lunch in a draughty bus shelter in Coverack, Richard silently studied the map and announced uneasily,

'Cadgwith is a bit further than I thought. It's a good seven miles and in this weather we'll have an early dusk.' We set off at a cracking pace, but in slippery mud, it was often one-step-forward-and-two-back. Serpentine rock was treacherous underfoot, and also slowed us down. Kennack Sands had vanished. It seemed however fast we walked we'd never get there.

'These are definitely Cornish miles,' I thought.

In the 17th century, a gentleman called Richard Carew noted the peculiarities of Cornish measurements, '*The Justices of the Peace have oftentimes endeavoured to reduce this variance to a certainty. It has been observed by strangers that Cornish miles are much longer than those about London.*'

When the elusive Kennack Sands hove into view, all set about with caravans, it was 4.15 p.m. and the mist was closing in. I cursed the Cornish mile and wasn't impressed when my informant told me about the unusual complexity of rocks here. 'Kennack gneiss, serpentine and gabbro as well as veins of asbestos and talc.'

'You're cribbing,' I said unimpressed. 'And Kennack isn't a bit gneiss.'

We hurried on, the mist wrapping round us like a shroud. Although there wasn't much wind, huge sinister rollers crashed on the rocks beneath us. It was a Spring Tide. The black serpentine rock gives the cliffs a very bleak look, and the dark remains of a quarry added to the gloomy atmosphere. The sound of crashing waves increased and we glanced nervously down a great chasm, where the white surf was churning ferociously several hundred feet below. This giant hole is caused by the collapse of a cave and has a dramatic natural arch at the bottom. It was like a Devil's Frying Pan, and I really thought the Devil was licking his lips that evening.

'Wait for me,' I yelled above the roar. Richard didn't hear. Feeling vulnerable, I increased my speed, aware that this was not the moment to turn an ankle. Eyes glued to my boots, I concentrated on where I put each foot, although this task was increasingly hard in the dimming light. The fisherman's look-out on the headland above Cadgwith was a welcome sight, and from here we peered down into the little harbour in the gathering dusk where Jonathon, our host, looked relieved to see us. We were twenty minutes late and it was nearly dark.

'I was just about to send for a search party,' he said. We all stood silently for a moment by the road, hypnotised by the powerful rollers, and thankful to be off the cliff.

We were grateful for a quiet evening and a good read . Richard devoured a book about the wreck of the Steamship Mohegan which foundered off the Manacles in 1898 with a loss of 106 passengers and crew. I browsed through a fascinating book on Coverack and didn't dream of the Devil having a 'fry up'.

At Lizard Point, the sun dazzled the lighthouse, the sea creamed and sparkled. For the first time we began shedding clothes. Being a Saturday, we even met a few other people enjoying the landscape and the sunshine. One man, face set to the warm sun, greeted us simply, 'Isn't it wonderful!'

Eating a frugal lunch of limp peanut butter sandwiches above Kynace Cove, we watched a great bank of sea mist rolling in at speed. It looked so like a Renaissance painting, I almost expected mythological figures to follow. We were soon pulling our clothes on again, wrapped in a cold mist and Kynance Cove looked mysteriously beautiful in its white shroud.

I called out to Richard. 'You go ahead. I'm going to take a photo.'

Arty farty photos take a while, and eventually I looked up to see Richard climbing out of the cove and hurried after him. When I reached the top of the cliff he had vanished. 'He might have waited,' I grumbled to myself, and set a cracking pace to catch him up.

Thick walls of mist are disorientating, especially for those whose sense of direction is minimal in good visibility. The path was not clearly demarcated. The sea was an invisble crashing sound somewhere on my left, and there was no sign of my vanguard navigator. Four letter words came to mind. Richard had the maps, names, phone numbers, thermos and even the space blanket. I stopped in my tracks and blew the little whistle my physio colleagues had given me for just such a moment. The feeble sound was lost as the lighthouse fog-horn blared its sonorous message. I seemed to be rooted to the spot for ages, my pulse rising with agitation, when a purple figure loomed out of the mist behind me.

'Where the hell have you been?' We cursed each other simultaneously. Richard had climbed over to a little beach the other side. When I hadn't joined him, he realised that I had gone on ahead.

'I didn't know you could walk so fast,' he said when the anger had cooled on both sides.

'Well, that makes a change,' I said, 'and it's wind-down time.'

A cup of tea restored domestic harmony. By the time we reached the cliffs above Mullion, the sea gods had rolled their mist away. Bereft now of fishing boats, the silent deserted harbour looked sadly empty, watched by the unblinking windows of the large hotel on the cliff on the far side. However, there was nothing sad about the little chestnut Goonhilly ponies that nuzzled us hoping for titbits.

Before we reached Porthleven, we walked across the infamous Loe Bar, a long bank of shingle, which formed when a natural sandbar dammed the River Cober in the 13th century. Many ships have foundered on this bar; a simple stone cross has been erected as a memorial to those who died when the frigate Anson was driven onto the sands in 1807. Over a hundred men lost their lives within a stone's throw of the shore. Among the helpless crowd of bystanders was a Helston man called Henry Trengrouse. He was so shocked by this wreck that he invented the rocket appartaus for throwing a line to a ship, a device which is still used today. The memorial also tells us that Trengrouse was given the scantiest of

financial assistance for this project, and having spent all his own
cash, died in penury. Yet his invention must have saved literally
thousands of lives.

Richard was a speck on the horizen and I hurried across the
sand after him, spurred on by righteous indignation for poor Henry
Trengrouse.

At Rinsey Head we saw our first signs of the copper-mining
industry. The National Trust has restored the engine-house and
chimney of Wheal Prosper as a memorial to Cornwall's mining
days from 1750 to 1870.

The mile-long beach at Praa Sands was a nightmare. 'This is
awful,' I grumbled to Richard. 'The sand's so soft it's like walking
through a ploughed field.'

'We've no alternative. To go inland it would take longer, and
you know how far we still have to go.'

I certainly did, and footslogged silently across the long soft beach.

A little further along lies Prussia Cove, so called because the
famous smuggler John Carter bore a striking resemblance to
Frederick the Great and was nick-named the 'King of Prussia'. The
cove is tiny, and the rocks which form a little natural harbour, are
deeply scored by the wheels of carts used to collect seaweed and
fish. The narrow path down to the cove is cut between high rocks;
it always reminds me of Daphne du Maurier's *Jamaica Inn*. Now
the fishing boats and the 'moonshine brigade' have moved out,
and the grey seals have moved in.

We climbed out and up onto the cliff at Cudden Point. At last
we could see Mounts Bay and St. Michael's Mount, welcoming us
like old friends.

It was nearly dark when we reached a friends holiday bungalow
in Perranuthnoe. Once illuminated, the place was sparkling white,
so clean you could hear the pips squeak.

'We can't take our boots in there,' I said. 'They'd contaminate
the place.' There was no door mat and no paper to lay the offending
items on. On the washing machine lay a phone book which made
an excellent shoe rest.

'Good old Yellow Pages.'

The owners were not in residence, and accustomed to baths,
tea and a big meal, we were a little disconcerted to find no heating,
or hot water.

'Good practice for when we're camping,' Richard said.

We changed our clothes and headed up to the local pub where we had a huge chicken curry and several pints of hard-earned beer. We had the first five hundred miles under our belt, so a celebration was due. The little bungalow was much more hospitable on our return and we crashed out early for there was another tough eighteen miler tomorrow.

We were up and off early, for an easy walk into Penzance, where we saw a sign to St. Just and Land's End.

'We've almost done it,' I said skipping along like a five year old.

In some ways it was hard to believe that we had walked all the way down here. Amongst the feeling of pride and satisfaction, a little voice was telling me that I still had another 3,800 miles to go, but I didn't let that spoil my delight.

As we sat above Newlyn's mediaevel quay, munching hot pasties, we were sad to see how much activity was taking place in the ship-breakers' yard below us. With the advent of continental ships flying 'flags of convenience' and E.C. fishing quotas, the industry is rapidly shrinking.

'Poor Cornwall,' I said. 'First the pilchards disappear, then the mines go bust and now the fishing industry is on its knees. Now they've only got the tourists, and I don't think they're too keen on them.'

As we walked around our coasts, we found the fishing industry a shadow of its former self in many long-established ports.

We climbed up the steep hill to Mousehole or 'Muzzel' as the locals call it. Buzzing with tourists in the summer, the snug little harbour was now deserted. It was hard to believe that it was Cornwall's main fishing port for many years, but lost most of its trade when Newlyn was developed in the 19th century. Apart from its convoluted harbour, set under the steep cliffs, the village can boast of being sacked by troops from three Spanish ships in 1595. 'Muzzel's other claim to fame comes in December each year when Christmas lights cunningly placed all round the harbour and even on some of the boats, make it the Oxford Street of the South West.

From Lamorna Cove the coast path became rocky, steep and muddy but we knew every stone and made good time. Spring arrives early in West Cornwall and jonquils grew along the path on our way down to Penburth, a fishing cove in a pocket between steep cliffs. Here are no concessions to cars, which means it's quiet even in the summer months.

Our destination was St. Levan just above Porthcurno, one of our favourite sandy beaches. Even in the gloom of a Winter's afternoon, the saxe blue sea, pale golden sand and saffron-coloured granite cliffs looked like a Newlyn School watercolour. No wonder Rowena Cade had chosen this spot for her outdoor cliff-top theatre, called The Minnack, opened in 1932 and still going strong.

Lucy and John gave us a hero's welcome. As we soaked our tired limbs in the luxury of their corner bath, big enough to swim in, the mirrors reflected first the bubbles, and then a scraggy creature who might have just emerged from Belson Concentration Camp. I'd never been fat, but now bones stuck out everywhere and I could easily count my ribs. 'Ughh' I thought as I dived under the bubbles, I emerged after a long soak and weighed myself, to find I'd lost over a stone. Richard also weighed himself, and had lost about the same amount, but didn't yet look half starved.

As we rounded Gwennap Head with its disused Coast Guard look-out, we paused. It was a significant moment. Richard's voice showed a trace of emotion.

'There's the Longships Lighthouse in the murk ahead. From now on we stop walking South West and start walking North East'

'Whoopeee!' I cried, and then bought out my little recorder.

'We have reached the big toe of Cornwall, half a mile from Land's End and are about to turn North.'

When I played it back I thought I sounded like a pair of nail scissors.

The old hotel, perched on the Atlantic Ramparts off Land's End, was given a much-needed face lift by Peter de Saveray in the early 1980's. It is now a theme park visited by a million tourists every year. We were due to meet our daughter Katie and the press there at 1 p.m. As we were early, we celebrated in the usual fashion, and then wandered out to find three people waiting for us by the 'pole', *the* Land's End signpost They had been waiting rather a long time. For once, neither Richard or I were clock-watching.

After interviews, food and more drinks, we set off for the last seven miles to our cottage at Cape Cornwall. Katie took our packs. Just outside the main entrance a very smart Land Rover had John O'Groats emblazoned on the side. I began to think my alcohol intake was wishing away the miles.

'Er, Richard,' I said nervously. 'Do you see what I see?'

'The same company owns both Land's End and John O'Groats,' Richard smiled. 'Were you thinking of hitching a lift?'

We set off happily enough, but after a mile or so I was finding it extremely difficult to put one foot in front of the other. They felt like lead. I looked ahead and saw Richard sitting down on a rock, looking like I felt. I crept up to him.

'I'm sure it's not just the beer. It's weird. I've never felt like this before.'

We crawled slowly on. We could have walked the path blindfold as we knew it so well, yet we could hardly make the last few miles. Mentally we had arrived; our minds had, as it were, switched off our physical 'engines'. It was our first taste of the powerful influence of mind over body, a phenomenon we should meet again many times.

When we eventually dragged our unwilling bodies into the cottage, Katie greeted us cheerfully. The fire was lit, the kettle boiling, and there was a delicious smell of toasted tea cakes. Full of tea, with our feet happily propped up, we opened our great pile of mail from family and friends. Congratulations and good wishes tumbled out of the envelopes. We felt we must at least have climbed Everest.

'What's all the fuss about?' I asked Richard. 'We've only completed just over 500 miles.'

Outside the wind whistled and shreiked, and rain lashed the windows intermittently.

'It sounds much worse when you're inside,' Richard replied. 'When you're out in it, you just get on and walk through it. There's no alternative.'

I was opening a parcel from my colleagues at the hospital. 'Shally's Shoe Box' It proudly announced. Out piled shoe laces, foot cream, rucksack-sized shower gels, chocolate teddy bears, plasters, lipsyl, insoles. Last but not least came two scones, reverendly wrapped in white serviettes. Our hospital bakes these giant scones daily, and they are my mid-morning fix. I was overwhelmed. The morale boosting good wishes of our friends and family played a big part in getting us through the low moments of the walk.

We spent five happy days at the cottage in a strange limbo. Richard busied himself giving the cottage some tender loving care. Tools and paintbrushes were soon in action, and B & Q's profits

were going up. I washed our clothes, did running repairs, wrote
letters and relaxed. On February 13th we left our granite haven,
and resumed our progress along the north Cornish coast, a dynamic
and dramatic interface between land and sea.

Chapter Five

Here where the cliffs alone prevail
I stand exultant, neutral, free.
And from the cushion of the gale
Behold a huge consoling sea.
 John Betjeman

Cape Cornwall has been referred to as the 'connoisseurs Land's End'. This rocky headland misses being the furthest point South West by a mere 1,000 yards. The Cape's little hill is crowned by a mining chimney; a reminder that in the 19th century this north coast was covered in tin mines and is still honeycombed with shafts. With 'heritage' the buzz word for Cornwall in general, and this part in particular, much of the coast here is owned and beautifully preserved by the National Trust.

West Penwith is for us the quintessential Cornwall. Rocky carns silhouetted against windy skies, great standing stones casting long shadows across the bare moor. Deeply scored granite cliffs, like tightly tied joints of meat, drop to a churning sea. In this pagan landscape spirits of the past are palpable. The light here has a special translucent quality which has inspired artists and sculptors for over a hundred years. The Newlyn and St. Ives schools of painting are well known, and Barbara Hepworth settled in St. Ives because she felt a real empathy with the area. 'I the sculptor, *am* the landscape.'

As for the Cornish people, like other Celts they are a law unto themselves. The old boys in their berets, who gather like starlings under the clock tower in St. Just, would still consider tourists and incomers to be 'furriners'. Cornish men with their long history of wrecking, smuggling and witchcraft, have a healthy contempt for the law. In 1718 a certain Mr. Edward Giddy wrote the following to an unknown peer of the realm:

I cannot help saying that perfidy, drunkenness, idleness, poverty, contempt of the laws and universal corruption of manners, are in this neighbourhood too prevalent . . .

I wondered if 'yours disgusted' came from Tunbridge Wells.

However, Richard Carew, a century earlier, was impressed with the climate, even if he was disgusted by the strange variations in land and water measures.

Touching the temperature of Cornwall, the air thereof is cleansed, as with bellows, by the billows and flowing and ebbing of the sea, and there through becometh pure and subtle and, by consequence, healthful . . .

We left our cottage after our welcome break, to face the hardest 'Cornish miles' of any yet. The north coast of West Penwith is one of the most desolate stretches of the coast. Boulder-strewn moorland, dark cliffs and rocky headlands. The few remaining engine house of Botallack Mine perch on the cliff edge; their workings ran six hundred yards under a sea that was once the colour of dried blood. Their empty shells have been preserved; and it is hard to believe that a hundred and eighty years ago it was the richest mine in Cornwall.

That evening I noted in my diary:

Coast breathtaking. Botallack mines spot-lit by low sun. The sea and cliffs look best in these winter conditions. Path hilly, stony, wet and muddy. Lost path once. Rugby-tackled by brambles.

'Sorry Richard, of course we didn't *lose* the path. It just disappeared for a mile or so!'

Finally we reached Clodgy Point (Clodgy, the guide tells us, is Cornish for *leper*). From here it is an easy walk into St. Ives. We paused for breath and to admire the view across the dark rocks to the gold sands of Porthmeor Beach, and St. Ives Head with its Coast Guard Look-Out and little chapel. While the living surfers rode the cold waves of this north-facing beach, tombstones scatter the hillside looking watchfully out to sea. Above the beach the inspirational new Tate Gallery is proof that the artistic community here still flourishes.

My aesthetic sense was well satisfied, but my stomach was craving for carbohydrate and I was on the look-out for a bun shop. Richard's thoughts were on more profound matters.

'Here's our friend Smeaton again,' he said. 'He built this stone pier in 1770, which helped St. Ives become Cornwall's biggest pilchard port in the 19th century.'

'Good for him,' I said, 'but I'm starving. There must be lots of shops here selling sticky buns.'

There weren't. St. Ives sleeps in winter, gathering strength for the summer when its little streets bulge with window boxes and humanity, and the air is heavy with the scent of frying oil.

I paused at Porthminster beach on the east side of the town. Here the golden beach was bordered by gardens where palm trees towered over spiky groups of New Zealand flax, and mesanbrethium jostled for ground cover with the fleshy green leaves of the Hottentot Fig. This was a welcome chink of softness, in an otherwise barren and rugged landscape.

Godrevy lighthouse was iridescent in the evening sunshine and a slice of rainbow momentarily pierced a cloud. I thought of Virginia Wolfe's novel 'To the Lighthouse', while trying to make my 'stream of consciousness' take my mind off hunger and fatigue. The setting sun gave a warm afterglow as we walked up the Hayle estuary, past the ancient church of Lelant and so back onto the road.

Our progress through Hayle was leisurely. The estuary was a mass of birds. Disturbed by us, a huge flock of dunlins rose with military precision and criss-crossed the estuary wheeling round in unison, undersides to the light, swerving and veering, rising and falling as one body, flashing the dark bars across their backs in balletic harmony. Though we saw many dunlins on our travels, this was the biggest flock and their aerobatics were a lasting memory.

Towan is Cornish for sand dune. We slid joyfully down the forgiving slopes to reach the huge deserted beach below, leaving a wake of footprints. After miles of having only a bird's eye view of the sea, it now seemed part of us, a turbulent travelling companion on our left. At this point the weather deteriorated. We climbed up to Godrevy Point in strong winds and pouring rain. With my hood drawn in, I am blinkered to the world, and felt vaguely uneasy at one point when I could see lashing waves on two sides of what appeared to be a narrow isthmus. The wind and rain can be very disorientating. I put my head down and best foot forward, thankful that the wind was now behind us, and headed for Hell's Mouth.

'What a perfect name,' I gasped, managing at last to catch up with Richard.

The pointed rocks in the bay look like huge teeth from the mouth of the black cliffs, battered by all the furies of Hell.

'Probably looks benign on a good day,' he said. 'But I think we'd better get out of this hellish wind and take the road into Portreath, it just isn't safe on these cliffs.'

We never like taking to roads, it seems an admission of defeat, but the wind was rising as we spoke. A disgusting porta-loo at the roadside was also hellish, and shuddered so much in the wind, I thought I would be caught flying with my pants down.

Lunch time saw us perched in the decaying bathroom of a derelict house amongst the shattered glass and peeling paper. Sitting on an upturned plastic bucket with a hole in it, I don't think I have ever seen Richard look more miserable.

'At least it's dry and windproof,' I said, brightly, from my perch on the edge of a battered bath.

The only reply was a slate crashing down from the roof.

The rain eased in the afternoon as we walked down into Portreath where we watched huge waves crashing over the sea wall before rejoining the cliff path to Porthtowan. In this weather it was the most dismal stretch of path I remember. Fearsome black cliffs, (all but two flesh-coloured stratas, known as Sally's Bottom) set off a scarred landscape.

'Sally must have been a sturdy wench,' Richard remarked as we climbed the black paths, which criss-crossed the cliffs-tops between blackened heather where the desolate remains of the mining industry, settling beds, smelters, and wired-off shafts could be seen. One of these had a skull and cross bones on it and was smoking quietly. The M.O.D dis-used airfield at Nancekuke added another sinister ingredient to the desolate scene.

'You know that was used for germ warfare until quite recently,' Richard told me gleefully, pointing to the hefty perimeter fence.

'Just tell me how much further,' I snapped. 'It'll be dark soon and I don't fancy a night out here.'

Half-an-hour later we were on a tiny road outside the huge aerodrome gates with 'STOP' all over them and welcoming notices telling us we would be arrested under the Official Secrets Act if we trespassed.

At this bleak moment a car drew up beside us.'

'Are you the walkers?' a friendly voice enquired.

Paul was concerned; it was now nearly dark and he had come out to meet us.

Next day, the sun was working its magic on the cliffs, transforming the dense blackness to reds, saffron, and verdigris, with a hint of sparkling quartz. We passed deep ditches made by the local Council to deter New Age Travellers from settling, and curious wired tent-shaped structures which we learned were to prevent birds and small mammels from getting trapped in the mineshafts. These shafts were the home of thousands of bats, including some rare species, and the wires were spaced to enable the bats to fly in and out.

'So much for the 'Great Chain of Being' theory, where humans were only second to God and the Angels. Now bats ruled OK and the Devil could take the humans especially if they were of no fixed abode,' I thought.

Once above Chapel Porth we hit the wind again. If it wasn't denting our eyeballs, it was certainly denting our buttocks. I was surprised that the Wheal Coates mine was still standing as I raced past. My pace became jet-propelled. I could no longer stay on the tiny path, and let the wind do what it would with me. Like a piece of spume I blew up the side of the hill, well ahead of my more stable companion. My feet felt out of control and I didn't care. It was an elating feeling, like falling off a cliff. 'Crash!' I was in the heather and none the worse.

Richard was nowhere to be seen. The wind propelled me towards a coast guards hut. Behind the sturdy building I was sheltered, and once again took control over my legs. To my amazememnt I saw a uniformed coastguard emerge, smiling. It was one of the few look-outs we passed that was still manned. I dusted myself down and, back on the path, braced myself for the next gust. It didn't come. Richard was calmly waiting.

'What's happened to all that wind?' I asked, feeling as though I had woken up from a dream.

'We've turned south slightly, just enough to give us some shelter.'

Sheltered it certainly was, and the sun felt warm on our faces. A huge sea hurled surf well up the sheer cliff face. We stopped to watch the fulmars billing and cooing. It was, after all, Valentine's Day. I picked a violet and gave it to Richard. In return he told me how to differentiate a fulmar from a gull, explaining that fulmars only have one chick which takes a long time to rear. As we walked round the coast we watched the fulmars rearing their slow-growing chicks, the last of all the seabirds to fly the nest.

'Fulmars have made a remarkable comeback,' Richard informed me as we returned to the path. 'A hundred years ago there were only a handful left in the country, now they're everywhere in large numbers.'

Jericho Valley was filled with ghosts of the past. Ruined engine houses and chimneys, heaps of spoil, settling beds, pit props and the foundations of derelict buildings, bore witness to a once-prosperous mining area. The wooded valley was warm and windless. The only sounds were the birds and a fast-flowing stream that had once powered the Jericho Stamp for the ingots of tin. The pungent smell of gorse filled the air. The silence here contrasted with the wind-driven cliffs. While the fulmars have increased, the miners are now nearly extinct. Standing here a hundred years ago, we should have been among a seething mass of men, women and children deafened by the roar of the engines, the clanging and banging, the shouting and cursing, the air thick with smoke and sweat.

Newquay sprawled wetly across several bays: large hotels, surf shops, amusement arcades, night clubs, damp beaches and big rollers. These rollers and the safe sheltered beaches have made Newquay the surfer's capital of Britain. The anachronistic late 19th century hotels, perched on the draughty cliffs, frown down upon the town where late 20th century youth is catered for and 'Surfing Willie' rules OK!

The rising wind and huge seas had deterred even the bravest of surfers. We paused a moment at the white-washed 14th century Huer's hut which looked more like a chapel than a look-out, perhaps because it had originally been a hermitage. It was the Huer's job to look out for the shoals of pilchards so prevalent in the last century. To celebrate the landing of a shoal, the fisherwomen would bake the 'Heva' cake, a hefty affair intended to fill their menfolk's empty stomachs which was served with a 'dish of tay'. Superstition was rife, and until as late as 1920 the fishermen's wives and daughters were locked indoors to prevent them from seeing the shoal of fish when the seiners went out. It was thought that if the women saw the fish before they were caught, the men would have a season's bad luck.

At Watergate Bay a local popped out of his house to warn us of 75-mile-an-hour gales approaching rapidly. When we reached the cliff top we realised that they had arrived, and we were quite unable to remain upright. We beat an ignominious retreat, finishing the day on a road where even the puddles had white horses.

As we left St. Mawgan, a watery sun shone behind the bare branches of the trees around the 13th century church where rooks 'cawed' soulfully. Back on the cliffs, the wind had moderated, and we had perfect views back to St. Ives, and forward to our destination at Trevose Lighthouse. With springy turf underfoot, we made good time, and I wrote in my diary:-

Found a sheltered spot in the sun! For the first time for weeks we didn't feel cold after ten minutes.

Spring was in the air again. Bedruthan steps, deserted at this time of year, was a dramatic sight. The great dark rocks emerging from the foaming water, were, legend has it, the stepping stones used by the giant Bedruthan. He must have had tough feet, as the rocks were very pointed. Now they are in the capable hands of the National Trust who were busy building a very smart vernacular pathway ready for the tides of heavy-footed tourists.

We had been booked into the Trevose Golf Club at Constantine Bay, a club patronised by Margaret and Dennis Thatcher, which may or may not have boosted the membership. We left our rucksacks in our modest cabin accommodation, and headed off for Trevose Head with its still-manned lighthouse looking magnificent in stormy seas, black clouds and an evening sun. Seals and surfers were out in force in Harlyn Bay (hard to differentiate them), and we completed our circular walk before dusk fell.

Back at our cabin, we luxuriated in privacy. Richard suddenly asked me for a 'marlin spike'. For a moment I thought he had lost his marbles.

'It's not my marbles I've lost, it's my stomach,' he said proudly. 'A corkscrew would do.' I watched mystified as he pulled his belt off and proceeded to make a hole in the leather, at least an inch away from its predecessor. Any trace of a beer belly was now history. He was leaner and fitter. We celebrated with another beer.

'D'you realise,' Richard said, as he drained the glass, 'the two stone I was carrying on my front, you are now carrying on your back. I'm carrying our gross weight loss of three stone on mine.'

'Wow. Makes you think doesn't it,' I said displaying the growing gap between my trousers and diminished waist line. 'I think I need a belt or these are going to fall off.'

We set off in good spirits for Trevose, where the black cliffs were scooped out and indented. It was a perfect place for choughs to breed. These are black birds, not unlike ravens, except that they have distinctive red beaks and legs. Now extinct in Cornwall, they were once so numerous they were engraved on the county emblem.

We turned into the Camel estuary, a broad sweep of sheltered sand now at low tide. Several horses and riders were fording the narrow strip of water, and I envied them for a moment. It was a long walk in to Padstow, and, anxious not to miss the ferry, we didn't have time to explore this little fishing port. Many of the indigenous population here are descended from Spanish immigrants who, in the 16th century, settled and intermarried. Surnames like José are still common today. Murray's 1859 Guide to Devon and Cornwall gives us some idea of what it must have been like in the last century: *This is one of those antiquated unsavoury fishing towns which are viewed most agreeably from a distance.*

As it was low tide we waited at Lower Beach and, feeling rather foolish, waved our hands at the tiny ferry on the other side. At least I waved my arms; I didn't notice Richard's moving at all. Much to our surprise and delight, the little boat responded, and on reaching us, pulled out hen-house type plank. We climbed in gratefully; this trip had saved us a twenty mile detour to Wadebridge. The ferryman turned the boat round, and then seeing some passengers waving from the shore, returned to collect them too.

At Trebetherick, on the Camel estuary, we discovered John Betjeman country. We made time to visit the little church of St. Enodoc which had been dis-interred from the sand dunes in 1863. For this reason it was formerly known as Sinkerninny church. It is here that the immortal bard is buried, while others are Summoned by Bells. The little church has a quirky list on the old spire, and a quirky history. Before it was exhumed from its sandy grave, along with a pre-historic village, the contemporary incumbent had a skylight built so that he could climb into the buried church and hold a service annually in order to retain his stipend.

John Betjeman spent happy holidays in Cornwall as a child, and returned to his 'prevailing cliffs' and 'huge consoling sea' as an old man. Walking the cliff paths in winter storms, Richard and I could empathize better with the poet's emotional response to this wild and rugged landscape.

Chapter Six

Coleridge received the Person from Porlock
And ever after called him a curse,
. . . As the truth is I think he was already stuck
With Kubla Khan.
Stevie Smith

We set off from Lundy Bay heading for Tintagel in overcast
conditions. The coast here is owned by the National Trust and
wild ponies graze the cliffs. What appeared to be a lone church
tower crowned Doyden Point above Portquin Harbour. A 19th
century 'gentleman' called Samuel Symmons bought the headland
in 1827, building this folly which he called Doyden Castle. The
drinking and gambling which went on within those walls was less
than holy. It was a perfect spot for the rake to make all the progress
he wanted.

Portgaverne's deserted harbour would once have been full of
working and fishing boats.

'How did they manage to get them in and out of this narrow
harbour?' I asked Richard.

'By warping out,' he replied having done his homework. 'They
pulled the boats out backwards by using ropes and chains attached
to the rocks. If you look carefully you can see the hooks.'

The steep road on the east side is called the Great Slate Road
(quarried out in 1807 at the expense of the Delabole Slate Company)
and we noticed that the rocks at the side of this narrow lane were
deeply scored from the slate-carts.

'That was how they slowed their descent,' Richard informed me.
My private guide was going well.

After enjoying several days of easy walking we were once more
into switch backs. Clearing skies had brought more wind, and as
we reached Trebarwith Strand we met a youngish couple in jeans
coming down off the top.

'Touch of wind up there,' the man warned.

We smiled and nodded. Not apparently the reaction he had expected.

'Can't say I didn't warn yer!' he shouted to our retreating forms.

It was a bracing but exhilarating walk. Tintagel church was clearly visible and the great slab of Gull Rock looked like a backward-leaning tombstone. The chiselled sculptures of the slate cliffs at Lanterne Quarry were stark silhouettes in the stormy evening light. I remember how long it took to battle along the cliff tops to that 12th century landmark of a church, and how good it was to sit quietly inside this stone and timbered haven. The moans and shreiks of a now muted wind accentuated the calm interior. We sensed some of the prayerfulness of this ancient place, thanksgiving for a safe return. I remembered Robert Louis Stevenson's simple lines in the epitaph he wrote:

'Here he lies where he longed to be
Home is the sailor home from the sea
And the hunter home from the hill.'

Tintagel has been a major tourist attraction since Tennyson linked the village with King Arthur and his knights of the Round Table in *The Idylls of the King*, a work the inhabitants of Tintagel must have blessed him for.

Although it was dusk and we were tired, Richard and I felt compelled to go and have a quick look at the ancient castle ruins, perched on the dark dramatic cliffs above thundering surf, before being swept back for bath and a dinner party.

From Tintagel to Bude was one of the worst days we had on this stretch of coast. We had 21 miles of tough walking, starting at 8 a.m. The hotel on the cliffs, a megalithic brick edifice, has been described as: *An elephantine monument to the directors of the London and South Western Railway,* who were neither slow nor timid about exploiting the Arthurian legend. Too large to be economic, yet too fabulous to destroy, it is the quintessential white elephant.

A damp and deserted Boscastle, must once have offered welcome shelter for boats on this long wild stretch of coast. A large black cat crossed our path, where a notice above the door said 'The Witches of Boscastle selling the wind'. Today it was rain they seemed to be selling. We fortified ourselves with chocolate ready to tackle Cornwall's highest cliff. The hundreds of steps built on the steep sections of cliff path were tailor-made for giants rather than mere mortals. No step is right for one stride, and it was tempting to abandon them. The incessant rain added gloss to the mud, which at times was shin-deep; the drizzle turned to heavy rain. Crackington Haven was memorably awful, with progress slowed by two families with small children who wouldn't let us pass. The cliffs of Pencannow Point rose to 400 feet and felt like it. At Widemouth Bay Richard took to the tarmac. It was nearly five o'clock and we were due to rendez-vous with friends at 6 p.m.

The good news was that we arrived just as the clock was striking 6.p.m. The bad news was that we couldn't find our hosts. The huge car park was virtually deserted. It was dark and wet, and we were tired and cold. I rang our contacts. There was no reply. Ever a survivor, I walked brazenly into the nearest pub, which appeared to be shut, and changed my clothes on their commodious doormat. I then heard the rustle of a newspaper from behind the bar, and a sandy-whiskered publican noticed me shivering on the mat. I was invited to sit by his fire. Feeling like Jemima puddleduck, I perched uneasily on small stool while Richard searched for our hosts. They had expected us to come down at the end of the coast path, and were anxiously waiting for us there.

Our hosts lived a good twenty minutes drive away and their car was cold. Richard was soaked to the skin. Conversation between chattering teeth became a problem. We staved off hypothermia with thoughts of a warm house and hot baths. At that moment our hostess was telling us how much she disliked over-heated houses. Their house was large and our bedroom very cold. The heating was then turned on for our benefit, and we soon warmed up in a very deep, very hot bath. A large wholesome meal washed down with beer, soon revived all the parts. Had we been stranded out on the cliffs that night, we should certainly have been in a state of hypothermic exhaustion.

Jill is a 'home-made' friend. Energetic in her early sixties, with long hair loosely swept back from her face, ethnic clothes, and leather mules which she designs and sells herself. She makes butter, cheese, yoghurt, cream, and grows her own vegetables.

Eric, now in his seventies, retains a wicked sense of humour. A farmer all his life, he recalled:

'I was the youngest of five children. I had to plough the land at only fourteen. My father never recovered from shell shock in the First World War. All of us kids had to work from an early age.'

His eyes were full of memories as he had a modest gulp of beer.

'We hadn't got a tractor then, and used horses. I remember the biting cold and the fatigue. The horses were changed at midday, but we went on until the job was done, with not even a lunch break.'

They were up early next morning to get us to Bude by 8 a.m. and then Jill insisted on taking our rucksacks to Clovelly. We didn't protest too loudly as we had another 22 mile day. For Jill it was a thirty mile round trip.

I wrote in my diary:

Set off in fresh wind with rough seas. Soon started climbing in earnest, at least ten big dippers (equivalent to Ben Nevis as each cliff was about five hundred feet high). Good views back to Pentire Head and Tintagel. Ahead, Hartland Point Lighthouse and Lundy very clear. Bright sunshine between the clouds brought out the colours in the cliffs. We felt elated with all this beauty, space and light to ourselves.

The dramatic landscape, in these conditions, proved the perfect antidote to fatigue. We felt sorry for anyone who was shut inside four walls and couldn't share this with us.

We passed the 'Hawker's Hut' and learned something of The Rev. Robert Stephen Hawker, the eccentric vicar of Morwenstow from 1834-75. A writer and poet of some note, he built this little hut of driftwood, and, wearing his cassock over a fisherman's jersey, he would write and meditate here, sometimes smoking an opium pipe. Tired of the superstitions still held by his parishioners, he once dressed as a mermaid and seated himself on a rock by the seashore. This bought the curious villagers out in force. He eventually revealed himself by standing up and singing the National Anthem! As if all this wasn't enough, it was Hawker who instigated the ever-popular Harvest Festival Service.

'I wish he was still here,' I said, as we paused to catch our breath in his little hut. 'I could do with a puff of opium to get me up these hills.' Clambering up these steep slopes, lungs and legs seemed to be in competition to see which would give out first.

We lunched sheltering among the spiky rocks of Welcoombe Mouth, sitting on the huge grey boulders and enjoying sun without wind. Behind us was a great cave, where a couple of pre-historic figures were enjoying a cooked lunch over a camp fire.

We walked endlessly up and down the 'big dippers', cliffs that plunged down into dark steep sided valleys or coombes. From the cliff-tops, the black corrugated rocks below looked like basking crocodiles. Time was getting on. Richard had the bit between his teeth. Keeping him well in sight, I thought I was doing well considering it was after 3 p.m.

'The book says it's only eleven and a half miles from Bude to Hartland. If that's correct we have only been walking at one and a half miles an hour. If we're not to be very late, we shall have to take the road from Hartland Quay.'

The going had been steep, but easy underfoot, and we had no packs.

'The guide is obviously wrong. The guy who wrote it must be Cornish, they're not English miles,' I soothed.

Reluctantly we joined the road at Hartland Quay. Then a bus drew up beside me.

I felt the Devil leering over my left shoulder.

'I wouldn't take a bus if you paid me,' I said to myself.

As we tramped along the road to Clovelly, I recorded into my tape how I felt at the end of the day -

I feel as if the whole of the lower half of my body has gone into automatic pilot, my legs don't want to, my feet don't want to, but they seem to go forward anyway, which is just as well.

I don't think I've felt this tired since we came into Torquay, but I forget that I have walked 22 miles and climbed vertical heights that would equal a stroll up Ben Nevis.'

Clovelly had to be bypassed. There is now a huge car park and a small aircraft hanger which everybody has to walk through and pay for the privilege of seeing this 'enchanting little village'. We explained that we were on foot, pointing to our packs.

'No. You have to pay. Everybody has to pay.' The lady at the turnstile was adamant.

We tried again. 'We're on a charity walk round the coast. Today we are going to Appledore. We do not want to see your village.' (Untrue).

Eventually she let us through if we promised Brownie's Honour we would just go along The Hobby Drive. She watched us carefully to make sure we kept our promise.

'That sort of thing makes me so cross. Whose pockets are lined anyway? Not the villagers' I'm sure,' Richard growled.

The three mile Hobby road ran through some beautiful woods and had been built by Sir James Hamlyn Williams to ameliorate local unemployment after the Napoleonic wars. Approaching Westward Ho! Richard, feeling warm from our best-feet-forward-pace, removed his over-trousers. This was a cue for the heavens to open. Richard decided it was a short sharp shower, but it was a deluge. His trousers squelched and stuck to his legs.

Westward Ho! was not the romantic place we had imagined. Charles Kingsley would have turned in his grave to see the caravan parks, holiday chalets, tacky shops and cheerless windblown, litter-strewn streets. Soaked to the skin, cold and very weary, our opinions about anything would have been biased at that moment.

We arrived at The Old Custom House, oozing fatigue and pouring water. We had been warned by our previous hosts that this was no ordinary household. Steve kept two women. Steve was not in, but Sylvia welcomed us to one of the most extraordinary homes we had ever seen.

We peeled off our outer garments in an attractive jasmine-scented conservatory, and were then shown the geography of the house. To reach the bathroom we went through a small anteroom complete with double bed. No bath, but a huge shower cubicle with three shower heads, which we were invited to use. The house was full of artefacts. Dolls, soft toys and teddy bears were lovingly piled into armchairs and onto sofas. Three large stuffed mice stood guard on the stairs holding batons. The walls and shelves were littered in interesting ethnic artefacts from Peruvian dolls to Guatemalan primitive statues, tribal regalia and penis sheaths. We learned that Steve, Janet and Sylvia travelled to some of the most primitive places in the world, and lived like the natives. They certainly had some stories to tell.

The four hundred year old house had been sympathetically converted. Downstairs a huge fire roared in the grate and the brass glittered on the hearth. A large simple mirror reflected the old wood and stone in the room, the chintz furnishings invited repose. After a drink, Richard and Steve went off to a Rotary Meeting, and I had a delicious supper with the girls by the fire. Afterwards they were happy for me to go into the upper room with its large observation window looking out to sea. I wanted to write my diary, but it was difficult to concentrate with the wind screaming round the house, and so many strange and interesting things to look at.

I wondered about this 'ménage à trois'. Ethnic-looking Janet was the quiet shy one and spoke in short stuccato sentences. Sylvia was round, blonde, cheerful and flirtacious. Both were in their late fifties or early sixties, understanding and hospitable.

I admired them for their exciting adventure holidays, carrying 40 lb backpacks and hiding their money in 'blood-stained' bandages round their legs. They always took a supply of cheap costume jewellery to give away if the going got tough. Steve had been held up at gun-point on a bus in Guatamala only last summer. He was a good-looking, weather-beaten man, very entertaining, and his girls obviously adored him. They were not afraid to be different, in what was historically a very provincial place. But then Appledore itself is something of a time warp. It has been alleged by Bideford folk that Appledore is 'the place they eat missionaries'.

'I thought Devon was a genteel place,' I said to Richard as we wandered through the brightly painted Georgian Streets of Appledore.

Bideford's tree-lined 17th century quay had several coasters moored there, giving the port some life, though this is a far cry from its hey day when it was one of the busiest ports in England with ships trading as far afield as North America. We crossed the old bridge with its twenty four arches which 'have spanned the Torridge since the Middle Ages'. It now glares at its contemporary counterpart further downstream. This thirty three metre high road bridge was opened in 1989 as an extension of the A39 to 'open up the West Country' for the devouring tourist.

'No wonder the Samaritans have got a plaque up. It's a good place to end it all if you felt in the mood,' I muttered darkly. Richard and I were having disagreements about the recordings I was making. He didn't like me recording anything he felt might not be strictly accurate; mid-flow I would be corrected.

'OK. You do it then,' I said, handing him the little black box. Richard shook his head and refused. Thereafter I made sure I was out of earshot before I recorded anything, or left the recorder running when Richard was saying something interesting.

The railway stopped at Instow, and goods were then sent by ship to Appledore across the estuary. Railway enthusiasts had restored the pristine signal box. Steve told us how the Lady of the Manor in Appledore used to order her grouse from the station master at Instow. He would then ensure they were delivered to her door, from the grouse moors, the very next day. Deferential 19th century Datapost was extremely efficient if you had blue blood.

'We're due to meet Fred, the Braunton Rotary Club president at Chivenor R.A.F. base at midday,' Richard warned me. 'We don't want to be late.'

This Rotary Club was looking after us in style at the elegant Saunton Sands Hotel. We had been warned, and had our glad rags sent from home for this occasion.

Fred was an easy-going retired bank manager.

'Er . . . um. Shall I lead the way?' He asked rather nervously.

'Please, go ahead, you're the local man'. Richard was happy to be led for a change.

Fred's orienteering skills were on a par with mine. Instead of taking the coastal path along the Braunton Burrows Nature Reserve, we found ourselves admiring roadworks on the outskirts of Braunton, and then in some rather bleak sand dunes with no sign of the sea. Fred got us to the hotel by the unscenic route.

The Braunton Club had laid on a Ladies Evening for us. Having arrived at mid-afternoon, we had time to make use of the hotel swimming pool and jacuzzi, and really dress for dinner in our sumptous quarters. The only problem was that Jo had packed my posh frock, and forgotten my posh shoes.

'I'll just have to wear my 'designer' Reebock sandals. Then I can tell the manufacturers they are as good on deep pile carpets as they are on the foothills of the Himalayas.'

'Really trendy. You look as though your recovering from a bunion operation,' was all the encouragement I could hope for.

We ate a delicious meal in a private room with about twenty Rotarians and their wives. The men were very friendly, greeting us enthusiastically, while their 'insignificant others' seemed to melt away. We were not introduced to a single wife, and in the bar after the meal things got worse. The men, grumbling at the high price of the beer, nevertheless consumed plenty. The question in debate was our route to Ilfracombe next day. Maps were produced, opinions were aired, voices rose.

'It's a long walk' said one. 'You'll have to leave out Baggy Point.'

'No. You could do that, but you can't go that way. Try this.' Stubby fingers hit the map firmly.

'I've walked it and that's not what I would recommend.' This 'walker' pulled the map from the others' grasp and clutched it possessively. Meanwhile the wives, clutching car keys and sipping orange juice, were having a quiet gossip on their own in a corner of the room.

It was the sun's turn to shine today and we had a memorable walk, eschewing Baggy Point and taking the cliff path to Croyde and Woolacombe. The Welsh dragon was quietly smoking along the coast of industrial South Wales. Lundy was an added attraction since Steve had told us the spicy story of the 'lusty landlady of Lundy' who was purported to have seduced the few men on the island, reeking parochial havoc in the process.

The guide book had warned us of steep gradients, some of 600 feet. This walk was 'not for the faint-hearted'. Yet the going underfoot was easy, the sun transformed the cliffs into sparkling quartz and we revelled in our new-found fitness. We reached Ilfracombe by mid-afternoon and regretted listening to local knowledge and missing Baggy Point.

In our modest B & B that evening Richard made an announcement.

'In another three days we shall have reached the end of the South West Coast Path. It will have taken us forty-two days.'

'How far is it, end to end?' I asked.

'Five-hundred-and-ninety-four-miles without counting the towns or the vertical height.'

'You mean 594 Cornish miles,' I replied.

'Nine-hundred-and-fifty-six kilometres if you prefer.'

'Mmm. Sounds impressive. I don't know whether I shall be glad or sorry to leave it.'

Ilfracoombe looks like a toy town from the view point at Helesborough. It nestles round its harbour and the houses play sardines as they cling to the steep hills. St. Nicholas' chapel sits on a little hill high above the town and has been a guiding light for sailors for centuries. Ahead we could see the mouth of the Severn estuary which meant Bristol wasn't too far. We were soon climbing up the notorious Great and Lesser Hangman, (maximum height 1034 feet above sea level) scrambling down the precipitous slopes of the Heddon Valley, and on to Woody Bay.

Although high, the cliffs along this stretch were softer than their Cornish counterparts, and the paths easier. We had panoramic views along the coast which now met the rolling hills of Exmoor. The guide gently points out that: 'A few roads wriggle seawards down deep, wooded coombes, but the best of the scenery is reserved for walkers.'

Lynton has a supercilious feel. Its large Victorian buildings look down on Lynmouth in the valley below. Lynmouth still seems to be in mourning for the victims of the 1952 flood disaster. The only sounds were the roar of the river as it hurtled down the hill and the crash of waves against the harbour wall. The rebuilt little street was like a stage set without actors. Closed notices everywhere were cheerless welcome for the tired walker. The place was pulseless. The restaurant-cum-B&B where we were supposed to be staying had a window-full of stacked chairs, and a closed sign hung limply on a piece of string.

'Let's try the back,' Richard suggested.

Reluctantly my feet followed. The doorbell was answered and we were expected.

'Come on in,' said Dave. We followed him up some creaky threadbare stairs to a simple family room. 'Bathroom next door. I'll bring breakfast to your room. If you want anything,' he pointed to a firmly closed door, 'that's where we are.'

It was as if we had woken him from hibernation. Nothing would have induced us to knock on the closed door.

'At least there'd be no singing for our supper tonight.' Richard sounded as relieved as I felt.

My feet were in militant mood and took me to the pub under suffrance. The place was cold and cheerless. The landlord looked as though his face would crack if he smiled. The seating was sparse and uncomfortable. A young woman sat by herself in a corner reading a book. We ate some indifferent food perched uncomfortably on dralon stools, and left. Our bodies craved to be supine.

It was good to leave the dank valley and climb Countisbury Hill. I had to admire the sheer muscle power of the lifeboat crew from Lynmouth, who, in 1899, unable to launch their boat due to huge seas, dragged it up this very hill to help a two-masted brigantine in distress in Porlock Bay. It was hard enough to drag myself up with a heavy pack on a good road, but on a poor road in the teeth of the gale - stuff that legends are made of.

Peering down through the trees at the tiny 13th century Culbone church, was like squinting through a keyhole into the past. The little clearing was a real Saxon 'den'. The cottages, farmhouses, and charcoal burners have drifted away like smoke. The thick woods, which once sheltered a leper colony, now only shelter the red deer. An empty silent stage but one on which passions had once run high. We learned that in 1280, Thomas, chaplain of Culbone was indicted *'for that he had struck Albert of Esshe (ash) on the head with a hatchet, and so killed him'*.

The Victorians left more than their footprints behind along this stretch. Not only their buildings, but also their plants and their poetry. Their buildings have stood the test of time; their floral legacy, in the shape of the Ponticum rhododendrons, has run amok. It is now a weed which threatens to poison all competition on the cliffs. Their poetry also endures. Exmoor's wild landscape was considered a suitable place for 18th and 19th century romantic poets like Coleridge, Byron and Wordsworth to seek inspiration. Coleridge might have been annoyed that his *Kubla Khan* was interrupted, but the 'Person from Porlock' has his own mythology, recreated by Stevie Smith. Coleridge was stuck with his poem, and the Person from Porlock, a mere scapegoat.

Meanwhile the contemporary persons from Porlock shelter smugly under their wooded hill. Neatly rowed in stone, brick and thatch, tasteful shopfronts sell trug baskets, green wellies and walking boots. The village is after all only a hill's fold away from flatter lands, and ever-encroaching swards of tarmac.

As we climbed Bossington Hill, first or last bastion of the South West Coast Path, Wales was both visible and audible. There is a Celtic flavour to the names along the Bristol channel, valleys are combes and pronounced like the Welsh 'cwm'. 'Mynedd' is a hill in Welsh. Wales was calling.

Minehead is the end of the South West Coast Path, or the beginning if you go the 'right' way round. Gleefully we hugged the pole which announces 'Footpath to Poole (Dorset) 500 miles', and posed for a photo. Two of the community nurses who had cared for my mother, had joined us for the day. They were happy to snap our moment of triumph.

Vast acres of pebbly sand stretched away into a flat distance. Plate-glass windows filled with last season's tourist tack, gaudy soft toys, smudgy rock, buckets and spades, plastic bric-a-brac. Then there was Butlin's Holiday Camp, hardly the 'stately pleasure-dome' decreed by Kubla Khan. 'More of a deserted prison camp,' I thought.

Our Rotarian hosts told us some of the downside of this pleasure dome.

'They're always having trouble down there with drugs and hooliganism. It's a focus of infection for all the undesirables. Terrible place, but it brings employment. They're even trying to open it in the low season. Conventions, evangelical gatherings, sex weekends, you name it,' he explained. 'Sex weekends are very popular,' he added darkly.

The best thing about Blue Anchor was Vic. We called in at his signal box to ask if there was anywhere we could have a cuppa.

Vic, resplendant in blue serge donkey jacket with orange shoulder-protectors and dirty jeans was playing signalman on the privately owned West Somerset Railway.

'Next train May 4th, 2 p.m. And the caf's closed.' His round face shone under the serge beret and his eyes twinkled behind dark-rimmed glasses.

It was sleeting and we were wet and cold. Vic was more than happy to have an audience. His lovingly restored signal box was warm and dry. Mugs of tea were soon brewed and we were having his life history.

'I've been on the railways all me life, like me Dad and Grandad. Now I'm retired but I've still got this.' His eyes swept the brightly painted levers, polished brass handles of heavy wooden boxes behind which lurked mysterious dials. There was a strong smell of stale smoke, oil, stewed tea and newspapers.

'Don't approve of all this privatisation,' Vic grumbled cheerfully. It'll never work. Everyone's too greedy. If I can manage on my pension of £7,200 to have a bungalow, two motorbikes, one car, and five holidays a year, no-one should grumble.'

I was just thinking of putting him up for Chancellor of the Exchequer, when he divulged that he lived with his parents, and had no family of his own.

The station was an Adelstrop, carefully crafted to produce nostalgia: the bold black and white signs BLUE ANCHOR and LADIES. The Waiting Room, with its dirty little cosy stove and peeling seats; the milk churns; the school trunks. I was back on the steam train to Swanage in the 1950's, in my ever-shortening Harris Tweed skirt, brown blazor and itchy lyle stockings. Brown felt hat squeezed into a smutty hand, I would lean out of the little window with the wind rushing past my face, all damp earth and bird song. My last whiff of freedom abruptly enveloped in clouds of yellow smoke and smuts.

I looked at Richard. His eyes were still dreamy with memories. It was my turn to clock-watch.

'Goodbye to all that,' I said, shaking his shoulder gently. 'We'd better not be late!'

March came in like a lion, and a powdering of snow lay on the hills and we headed off for Watchet, East Quantox Head and Highbridge. For the first time for weeks we were back on roads, which neither of us welcomed. In Watchett there was no sign of the Ancient Mariner or the albatross to entertain us. The rolling hills let us down gradually to the flat lands of the Somerset levels. With no bridge across the Parrett estuary, Richard decided that we should walk to Nether Stowey and cover the dreary miles to Bridgewater and Highbridge on a bus. A good dose of sleet and snow made this decision easier.

Shivering by the bus stop in Nether Stowey, we found ourselves outside the house where Coleridge stayed from 1787 to 1800. Closed of course. A young man with gently curling dark hair and steel-rimmed glasses joined us on the bus.

'I am ah French stoodent from Paris, on a sahnweech year from Bristol Universitay.'

'I study your romantic poets. Zey are forrmeedable. Sad zat Coleridge's 'ouse ees closed today.'

His blue eyes shone. He enthused about our poetry, our countryside and our walk while the empty old bus splashed noisily through the tarmac.

'Vive la France!' I thought.

Bridgewater bus terminal looked like the end of the world. A sprawl of brick, tarmac and concrete, dotted about with draughty shelters, soft-focused in the freezing rain. An uncoated schoolgirl waited with us for the bus to Highbridge, bare legs blue to her ankle socks, bored face red and dripping.

We were early. Unaccumstomed to bus miles, we had an hour or so to spare before our Rotary contact expected us. Highbridge was inhospitable and bitterly cold.

'Sorry luv, we're closing,' was all we could get out of the only café along the dismal street.

'Any ideas?' I looked at Richard's frozen face and decided there weren't.

'Come on. We'll just have to a long slow shop. At least it will be warm and dry.' Norman's warehouse became a haven for an hour.

I described Highbridge in my diary as '*A town without a past, without a present and without a future*'. It merges into Burnham-on-Sea whose Victorian front looked pleasantly well cared for in the bright cold sunshine. Hinckley Point, our first nuclear power station, loomed across the bay, steely grey and rather menacing. The wide expanse of sand stretched all the way to Weston-super-Mare. Rivulets of blue water ribboned into the distance. It was good to be outside on these lone and level sands.

Grinning, Richard stopped under a sign which read 'Speed limit 15 m.p.h.'

'Read, mark, learn and inwardly digest,' I laughed, pulling out the camera.

A lone man passed us exercising his dog. Glancing at our packs he said simply,

'Lucky you!' We were.

It was strange to be walking on the flat after all the ups and downs. A dramatic black sky and brilliant sunshine lit the Bristol Channel bringing the snow-covered Welsh coast and the islands of Flatholm and Steepholm into sharp focus. A two hour detour, to cross the River Axe, took us through the green flats of the Somerset levels where we saw four 'mad March hares' only yards away, quite oblivious of our presence. They were cavorting in the sun, a strange ritual which looked as if Mohammed Ali was sparring with Carmen.

'Lewis Carrol's mad hatter had nothing on this,' I murmured quietly as Richard passed me the binoculars. Further on a pair of wild swans flew low overhead, honking mournfully. There was a welcome, but strange, absence of wind.

The following day rivers again kept us inland, this time squelching through boggy fields and crossing the M5 twice. Our hate level for roads and cars was rising. Weston-Super-Mare at least had a pier to commend it, but Clevedon had nothing. We sat in a cold park behind the sea wall among the swings and roundabouts, toy trains and bouncy castles. The last few miles into Portishead were on a real coast path again and immediately easier than the level tarmac.

I had begun using my tapes and radio, to take my mind off aches and pains and Richard's retreating form. The only snag was that my earplugs fell out a frequent intervals. Obviously got the wrong shaped ears I thought dismally. Oh well, not one but three whole rest days were coming up I told myself. Come on feet, you're in for a treat!

I can't remember exactly when this habit of talking to myself started. But when things were not going too well I would bring out my alter ego. A very sensible person who knew all the answers. Calm, realistically optimistic and one who believed in me totally. This inner travelling companion was to be a great help later in the walk.

Our bodies revelled in the rest which Richard's sister gave them. She met us in Portishead with flasks of tea and hot water bottles.

We felt as though we had just been rescued from the north face of the Eiger and continued to enjoy being spoiled. We just ate and slept for three days. When we set off again on March 8th, it was with reluctance that our bodies propelled us over the Bristol Channel on the Severn Bridge.

Chapter Seven

It is spring, moonless night in the small town, starless
and bible-black, the cobblestones silent . . .
down to the sloeblack, slow, black, crowblack
fishing boat-bobbing sea.
Dylan Thomas

Long road bridges are so much the domain of the car that people were surprised we had been able to cross them on foot. The Severn bridge had a side track for service vehicles and pedestrians, and our forty-five minute crossing was a vibrating experience. Never having taken the slightest notice of bridges before, I was suddenly aware of the magnitude of them, their delicate strength, the height and precision of the stays, and the huge span which shook like an aspen leaf each time a car raced passed. We crept across like tiny terrestial insects hovering above the vast expanse of air and muddy brown water.

The New Severn bridge, due for completion in 1996, looked like unfinished lego. Once more on terra firma and across the River Wye, we were welcomed to our second foreign land. 'Croeso in Cymru'. From now on every signpost was in Welsh and English and we really were foreigners. Welsh is a beautiful language to listen to but more incomprehensible than many European tongues. We spent many happy hours walking along attempting to pronounce the string of consonants before our eyes, but all the gargling, glotallizing, spitting and tongue clicking, only bought on a thirst. Perhaps this foreign tongue is all part of the charm of a land which is so steeped in mists, myths and legends.

Our Welsh 'Croeso' wasn't all that kind. As we approached the new bridge we were told we couldn't continue along the estuary without hard hats as it was now a construction site.

'Fine'll cost ya £500.' The security guard wagged a warning finger at us. 'If ya try and go through motorway construction site, same rules apply.' We had a dreary three mile detour before we were back on the dyke path.

Barry, a Rotarian photographer, was a mine of local knowledge.

'This area,' he said waving a hand across the flat green landscape, 'was seething with Romans 2,000 years ago. They've dug up remains everywhere. Caerleon was as important as Chester and the name means "Fort of the Legion".'

He produced another lense from his commodious pack, and focused on us.

'Hold hands and look happy! That's great. I've got the new Severn bridge in the background. Just what I wanted.' He shook hands with us, and watched our retreating forms marching as briskly as any Roman citizens, towards the sea wall and Newport.

Turning inland again we plodded on towards the belching chimneys of Llanwern steelworks and Newport's urban sprawl. Sitting wearily on a culvert for some tea, we were diverted by a cheerful farmer in green barbour and wellies, chewing his pipe like a cow chews the cud.

'Did you know the land hereabouts is between four and six metres below sea level?' he said proudly. 'Very prone to floods.'

'We had noticed that the old church at Redwick had a floodmark at 20 feet dated 1666,' Richard replied.

'My family's been farming round here all me life.' The pipe shifted easily to the other side of his mouth while his arm described a great arc showing how much land he and his brothers and cousins owned.

'We're known locally as the Mafia, only in Wales that's the Tafia.' He grinned and pushed his cloth cap further back on his head.

'He seems happy enough,' I said as we set off for Newport in an early dusk. 'But I couldn't live six metres below sea level however much land I owned.'

We plodded on into the big city with only a cursory glance at the famous transporter bridge (one of only two left in the country). It was after 6.p.m., we had walked twenty one miles. Richard was in the fast lane, and in the bewildering outskirts of this deary city, I had a job to keep him in sight. At each crossing I prayed the lights would be red, or that a stream of traffic wouldn't block my view of his flapping trousers and large purple pack. We tried the very first B & B we came to. The door was opened by a petite blonde lady of uncertain age with peroxided hair swinging jauntily in a pony tail. What she lacked in stature she made up for in personality.

'Allo Sveethartz! Don't stand zare, kom in please. Kom, kom!'

Her thick German accent was overlaid with a thin veneer of Welsh.

'I ave just ze family room left.' She glanced at our feet.

'Please leave ze muddy boats in ze hall. Kom. I show you ze room.'

It was a fair sized room with one double and two single beds. The white wrought iron bed ends were full of curly-cews, the pink patchwork bed sets flounced everywhere, and the pillows were carefully angled. Red velvet curtains were drawn behind the double bed which had pride of place in front of the large bay window. A hairy pink blancmange rug was laid to rest at a jaunty angle. The room smelt of thinly disguised smoke. I wouldn't have been surprised to see a stuffed mouse with a lace mob-cap sitting up in the bed.

'How much is it?' I asked.

'£32.00 sveethart. You see zar is a power shower and zatellite T.V. Ze teasmaid, I show how it vorks.'

I explained that we were on a charity walk and couldn't afford £32.00.'

'You are choking!' she replied. 'Earlier I turn a lady away. She said she had left her uzband and ze man wiz her waz her son.' She glanced at Richard. 'I don't want trouble.'

I grabbed Richard's arm and introduced him formerly as my husband.

Her face became wreathed in smiles and the room was ours for a mere £30.00.

'Call me Rita,' she said, looking at Richard.

Two balding grey towels were reluctantly produced and Rita told us not to eat chips in the room.

'Breakfast at 8.00 sharp sveetharts. Don't be late!'

'That bed looks as though it means business,' Richard said. Sadly we were too tired.

We were just on time for breakfast. Two lodgers had already eaten and one further place was laid. The last guest appeared at five minutes past eight.

'Gud afternoon sveethart,' she said sarcastically. The travelling salesman in question shuffled his feet apologetically and sat down silently.

'You must have ze English breakfast. Egg, bacon, tomato, fried bread, sausage, beans, black pudding,' Rita said firmly. 'I cook very good.'

Having learned that my stomach doesn't perform too well on a Rita-type breakfast I left two sausages.

Rita was mortified. This was a personal insult. First I beat her down in the price of her room, and now I dared to leave her food.

'You eet zem,' she ordered, her pony tail swinging angrily from side to side.

There was no alternative. As I ate, I remembered the peel in bread-and-butter pudds at school which I would leave in a pile on the side of my plate. The same order had come then, and I had been just as compliant.

'That's my girl,' Richard smirked, enjoying my ignominy hugely.

Newport's decay depressed us. The great brown river Usk is all set about with death and decay. The demise of the coal industry had left a trail of derelect buildings and industrial detritus, gaping litter-filled spaces, and rotting cars. The transporter bridge was, we were relieved to see, being given a reprieve thanks to E.E.C. funds.

It was a relief to shake the dust of Newport off our feet along another stretch of sea-wall.

The islands of Flatholm and Westholm sat hazily in the Bristol Channel, and we could just make out Weston-Super-Mare and the South West Coast Path. Looking at them now from the other side, we felt we had achieved something.

'Come on,' Richard encouraged. 'Cardiff next stop.' And he set off resolutely across the flat green patchwork of wetlands dotted with churches which lay between us and Cardiff.

Our approach to the city was via a huge land-fill site. We found ourselves on a muddy path hemmed in between a high wired fence and a mass of brambles. The mud was like potter's clay before it is baked. Both brambles and clay left their mark. We shambled in to Cardiff station where we were greeted by daughters, boyfriends and cousins. A lightening tour of city, squeezed into a tiny mini, enabled us to see a few of the sights in general and number 19, Cressy Road, Roath Park, in particular.

Auntie Gladys, Richard's godmother, was one of this world's saints. A devout Christian, she shared an unpretentious Victorian terraced house in Cressy Road with her sister. Both ladies were spinsters of the parish. Defying the laws of nature, Gladys had survived both diabetes and T.B. spine long before these diseases were curable. Years of immobility had turned her body into a question mark. Undaunted she remained an active member of her church and an active godparent. Every birthday and Christmas Auntie Gladys' parcel would arrive. Recycled gifts from the church sale, lovingly wrapped in recycled paper serviettes and placed in a much-used brown envelope that Friends of the Earth would have been proud of. Deep inside would be a letter on faded paper, full of caring and cheer with never a moan.

One Advent service at her local church, Auntie Gladys was processing, candle in hand, down the aisle in her best jumble sale hat piled high with net trim. As her spirit soared ever-upwards to the heavens, her head bowed ever-downwards to her guiding light on earth. Best hat and candle met, and theirs was an holy combustion. Needless to say Auntie Gladys survived this trial by fire unscathed. But the incident must have done much to enhance her saintly reputation.

A wet Welsh mist wrapped round us as we left Penarth, where buckets and spades and parks and gardens have replaced cranes and trains that once transported the coal from the Welsh valleys. Disembodied jets roared and screeched through the low cloud at Cardiff airport, and one coal-laded train roared, puffed and clunked its way through a damp and dirty cutting, like a Welsh dragon in flight.

When we reached the Thomas' home near Aberthaw we felt we were really in Wales. Both Elgeva and Alan were Welsh. Elgeva (soft g) told us proudly that she had been named after King Canute's Saxon wife. I don't know whether his Saxon wife was a good mimic and raconteur, but this Elgeva certainly was. The local churchyard at St. Hilary's was, we were told, filled with Thomas' tombstones. We listened spellbound to her amusing stories of an eccentric American called Cloyd, who collected oriental rugs and exotic candlestands and baked his own bread before breakfast. Her accent moved easily from American to Welsh. Alan, a quiet and dignified ex-District Govenor of Rotary, told us of his wartime voyage to the States in the Queen Mary. His travelling companions were a bunch of German P.O.W's, Churchill, Beveridge and members of the War Cabinet. Such diversions were the perfect antedote to our dreary walk through the decaying industrial ports of South Wales.

Porthcawl welcomed us in full regalia. Chains of office, cream tea and the 'honeymoon' suite at the Atlantic Hotel. Time had slipped pleasantly passed at midday as we sampled some local brew with Katie and her boyfriend at a pub near Ogmoor. We rang to let our Rotarian host know we should be late.

'Six p.m. is rather late for tea,' I worried as we walked along the front at Porthcawl.

It was, and we were swept straight in without a moment to wash our hands or collect our thoughts. Our discomfort was soon forgotton with the warmth of our reception. Tea was followed by speeches. Richard's thanks were so profound there was hardly a dry eye in the house. He was able to tell them that not only were they giving him a cream tea on his birthday, but that I was born in Porthcawl, which somehow makes me Welsh.

The ladies clustered round chattering like Welsh sparrows, while our bodies yearned for their daily soak.

We slept soundly in the great brass four-poster bed, and were woken by a perfect sunrise over the sea. I made tea, handed Richard a cup which he rested on a heart-shaped cushion on his bare chest.

'Smile.' I snapped the moment. It was a good start to the day.

On our walk to Pyle in brilliant Spring sunshine we passed the ancient town of Kenfig.

'That was a thriving community 800 years ago,' Richard informed me. 'Now, all that's left of the mediaeval settlement is a ruined castle.' In the distance we saw the high-rise buildings and smoky chimneys of Port Talbot, which looked like the Coketown of Dicken's *Hard Times*.

The evidence of the rise and fall of villages, towns and cities was a recurring theme as we progressed round the coast. The latter part of the twentieth century seems have bought more fall and less rise. On the upside, the natural world has a greater chance when industry lies fallow.

We'd had enough of walking round industrial estates on hard pavements, so we caught the train to Swansea, giving the 'Coketowns' of Port Talbot and Neath a miss.

Pyle station consisted of two platforms backed by high brick walls, a double rail track with a bridge over it and a large sign saying BEWARE OF THE TRAINS. Sun and shade were geometrically demarcated. Two sets of railway lines shimmered in unseasonal heat. The only sounds were some bored youngsters playing ball and using the station as an obstacle course, scaling the brick walls and swarming over the shiny rails like monkeys. A dog barked. Occasionally a train would thunder through, shaking the ground beneath us and causing a mini whirlwind. We lay prostrate on the sunny platform for over an hour, just pleased to be stationary.

Swansea's marina glistened in the afternoon sun. Brand new, and totally deserted, it looked as though it still had its price tag on. The broad sweep of the bay was equally deserted. We took off our boots and let the warm sand run through our toes. The rocky headland on the far side of the bay silhouetted in the sunshine, beckoned invitingly.

'The Mumbles, look!' I said happily, swirling my tired feet in the warm sand. 'Gateway to the Gower. Look out St. David. Here we come!'

Neither of us knew the Gower peninsula. It was a prehistoric time-warp as yet devoid of visitors. In the low cloud and swirling mist we wouldn't have been surprised to see a mammoth lumbering towards us. The carboniferous limestone cliffs have been whorled and wind-whipped into bizarre fluted shapes, as though piped through a forcing bag. Caves near Port Eynon would have been further inland when our stone-age ancestors lived in them making a 'des res' cave estate for the Flintstones. The Gower is littered with ancient hill forts, stone hut circles and burial chambers. Golden sand rims the curved bays, and the great hump of Worms Head could easily be the back of a half submerged prehistoric monster. The name Worms means *sea-serpent* in old English.

'Look down there.' Richard pointed to the skeletal planks of a large ship wreck, now entombed in the long line of golden sand at Rhossli Bay.

'It could be the carcass of a dinosaur,' I replied, my imagination still buried in the mists of time. Ahead we could see the ruins of the ancient chapel of St. Cenydd, a 6th century hermit.

Walking beneath Weobley castle in the evening light, we passed through a field of ewes and lambs. The sheep panicked as we approached and made off, leaving one tiny lamb stranded, unable to cross the vast tract of mud. I picked up the tiny bundle of hearbeat inside a thin curly coat, marvelling that something so light and vulnerable could survive.

Roy and Gwyneth had lived near Dunvent for many years. Everything about Roy was big. His figure, his voice, his beautifully told stories, his boundless enthusiasm. Both he and Gwyneth were in local choirs, and when we expressed interest, he arranged for us to attend a rehearsal of the well-known Pontydulais Choir.

It was an unforgettable experience. The rehearsal was held in a primary school classroom, and there amongst the blackboards and chalk, the seventy strong males appeared something of a rabble.

Most of them were the wrong side of fifty, and as they chatted and laughed amongst themselves, it was reminiscent of Saturday night down at the local. Suddenly the conductor raised his baton,

'Straight in now boys . . . one, two, three.' And away they went. Precision singing as perfect as dunlins in flight. Their deep voices soared and dipped, roared and whispered, legatoed and stuccatoed with controlled enthusiasm. The conductor would occasionally beat the desk with a witty reprimand and then 'OK boys, once more' . . . When the baton was raised we could have heard a pin drop. Best of all were the hymns, sung in Welsh and the finale.

'A-Aymen, Aymen, Aymen!' Those powerful voices reached a tremendous crescendo on the final notes. They were still using the so / fa / do / ray system. Sankey and Moody would have been proud of them.

The controlled power and deep-seated camaraderie was palpable in that classroom. I once heard a story about some miners, who had to crawl several miles every day to reach the coal face. They were not paid until they arrived there. At the end of the day, physically exhausted, they had to crawl back. Then they would sing to keep their spirits up in that living grave. Every day the miner lives on the edge and relies on his comrades in a potentially life-threatening situation. This bonding can't be shaken off like coal dust when they surface; they need to congregate and continue this bonding in a more relaxed atmosphere. To their credit, the Welsh wives seem to understand and tolerate this need.

As if we had not had enough, those Welsh choristers had a whip-round for us and collected the staggering sum of £53. In an area of high unemployment, many of these men were out of work or retired. Their generosity found us at a loss for words. The tape of their choir was another gift, which kept my feet moving for many a mile. By the time we reached Cardigan I was humming *Calm is the Sea*' and '*Speed your Journey*' for all I was worth. Luckily no-one was within earshot, for my voice rivals my sense of direction.

When you breakfast with a Welshman who is a good raconteur you don't get off to an early start. Roy eventually drove us back to Llanhidran, but en route took us to a exclusive Victorian hotel to show us where his family go on special occasions.

'The owners are friends of mine. They'll be delighted to see you.' He beamed.

The imposing house was on a hill with a view of the Laughor estuary. We drove up to a business-like pair of wrought iron gates. The lady of the house was gardening nearby with her trusty doberman beside her. Roy made himself known, and we waited a long time for any response. The barred gate had a picture of a doberman and the wording:

'This dog will reach you in fifteen seconds.'

This dog was now sizing us up. Only two feet and an iron railing was between us and his slavering jaws were shaking in joyful anticipation. I was wishing I had stayed in the car. Slowly the owner attempted a luke-warm welcome and disappeared to shut the reluctant dog up. A disembodied voice called,

'It's safe now.' We had a quick peek in the hall of the house and never saw the owners again. It was a case of beating an ignominious retreat, tail between legs. We piled thankfully into the car, hoping for a quick get-away but Roy had to reverse down a quarter of a mile of twisting drive. His neck mobility, not being what it was, prevented him from seeing where we were going. He managed a few yards, and then found the car locked against the unfriendly wall on one side, or the precipitous slope on the other. A chorus of 'Right hand down, a bit of left now, straighten up - whoopse!' Did little to help. The car tacked and stalled down the hill, watched by the released slavering doberman. I imagined a twinkle in his eager bright eyes.

Llanelli had bitten the dust like Newport and Barry. The pavements seemed to have more than their share of dog shit and litter. The wind whistled round large boarded-up buildings with rotting window frames and peeling posters. Only weeds flourished in the cracks of empty parking lots. It smelt of industrial decay.

'I'm glad to be out of Llanelli. Poor sods who have to live there.'

'Thchlanechli,' Richard gargled accurately. 'It's not a female version of lanolin.'

Eirey was herself a physio who had seen an article about our walk in the physiotherapy journal. On the strength of this she offered us hospitality. I felt a twinge of guilt when she went off to work in her uniform next morning, but on the whole neither Richard or I felt guilty about not being at work. As far as we were concerned we were working, a nine to five itinerant commitment which was often as much as we could manage.

Burryport was little better, but it at least had a beach and a marina. It was here that we were interviewed by our man from

The Evening Standard. He was late. Clive, their intrepid photographer had to drive down from London. Tom, who looked as though he had just emerged from public school, slumped himself in an armchair, cocked one leg over the other and started the interrogation.

'How's it going? Any problems? Have you kept fit? Are you still on speaking terms?'

'Fine. No. Yes. Sure,' we replied.

'A few blisters. Too much weight on our backs. A bit of weather. Wonderful scenery. Kind people.'

Tom scribbled diligently with his left hand, pausing occasionally to push his forelock back from his eyes.

'Sure you haven't had any real problems?'

'Sure. We've been lucky.'

His face fell a little. 'Over to you, Clive,' he said to the photographer.

A few minutes later we were out on Burryport beach in a gale. Sand blew in our eyes our ears and into Clive's lenses.

'Walk this way, I'd like the lighthouse behind you.' We strained forward against the wind while Clive ran backwards into it. Unused films fell from his pockets like coins from a jackpot.

Tom stood on the sidelines, hands in pockets, shivering miserably in his thin London jacket.

'Take your hoods off,' Clive shouted, still running. The wind tore through our hair and took our breath away.

'Right. That's the third film. I think that'll do. Last week it was the Queen on her Irish visit. I was fighting umbrellas then. Got any exercises for my neck?' He asked me.

It was now so late, that, had we walked our intended mileage, we shouldn't have reached Carmarthen until after dark. Richard, for the first and last time, asked for a lift to Kidwelly. Clive was happy to oblige and regaled us with stories of his cross-channel flight in a hot-air balloon with no basket strapped to the cylinders.

'See you at John O' Groats.' Clive roared off back to the metropolis.

'Clive's adventures make ours seem very tame,' Richard commented as we turned into the head wind on the Carmarthen road.

The Evening Standard thought likewise. We hadn't been benighted on the cliffs, broken an ankle or even fallen out with each other. There wasn't a story.

It was St. Patrick's day and the pubs of Carmarthen were lively. We found a respectable-looking B & B on the outskirts before celebrating everything we could think of in the local pub. On our return, we heard our host calmly dealing with a suicidal man. Their disembodied voices rooted us to the spot as the crazed man railled against all and sundry. His voice rose to a terrible crescendo until it finally broke down. We crept quietly upstairs and later heard the police arrive.

Next morning as we sat down to breakfast a young man emerged with his arm in a sling. He had been sleeping on the settee in the lounge. He nodded curtly, put on his coat and left.

Our host produced breakfast as if nothing had happened.

'If you're off to Laugharne you'll be visiting Dylan Thomas' boathouse. My father went to school with Dylan. Terrible bully he was. Strange man.' He shrugged as if trying to be rid of something unpleasant.

We talked a little of the Welsh language.

'When I was a boy, my parents didn't want me to speak Welsh. It was to England we looked, see. Now it's divverent. The kids learn Welsh in school. If you speak Welsh there's better chance of a job.'

Camarthen was a bustling market town. The unsophisticated Georgian houses gave it a very English look. We were constantly being reminded that this southern strip of Wales is known as 'The little England beyond Wales'. The Normans invaded South Pembrokeshire in the 11th century and wasted no time in building a frontier of castles which was known as the Landsker. This invisible line made a linguistic and cultural divide between North and South, a divide which is very evident to the traveller. The Georgian towns of Carmarthen, Laugharne and Tenby are so anglicised that the locals apparently don't even speak proper Welsh. When I asked our landlady in Laugharne to translate a few words for me, she was interrupted by her indignant husband.

'It's no good asking *her*, *she's* not Welsh, she comes from Laugharne.'

At least we learnt that the Welsh are alive and well in Carmarthen.

'Don't leave your packs there, boyo,' Richard was warned as he waited for me to emerge from the Ladies.

'A light-fingered little Welsh bugger'll nick 'em!'

'He certainly looked as if he had itchy fingers.' Richard was highly amused by the little incident. After that, anything we didn't approve of was the fault of 'light-fingered little Welsh buggers', like the footpath sign that pointed into a dense hedge.

The road to Laugharne moved easily through fertile undulating farmland. The sound of the sea was replaced with the bleat of sheep and lambs. Drifts of snowdrops lay thickly under the hedges, celendines and primroses promised Spring. It was good to be alive and out and about in our 'green and pleasant land.'

'If in Bath they put a hanging basket under every lampost, in Wales they put a castle on every hill,' I observed as we admired Llanstephan's 12th century castle, visible yesterday from Ferryside on the other side of the Tywi estuary.

'This is where the River Taf meets the Twyi. A little further round and we'll be able to see Worms Head on the Gower.' Richard, as ever, was patiently helping to orientate me. He looked carefully at the castle entrance.

'See that chute in the stone up there. I'm sure that was for boiling oil or water to deter any little Welsh buggers that might have been trying to batter the gates down.'

It was Saturday, March 18th, the day of the Wales v Ireland rugby match. If Richard was missing viewing the match he wasn't showing it. A very long steep hill at the end of a long day, and we were only a mile downhill from Laugharne. A convenient seat gave me a puff stop, and an old boy emerged from a nearby house and joined us.

He had a deeply-lined weather-beaten face and looked in dire need of a dentist. Richard asked him about the rugby.

'Terrible. I dunno what happened to rugby nodays. Wales lost again.' He shook his old head sadly, remembering better times at Cardiff Arms Park.

In our cosy B & B Richard was as usual pouring over the maps.

'We've just completed our first 1,000 miles.' He announced with a hint of a smile.

'That works out at ten pints each. Come on. We better start drinking!'

We joined the gloomy Welsh in a pub that was playing Irish music. Strangely nobody seemed to mind.

The Welsh bitter was good. Feeling this was something of an occasion I gave Richard the following instant doggerel:

There once were a staunch pair of walkers,
Who really aren't telling you porkers.
They've now walked to Laugharne
Where they're sipping Welsh balm.
Three cheers for one thousand-mile scorchers!

Richard's eyes rolled to heaven. 'Dylan Thomas pipped you to the post,' he said with heavy sarcasm. 'I think it's time we made tracks. We've got the Pembrokshire Coast Path to tackle next.'

Dylan Thomas' whitewashed Boat House nestles under the cliff. That *'unshaken house on a breakneck of rocks'* was now garnished with daffodils and sparkled in the Spring sunshine. His little writing shed (*'water and tree room on the cliff')* has been lovingly preserved. Here he wrote his radio play *Under Milkwood.* He called Laugharne, *Llareggub.* If fluent in Welsh or Dylan Thomas, the reader will know this means *bugger all* backwards. The panoramic view from here included both the estuary and Sir John's *'elmed hill'* and the *'crystal harbour vale . . .'*

To us, *Llareggub* seemed to have everything. Tree-clad hills, boat-seated mud flats, faded Georgian houses, a near-perfect castle and *'a heron Priested shore'.* Small wonder that the poet himself just came for the day, and never left.

Time was getting on. The long arm of Marros Sands was bathed in late afternoon sunlight. We could see our destination of Saundersfoot several miles ahead. Tenby where we should be the next day beckoned in the distance. From Amroth the mellow sands were the start of the 181 miles Pembrokeshire Coast Path. The low light warmed the wood of a fraying wreck. It grinned widely in its sandy tomb like the rotten tooth-filled mouth of vast dog fish. Further on we came across decaying tree trunks, with roots shaped like the heads of prehistoric creatures, embalmed in the sand.

'That's the remains of a preserved forest.' Richard informed me. 'This area had a lot of coal measures and coal used to be exported directly from the beach until they built the harbour at Saundersfoot in the 19th century. Pembrokeshire anthracite was much in demand then.'

Richard had been studying our enlightening National Trail Guide for the Pembrokeshire Coast Path. I was going to learn a lot in the next two weeks.

I had a bad night with a thumping migraine, and was not relishing the thought of a long walk to Manobier. For once I accepted the offer to have my pack taken on ahead to Tenby, where we were staying the night. Dosed up and out in the fresh air, my head cleared and spirits soared at the prospect of miles of designated footpath. In this immensely ancient coastal landscape, all the rocks underlying the land surface are more than 300 million years old. I wished I knew more about geology. All I could do was admire these grained, pock-marked sliced remnants of the Ice Age. There is something very humbling about cliffs. These Pre-Cambrian rocks once created a gigantic mountain range along the contact of the two colliding supercontinents of North America and Eurasia.

'Don't you sometimes feel like a two-legged insect, here today and gone tomorrow?' I was addressing a rapidly retreating back. It was time to stop philosophical and physical meanderings, and hit the trail.

Chapter Eight

The sea washes away the ills of man.
Euripedes

Tenby is thickly wrapped in history. Sited at the end of a rocky headland pointing into Carmarthen Bay, it begged a castle in the 12th century. Once inside the ancient walls, the visitor is treated to layers of Georgian and Regency architecture graciously draped round the four sandy bays, and perched above the old harbour. The town flourished as a busy trading port in Tudor times and was used by wealthy Bristol merchants as a holiday resort in the 18th century which accounts for its classical elegance. The 19th century is represented by the Napoleonic Fort, known as Palmerston's Folly which crowns the little island of St. Catharine.

Richard nodded to an impressive Regency hotel on our right.

That'll be our pad for tonight.' Graham, the proprietor, also owned Palmerston's Folly.

'I'm trying to get it converted into an art gallery for the Graham Sutherland Trust. It should be an asset not a liability,' he told us earnestly.

Caldney Island lay like a basking whale a mile or so off the coast. It is virtually uninhabited except for the monastery, where some twenty Cistercian monks still continue their ascetic existance. However, they too have to survive in a commercial world, and do a good trade in honey, chocolate, cream, yoghurt, herbs, and probably anything else they can flog. During the Summer months boats ply to and fro with their cargo of tourists. Now the little island lay meditating in the calm waters of Carmarthen Bay.

Manobier sounded very Norman, and from the coast the well-preserved 12th century castle and simple stone church looked like something out of *A Nursery History of England*. All it needed was the knight in shining armour, with the red Crusade Cross emblazoned on his back, to complete the scene.

'It is quite a special castle,' Richard said. 'Giraldus Cambrensis was born here.'

'Er. Yes. OK. Was he a light-fingered little Welsh bugger?'

'You could say that. He was a 12th century writer (and there weren't many of them around) who toured the country with an Archbishop trying to raise money for the Third Crusade.'

Richard's head was in the book as he read, 'His Chronicles give a detailed portrait of life in the Middle Ages.'

'Shame. The beginning of the end for all those myths and legends.'

Undeterred Richard read on 'Gerald called this castle, *the most delectable spot in all Wales.'*

We thought the whole coast on this stretch was very *delectable*. The cliffs were a surprising mixture of red sandstone and carboniferous limestone, layered, scored, twisted and gouged into wonderful patterns and shapes. We stumbled across Neolithic quoits, Iron Age forts, natural arches and blowholes. We nearly stumbled into several fissures in the ground. These giant chasms looked as though the giant had thrust a knife into the cliff, to see if it was cooked. The 'gashes' were only a few feet wide and their sheer sides plummeted down to the sea 100 feet below.

'I'm glad it's light,' I said. 'I wouldn't fancy putting a foot down that one.'

'It does tell you to be careful,' said my Trail Guide.

At Stackpole Head Richard was scanning the cliffs with the binoculars.

'Look out for choughs. This is one of the few places we might see them. 'They're like crows only they have bright red legs and beaks.'

We not only saw a flock of choughs, we also saw a flock of geology students in bright yellow plumage and shiny heads, perched on the cliffs clasping clip boards, hammers and sandwich boxes. Stackpole Quay made a good spot for lunch and we had time to admire the National Trust's restoration work on the old quay built by Lord Cawdor. From here limestone was exported in the 18th and 19th centuries and coal imported, primarily to keep his lordship warm at Stackpole Court.

The next bay at Barafundle was, we felt, *the* most delectable spot. Sheltered and unspoiled, it must have been a private paradise for the Cawdor family. The arch and steps they built, to make their crinolined descent easier, are still intact. The sun shone on the warm, sand-backed dunes where only the soaring skylarks broke the silence.

Crossing the lily ponds at Bosherston on a Monet-type footbridge, (more of the lavish Cawdor estates) we returned to the road and headed for the pub Richard had looked out at Castlemartin.

The landscape was suddenly bleak and windswept as we skirted another M.O.D. Danger Area. It had been a long walk and it was getting late by the time we reached the village. Our pub for the night was now an art gallery and firmly closed. Spirits nose-dived and feet ached as we looked for a bed and breakfast in the dreary one-street village. I raised my eyes to one bleak grey building which was called simply *Cold Comfort.* Rounding a bend we came across a no-nonsense farmhouse advertising B & B. Mentally I was already in the warm bath clutching a cup of tea.

'Sorry. We're full up. There's a lot of work going on just now at the Texaco Oil Refinery. They had a nasty explosion there last year. Now the plant is being overhauled and the contractors are in any accommodation they can find.'

The farmer looked genuinely sorry to have to turn us away. I was doing something of a wilting act on his front wall. I had got as far as removing my rucksack, but hadn't yet undone the boots.

'Where have you walked from?' Enquired his small daughter politely.

'Manobier today,' I replied.

'Is that in England?' She asked gazing curiously at us with eyes full of pity.

Reluctantly I heaved my pack back where it belonged and we set off along the dismal street in the vain hope that we should find a bed. Several minutes later a car hooted behind us.

'I've rung some friends who live at the far end of the village' said the farmer, winding down his car window. They do have a room and are expecting you.'

His small daughter continued to gaze at us through a screen of dishevelled blond hair.

Castlemartin was looking up. Watered and washed, we just made the half mile to the Welcome Inn. The journey back was a lot easier. We had a good view of the 'tongues of flame' issuing from the lean chimneys of the American dragons at Milford Haven. The Texaco Oil Refinery was lit up like a forest of Christmas trees. I had strange dreams of black people with red legs looking through binoculars at multi-coloured birds in crash helmets hitting themselves over the head with hammers.

Munching sandwiches, we sat in a warm hollow on the cliffs above West Angle Bay, watching a car ferry from Ireland making stately progress down this great tentacle of water, trailing its white wake. The strong bleat of ewes now replaced the roar of waves, echoed by the high-pitched wobbly sounds from their tiny offspring. The fecund smell of lanolin and sheep's dung tinged the air. Skylarks caterpulted their soprano voices into the blue with a rhythmic 'cark-cark' in the bass from a solitary black-backed gull. The spring sun warmed us within and without, giving a surge of well-being that stirs something primeval deep within us. Richard lay with eyes closed, a look of ecstasy on his face. I picked a daisy and gently shed the petals one by one over his upturned face.

'He loves me, he loves me not, he loves me . . .' I thought I saw an eyelid twitch, but the face remained impassive.

A steady trickle of oil-laden super tankers slipped in and out of Milford Haven. From our vantage point on the cliffs they looked like harmless toys, a little entertainment for the walker. As I write one year later, the Sound is more black than blue, the tides no longer wash clean, but deposit layers of black crude oil upon cliffs, beaches and islands. These cliffs, a haven for sea birds, are now a death trap. The single-hulled oil tanker 'Sea Empress' ran aground near Mill Bay on February 15th 1996. Much of her lethal cargo haemorrhaged as she hit the rocks. A blanket of oil spread over a uniquely beautiful stretch of coast.

I remembered the sea water baths in Tenby, built by Sir William Paxton in 1811, which are preserved for posterity with the ironic message from Euripides over the door *'The sea washes away the ills of man'*.

Angle village lay unmoved by 20th century technology. The fields on either side of the village follow the lines of ancient mediaeval field systems. Rotting hulks are visible in the mud. Only sixty years ago the women of Angle used to collect seaweed from Freshwater Bay, dry it in special rustic huts near the beach, boil it and sell it as larva bread. It was then considered a delicacy, but even rolled in oats and fried like bacon, we thought it was like eating a pair of our worn down boots.

We picked our way over the mud and rocks of Angle Bay like a pair of waders. Milford Haven sprawled hazily across the water, seemingly dwarfed by the slow-moving super-tankers. The Norman church at Rhoscrowther and a clutch of old houses, looked like a model village beside the giant stacks, pillboxes and steel rigging of the Texaco Oil Refinery, towering and belching above it.

'I'm sure that church will still be there long after the refinery has been dismantled,' Richard remarked as we pondered on the change in the outward and visible emblems of power in the past fifty years.

We had hoped to reach Pembroke early enough to ensure a bed for the night. The day, however, had been too good to hurry. It was nearly 6 p.m by the time we reached our destination. We then systematically knocked on every hostelry door the length of a very long high street. There was, it seemed, no room in any inn.

'We must look like a pair of tramps. I think the landlord in that last place thought we might contaminate his beastly pub,' I said, running a broken comb through my tangled hair.

'I'll ask in this pub if they know of anyone we haven't tried.' I was getting desperate.

'Three hundred yards over the bridge on your left. The pink house.'

The little terraced house had steps up to the front door. I rang the bell nervously.

'Come in,' said a friendly voice. 'If it's a bed your after I've just let my last room ten minutes ago.'

The friendly voice appeared and a young woman eyed me up an down. 'I'm sorry I can't help.' She paused a moment taking in my long face and drooping shoulders. 'You look all in. Wait there, I've a friend down the road who might just have a room.'

I sank into the nearest chair, straining to hear her telephone conversation.

'Hello! I've two tired walkers here . . . Busy . . . Really? . . . Oh dear . . . Yes . . . Good . . . OK . . . Bye.'

A small boy with big eyes and a dirty face, appeared from the garden. He regarded my wilting frame with some hostility. 'You can't stay,' he said defiantly. 'Mam says we're full up.'

I was just wondering if there were any decent bus shelters in Pembroke, when Mam appeared beaming.

'You're in luck. My friend says an engineer has just had to go home for family reasons. It's the black and white Guest House half way up the High Street.'

Richard rejoined me at street level.

'We've already been turned away from that one,' he observed gloomily.

'I know. Let's just hope it's the wife this time.'

We were made welcome. Our landlady was as solicitous as her husband had been disinterested, as polite as he had been rude. We were led up some rickety stairs to a poky room. It might have been the best suite at the Savoy.

'Word of mouth works wonders,' I said lying on the small bed with my feet twitching happily above my head.

* * *

The great toll bridge across the Daugleddau estuary, (completed in 1976), took us from Pembroke Dock to Neyland and Milford Haven. Before crossing, we paused to gaze out over this 24-mile stretch of navigable waterway and reflect on the miscellany of craft that had plied these waters over many centuries.

'Marauding Vikings, Celtic Saints, Norman conquerors, Flemish settlers . . .' Richard reeled off the list of names from an information board. 'And that's just for starters.'

'Tudor conquerors like Henry II, Strongbow, Earl of Pembroke, Cromwell. You name them they've all sailed from here.'

The history lesson continued.

'Pembroke Royal Naval Dockyard was built by the Admiralty to cock a snook at Charles Greville's inflated prices at Milford Haven during the Napoleonic Wars. Apart from the usual ships they also built four of the Royal Yachts there. Then of course there was Brunel who built the railway and moored his steamship *The Great Eastern* at Neyland. Milford Haven had one of the largest fishing fleets in Britain in the last century.'

Richard paused for breath and the lesson ended. We both stared silently at the great waterway, now dotted with a few pleasure craft, a lifeboat, the odd tug, and several super-tankers. Gone are the railway, the ferry, the fishing boats, paquet boats, ketches, schooners, Men O'War, long ships and coracles.

'The Ice Age carved out a large chunk of history as well as this waterway,' I muttered.

A pall of sterile silence seem to hang in the air like the heat haze. It was one of those rare moments, when mentally and physically we could sit and reflect. Neither of us wanted to break the spell, but there were still many miles to be walked.

'Time to move,' Richard said, shouldering his pack, adding, 'I wonder if they'll charge us super-tanker fees on the bridge. I don't know what draught I'd draw in the water, but it's certainly a lot less than when I started.'

We threaded our way round early 20th century gun emplacements, 19th century Napoleonic forts and late 20th century oil storage tanks. We ducked under half-dismantled piers and crept above the silver spaghetti of oil pipes in wire cages like a pair of overloaded monkeys. It was a relief to leave the last refinery and head off for St. Anne's Head, although it was a long time before we finally lost sight of the towering inferno's of the refinery chimneys. A quote from my crib book on the coast is worth noting:

Milford has now found a new lease of life as a base for one of the largest oil ports in the whole of Europe. It seems as if the fortunes of this little town, which as well as its harbour facilities has a wide range of seaside attractions for holidaymakers, are assured at last.'

(AA Illustrated Guide).

'Mmmm . . . I wonder.'

Walkers beware of tidal rivers on the way to Dale. If a long detour is to be avoided it is necessary to get the tide right. We managed to cross the river at Sandy Haven on four wheels as the tide was up, but The Gann was not so easy.

'We'll just stop here for elevenses and wait for the tide to go down,' Richard suggested.

It was pleasant bird-spotting and dozing in the sun. When I opened my eyes the river was higher than ever.' Richard was smiling ruefully.

'OK. Best foot forward. It'll be the long way round today.'

As we set off inland to Mullock Bridge he told me the story of the farmer who lived here in 1485 and had just heard that Henry Tudor had landed at Mill Bay.

'He'll cross my land over my dead body,' the farmer boasted.

Next day he was out with his gun, ready to defend his country, when he spied a huge army of 2,000 men approaching. A sudden wave of pragmatism washed the high moral ground from beneath his feet. He hid under Mullock Bridge until the army had crossed. Then he emerged and joined the rearguard on their way to victory at Bosworth.'

'If you can't beat 'em, join 'em. Farmers aren't stupid,' I said.

My diary entry for March 26th reads . . .

Rest on Mothering Sunday! Put clocks forward so no lying in. Huge plate of porridge and boiled eggs for breakfast. Wonderful cards from Katie and Jo. I'm a lucky mum.

Broadhaven Youth Hostel, for a modest charge, had given us the luxury of a family room with ensuite facilities, comfortable mattresses and bed linen. The ethos of the 'youth' hostel seems to have changed. Central heating, comfortable television room, high tech. kitchen, and meals provided if you didn't feel like cooking your own, are now the norm. We shared the smart new building with a handful of German students who arrived and departed on four wheels.

'We're the only ones with proper packs and muddy boots. Youth Hostels are now in the B& B market. I'm not sure that I approve.' Richard sounded a little smug.

'Maybe we have a masochistic streak in us, a hangover from those cold school dorms with horse hair mattresses.'

As I spoke my mind raced back to school days when the dorms were unheated, lino covered the floor, and there really was ice on the inside of the window. The proliferation of chilblains was in direct proportion to the descending temperature, doubtless fostered by hugging the cosy stoves. I don't think my circulation ever recovered.

The coast here is a mass of rockpools, sandstone and slanting shale cliffs. The 'dream' islands of Skomer and Skokholm are (or since the oil spillage should I say were) famous for sea birds. Skomer is described as 'An island steeped in history and mystery.' Prehistoric Gateholm (cut off from the mainland at high tide) had been a teeming metropolis. Long, thin and rocky, to contemporary eyes it looks only fit for seabirds, yet in Neolithic times it supported no fewer than 130 hut circles. These must have been the first generation of terraced dwellings with panoramic sea views, for no extra charge. Celtic saints, several centuries later, also fancied the inhospitable little island.

'Paranoid lot, weren't they?' I said, mentally trying to imagine how you could fit one hundred and thirty hut circles down the spine of such a rocky fortress.

'It was like a natural castle. In those days people needed all the protection they could get. Even the early saints built earthen embankments called *llan* round their churches. These became religious settlements.' Richard shook the last few drops of coffee out of the thermos. 'Now you know why so many Welsh names are prefixed with *llan* which is often followed by the name of the saint.'

Once again I was impressed by Richard's fund of general knowledge.

'Well done clever clogs'. I said passing him another piece of chocolate. 'You couldn't put your gloves on could you?'

Richard's hands had turned a cadaverous yellow colour as they always did when we stopped. Before the walk, Richard was the one with a good circulation. He had spurned thermals and only wore gloves when there was a frost. I was the reverse. Now he would frequently lose the blood from his hands, while mine remained warm and sociable.

'It's only because I have lost so much weight. My fat kept me warm before,' he would say.

'You never admitted to having any superfluous fat before,' I muttered, quietly worrying about peripheral shutdown due to an overstrained heart, a theory I quickly discounted as I watched Richard roaring up the hills ahead of me.

St. Bride's Bay lies like a big mouth between two jaws. Today the beaches and cliffs are enjoyed by walkers, horse-riders, surfers and the bucket and spade brigade. In the last century the once rich coal fields provided wealth and employment for the residents of Newgale and Nolton Haven. We found ourselves scrunching over black paths and stumbling across chimney stacks and the base remnants of engine houses, reminiscent of Cornwall. The little port of Solva tucks neatly into a long deep natural channel, and an army of limekilns show it's importance as a lime-burning centre in the last century.

Here we came upon this little gem from the 17th century.

'*A man doth sand for himself, lime for his son, marl for his grandson.*' Marl, our plastic informant explained, was a clay material.

The ancient quay lay sleeping peacefully; a little Welsh fjord. A couple of yachts and a motor boat were the only visible craft. A few well-tended old houses and a woollen mill were all that remained of the village.

'How far to the Youth Hostel at Pen-Y-Cwm?' We asked in a shop selling expensive knitwear and home-made chocolates.

'O not far. It'll only take you about twenty minutes.'

A hilly hour an a half later, we arrived at the Youth Hostel.

'Those were car miles,' I said bleakly.

I recorded in my diary that night:
Article in paper says it has been the warmest and wettest winter on record.

We met St. David's in perfect Spring sunshine. We were now in the land of Holy Wells, myths and miracles. Celtic saints might have had their day, but they certainly left an aura behind them. The Passionate Fathers thought so too, for in 1929 they built a retreat above St. Non's Bay, where St. David is reputed to have been born c. 462. The arched and convoluted cliffs plunged seawards, grey, and purple, with fluted sides and rocky feet. The air was warm and windless. Calm water softly licked the toes of the great cliffs. The green turf was springy beneath our feet.

Ramsay Island looked near enough to touch and the water roared past in a fearsome tide race, eddying and whirling round rocks aptly called *The Bitches*, rocks responsible for many a shipwreck. Back in the 5th century this did not pose a problem for St. David's buddy St. Justinian who lived an ascetic life on Ramsay Island. The islanders felt he was a lazy sod, just sitting in his cave all day meditating, so they chopped off his head. Undeterred, Justinian popped his head under his arm and strode across Ramsay Sound to the mainland, possibly to see if David had any glue. History does not relate the end of the story, but the spot where he and his head landed, is called Porthstinian (St. Justinian) and the ancient ruins of his chapel can still be seen.

St. David's must be one of the smallest cities in Britain, and one of the most unusual. As we approached in the low evening sun, the 'city' seemed to dominate the chunky cathedral which was built in a hollow to avoid the beady eye of marauding Vikings. The little tree-lined square was alive with vociferous rooks whose droppings had whitewashed the pavement beneath. There was a pleasant smell of home-baked bread and the locals were busy whitening their shops ready for the season. The sleepy city was stretching its historic limbs, ready for the incoming tide of tourists and contemporary pilgrims.

We rang the bell of a an unpretentious-looking B & B next to the pub. A large notice in the window advertised VACANCIES. A graveyard cough could be heard coming to the door which was opened by a bowed rather tubby man wearing a lilac T-shirt and shell-suit trousers. He had greying hair, a deeply-lined face and atrocious teeth. We were shown upstairs. The very tall, very dead house plant, did not auger well, but the cluttered room was fairly clean and had a lovely view of the cathedral.

'Bathroom's next door.' Our landlord was a man of few words.

'We'd like the room for two nights please.'

He grunted. 'If you want me I'll be downstairs.'

The room was filled with furniture. A double bed, settee, wardrobe, two bedside tables, a huge chest of drawers, (where a television and hi-fi stacking system perched), and a lace-draped dressing table that would have been more at home in an Edwardian dolls house. Nothing had been forgotten. Two clean but stained towelling dressing gowns hung behind the door and there was even a hair-dryer. Lace doilies covered every surface.

Richard was studying the menu behind the door.

'Breakfast,' he read, 'eggs fried, poached or scrambled with beans, sausages, potato waffles, tomato, mushroom, bacon and fried bread.'

'Evening meals, from £2.00, cod, chips, peas or salad, moussaka, cottage pie, spaghetti, macaroni with same veg. Mmm . . . sounds like walkers' food.'

It was a gratifyingly filling plateful. If the moussaka looked like brown gravel under some dirty snow, it tasted good and there were enough walker-size chips to feed an army. Our host had donned a starched waiters jacket which he had buttoned down the front. The only trouble was, the jacket was too small and reminded me of Peter Rabbit.

He remained monosyllabic and we wondered whether his English was not so fluent. After all, we were now North of the Landsker Line in Welsh Wales.

The chunky simplicity of St. David's cathedral, paradoxically uplifting in its very down-to-earthness, appealed to us both. Founded by St. David, patron saint of Wales, in the 6th century it has had a chequered history. The original church burned down once and was raided twice by marauding Danes. The tower collapsed in 1220 and the foundations were badly shaken by an earthquake in 1248. Now the Norman arches slope drunkenly backwards. It was built in a hollow on marshy land and slopes dramatically from East to West so the visitor walks uphill to the alter. The cathedral was plundered by Henry VIII and later vandalised by Cromwell, who is supposed to have ridden his horse up to the altar and broken some of the mediaeval floor tiles. Finally, in 1863, it was lovingly restored by the Victorians, who completely rebuilt the West Front with sandstone we'd seen quarried on the nearby cliffs.

That Sunday evening, Richard and I sat, transmuted, inside the beautiful oak-carved screen of the choir listening to the divine voices of the cathedral choir at Evensong. The girls and boys looked as though their faces had been scrubbed by Mrs. Ogmoor Pritchard herself; their cheeks like rosy apples, not a hair out of place.

There is something very moving about an Evensong service. Enclosed in this fretted sanctuary we felt an integral part of the cathedral. We floated on a higher plane, borne along by the tuneful voices. For a moment there was a sense of timelessness; we were privileged members of the Church Triumphant tasting a morsel of tradition. 'Lord now lettest thy servant depart in peace according to thy word. For mine eyes have seen thy salvation . . .' We knelt down and I shut my eyes . . .

I am back at my prep school. The great Welsh dragon is draped across the dais where the Williams sisters hold court. I rise from my small knees, and admire the worm-like imprints the floorboards make on them. The school is called St. David's and run by the Misses Celine and Margaret Williams, who are firmly rooted in the 19th century. Along with the three R's we are taught that 'manners maketh man', or at any rate a woman. We learn to curtsy, carry books on our head, sew, garden, play murder in the dark in the winter, and Robbers and Merchants in the summer. On March 1st every year we learn about St. David.

In true Welsh tradition, the Misses Williams are good orators and hold their young audience captive as they took us back to the Age of Saints and the cradle of Welsh Christianity.

Lucky St. David, I think enviously, had everything. Tall, good looking, clever, a linguist, he not only had a pet dove, but also a guardian angel. As if this isn't enough, he can turn his hankie into a hill (Carn Llidi) so the people hear him better. I blow my nose on my rather snotty rag, and feel St. David's must have been a very clean one. All he ate was bread, herbs and lashings of watercress. I hate watercress. We sing the Welsh National Anthem and skip off to lunch where there are daffodils on the tables and gritty leeks in a white sauce. I'm glad it's not watercress. Afterwards we go to Miss Williams drawing room and play card games or be read to. In the large drawing room there's a bust of St. David with a dove on his shoulder. I stroke the dove when no-one is looking, in the vain hope that it will give me miraculous powers.

' . . . World without end . . . A—men.'

The view from Carn Llidi was marvellous even on a dull day. Whitesands Bay, Ramsay Island with its roaring Sound, St. Bride's Bay to the south and Cardigan Bay to the north. Inland the peaceful city of St. David's, cradles the patron saint at its feet. Up on the Carn we were surrounded by pagan symbols, Iron Age forts, hut circles and burial chambers. Around the cromlech lay a largely unaltered Ice Age landscape, with glaciated slabs and massive erratic boulders. If you shut your eyes to the caravans and polythene-covered potato fields, we were in a pre-historic landscape.

If the good Lord did advocate a day of rest, he hadn't considered long-distance walkers. Weighed down with potato waffles and shepherds pie, we suffered from a bad dose of lead legs. Although on an afternoon pace in the morning, I was surprised to find myself in the lead. Richard then admitted to a touch of runny tummy or Celtic Revenge and needed frequent stops. When he asked for herbal tea instead of his usual fix of coffee, I was quite anxious, and we were both relieved to reach journeys end at the Trevine Youth Hostel.

The patient declared himself better after a long night. It was April 1st and the sun was shining with real warmth. Amongst the pretty cottages of Trevine village, was a modern bungalow with the red Post Office logo outside. A far cry from Dylan Thomas' description of Willy Nilly the Postman's, *dark and sizzling damp tea-coated . . . kitchen.* I could imagine this Post Mistress quoting Mrs. Ogmoor-Pritchard's words, *'Before you let the sun in, be sure it wipes its shoes.'* I had been listening to Dylan Thomas' *Under Milkwood* on the road to Laugharne and couldn't get his characters out of my head.

Richard pointed out the remains of the Old Mill which served the farming community in this area for 500 years. It closed in 1918 when better transport enabled cheap grain from overseas to be brought to the doorstep by road.

'It's like Cornwall again,' I said. 'Just the skeletal remains of industry left as curios for visitors. I wonder why industry is so much more attractive in retrospect. Why do you think we feel so nostalgic about it?'

'Because it represents a community of people who made their livelihood by it. Besides, the past is always more romantic.'

The mellow brick of the mill-house was sunk in dead bracken and strangled with ivy, but the mill stream still roared energetically down to the sea, its banks white with snowdrops. The old quarry at Abereiddy had a deep pool of green/blue water beside the neatly sliced granite cliffs. Ruined houses, a slate/shale quarry, a tramway cutting, and an old weigh bridge were just some of the memorabilia of Pembrokeshire's short-lived industrial revolution that lay scattered along these beautiful cliffs. Porthgain appeared to have been frozen in time. The old quays, brickworks and sheds of the port were deserted. A single fishing boat was drawn up on the mud. The quarrying finished in 1932, yet so much remained intact, it seemed as if the workforce had just gone off for lunch.

The boulder-strewn moor land was dotted with farms and lined by stone hedges. Spring was making itself felt. The dead bracken warmed in the sunshine. Gorse was blazing, blackthorn bursting, and the dark fields throbbed with ploughing tractors drawing their wake of seagulls. Richard and I, sheltered from the wind and any prying eyes, dared to expose our white legs to the friendly sun.

Strumble Head's ultra-white lighthouse beckoned to us over the cliffs, long before we saw it sitting at the end of a little chain of islands. White vapour trails above, and the wake of the Irish ferries below, made us aware that we were among many travellers in a shrinking world. This was re-inforced when we passed a massive field wall, cemented down and topped with huge boulders. The weary builder had written THE GREAT WALL OF CHINA on it in the cement. It certainly was one of the wonders of Pembrokeshire.

Striking off inland for Goodwick, Richard noticed a large memorial stone at Carreg Goffa which we paused to read. This was the scene of the last 'invasion' of Britain. On 22nd February 1797, a certain American Colonel Tate led an expeditionary force of some 1,200 French to start a Peasants' Revolt in England. Bad weather forced him to land in Wales, where he had to reckon with the Welsh women. Dressed in their red shawls and tall black hats, Tate mistook them for soldiers. Jemima Nicholson goes down in history for helping to defeat this invasion. Unlike the farmer at Mill Bay, she and a crowd of local women stood their ground, and repulsed the enemy. The heroic Jemima is supposed to have captured a number of Frenchman single-handed by using a pitchfork.

It was a long hard day's walk from Trevine to Goodwick, but there was so much to see we couldn't hurry. By the time we turned inland it was already 4 p.m. and we had a very hilly four miles to

Harbour village. Our hosts had planned to take us to a Rotary Race meeting, but by the time we arrived, twenty minutes late, we had had enough of racing. They kindly left us with a delicious supper and bottle of wine followed by an even more delicious bed. Our aching limbs and throbbing feet were so grateful we lost conciousness long before the Race Meeting was over.

Fishguard, first a busy trading port, and then one which rivalled Liverpool as a terminal for transatlantic liners, now sleeps quietly beside the giant arm of North Breakwater, best remembered as the film set for Dylan Thomas' play *Under Milkwood*. We left the peaceful harbour to the sounds of church bells intoning matins, and headed off for Newport via Dinas Head. This great lump of rock sticks out like a piece of jigsaw dividing the bays of Fishguard and Newport. At the isthmus of this headland, we came across luxuriant trees and shrubs with rock gardens in premature bloom; a surreal disembodied church with bell-tower, perched on the sea wall.

'It's called Cwm-Yr-Eglwys, or *valley of the church* and it's sheltered from the prevailing winds so things can grow really well. It sounds like a naturalists paradise. You're supposed to hear crickets here in August.' said Richard from the book.

'Whatever happened to the church?'

'Hang on, I'm coming to that. Mmm . . . The church was destroyed by a great storm in 1859, a storm which wrecked more than 100 ships in a single night off this coast. Before that the church was well inland which explains these massive sea defences.

We sat among the ancient tombstones, gazing at a limp grey sea that looked as though it wouldn't melt the butter in our sandwiches.

A Newport supermarket gave us a taste of real Wales. The shop assistants slipped easily from Welsh to English to suit their customers, but they were most at home in the vernacular. The day was overcast with a hint of drizzle.

'Good day for walking,' the check-out lady said brightly. 'Not too hot and then there's no wind. It's a very tough path to Poppit Sands though.'

We bought an extra bun each on the strength of that comment.

'Do you think her platitudes about the weather show how bad it usually is, or are the Welsh a very positive nation?' Richard was concentrating on getting us onto the right path, rather more important than discussing Welsh traits.

'You never said anything about this stretch being the toughest yet,' I admonished.

'It does say it's taxing and we climb some of the highest cliffs in Pembrokeshire. It also says, Richard read from the guide, *'If you are not particularly fit, allow a good long day and assume that it will take you more than eight hours.'*

We must have been fit, for we arrived at Poppit Sands in six and a half hours. The scenery was hypnotic with the sheer cliffs looking as though they had been gnawed, chewed and spat out by a vengeful sea. Marine erosion had slumped, sliced and folded the different rock-types, producing whirls, anticlines, vertiginous drops and collapsed caves. It was a tremendous finale for the Pembrokeshire coastal path which had given us some of our best walking in the best weather so far.

Chapter Nine

Light now inspects the fold of far hills;
Shadows dumb out the known shapes . . .
how soon their world could be denuded.
Stripped to molton ash, melting stone
new nameless mountains moulded
beneath disinterested stars.
G. M Coles - *The Glass Island*

Inevitably the flatness of Cardigan Bay was going to be an anti-climax. But we were entertained by watching a flock of sheep being driven into a large truck by a short-tempered Welsh farmer, who had few words of English, and no time either for incomers or his wayward flock.

'Ge 'orth wi'ee,' he repeated angrily to us several times in rising tones.

His large four-wheeled-drive blocked the road, while his farm hand was attempting to get a very lame ewe over a ditch and onto the tarmac. After much pushing, pulling, cursing and swearing in Welsh, he jumped into his car and drove after the sheep hooting loudly and cursing roundly. It was obvious that the ewe had broken her leg. She had no choice but to hobble painfully towards the truck which straddled the lane like some great pastoral hulk, a heaving sea of white wool emitting a cacophany of bleats. An elderly sheepdog just wagged its tail and looked bewildered. A farm hand near the lorry was holding a stray lamb in his arms. Just before the rear gate shut them in, the lamb was tossed like a pebble onto that woolley surf, and the truck drove away.

'Talk about lambs to the slaughter.' At that moment I felt like joining an animal rights group.

'Maybe that's real farming. We're probably too soft and sentimental these days. After all they do have to be taken down to the farm to lamb.' Richard's voice trailed away. I felt he wasn't convinced.

It is surprising how much a list of harbour tolls can tell the reader about the mores and customs of the port dwellers. In New

Quay the 'List of Tolls and Dues' have been left on the old Harbour Master's Office with their prices:

'*All foreign vessels loading or unloading within the limits to pay for every ton of their burthen - 8s. (shillings).*

Coal/ limestone - 4s.

Slates/tiles or glazed bricks - 1s.

Millstone/tombstone or monument - 1s.' (A marble one would have cost you 5s.)

The list went on with the sort of groceries which would be imported, dried fruits, sugar, tea and, of course, salt at 1/6d a ton. Dried cod and herrings were exported, and interestingly, a bushel of oysters paid a mere tuppence; in those days oysters were not the rich man's delicacy they are today. While a butt of beer was only 2s a barrel, wine was a luxury item at 5s. A bushel of potatoes was only a one penny; these must have been an important part of the daily diet.

'Malt, peas, tares, mustard seed - that sounds really biblical doesn't it? Listen to this,' I went on - 'Plough and harrow 6d. Wagon or cart 2/6. Now you really start paying over the odds for your luxury items. Sofa, pianoforte or barrel organ 5s. Dues payable to - Thomas Davis, Post Office, New Quay. See Denem Evans Solicitor.'

'Fascinating. Social history in a mustard seed.' At that moment our attention was diverted as the rocket fired a salvo for the lifeboat launch. It was the first we had seen.

Richard's Celtic Revenge was still vengeful, so in Cardigan I had purchased some kaolin and morphine. We got some rather old fashioned looks from passers by as I ladled it down his throat in the High Street.

'I reckon our status has sunk from New Age Travellers to junkies. I don't know where we go next,' I said, relishing the situation.

For the next 24 hours Richard called for his 'fix' at regular intervals and by the time we reached Llangranog he pronounced himself cured. Then of course it was my turn. By the time we reached Aberaeron, where again our mobile home was waiting, I was hooked on the 'fix' and suggested our berth for the night should be outside the public loos. From this pragmatic vantage point, we had good views of the neat rows of colour-washed Regency houses grouped round the deserted quay.

At Llangranog we met my intrepid father who had bought his motorised caravan down the narrow winding lane to meet us on the beach. With a dirth of campsites we spent the night on the bare cliff-top near the 700-year old Church of the Holy Cross at Mwnt. The simple white-washed chapel, looked more like a croft with a bell-tower than a church, standing alone on a grassy sward above the beach, surrounded by a neat stone wall. We were back in the Age of Saints, and the weary pilgrims must have enjoyed the peace and shelter of this little place as much as we did.

After the convolutions of the Pembrokeshire Coast Path, we seemed to gallop up Cardigan Bay. We had been warned of the sprawls of static caravans, but apart from a metallic blot near New Quay, our path had been attractive cliff tops and unspoiled ports and villages. Richard, attempting to avoid the road, ventured onto the grey pebbles of Aberarth beach at low tide, beneath the crumbling boulder-clay cliffs. The coast path proper had been eroded. It was a misty grey morning which toned with the grey boulders, limp grey sea and great grey buttress of the cliffs. There was an eerie silence broken only the trickle of stones falling off the cliffs and the slow slap of the sea. Scrunch, scrunch, scrunch . . . ' Our footsteps on the shingle intruded the greyscape.

There was a nauseating smell of rotting flesh and looking down we saw dead dogfish everywhere. The tide was coming in. Richard was a dot in the distance. I stopped and hoped he would notice and retrace his steps. While the gap between us widened, I thought of Ted Hughes' poem *The Relic*:

> *I found this jawbone on the sea's edge:*
> *There, crabs, dogfish broken by the breakers or tossed*
> *To flap for half and hour and turn to a crust*
> *Continue the beginning. The deeps are cold:*
> *In that darkness camaraderie does not hold.*

Richard decided that caution was the better part of valour, and we retraced our steps to the relative safety of the main Aberystwyth road, where cars roared past our elbows leaving us reeling in a cloud of exhaust fumes.

'I'm glad I'm not made of boulder clay. I should erode pretty quickly on this road.'

'I thought your feet were,' Richard replied.

'Thanks a bunch. How much more of this road?'

My Celtic stomach was still in turmoil and I was not a happy chappie.

'Only a few miles. Have some more 'fix'.'

Soon we were able to see some of the mountains of mid-Wales including Cader Idris and the hills of Pumlumon. Spring was in full flood again as we approached Aberystwith, along the fast flowing river curving gently under the steep hill called Pen Dinas.

Aberystwyth is an exceptional town. Its roots go back 4,000 years BC. Our Iron Age ancestors put themselves on top of Pen Dinas, and the now-ruined castle was built in 1277 by Edward I. Not only is it the principal seaside resort of West Wales, but it manages a homogenous mix of town and gown. The Victorian Gothic university proliferates turrets, towers, elaborate chimneys and pointed windows, and stands proudly at the end of the bay. It was built as a luxury hotel in 1860 by a railway pioneer. His venture failed, and the building became the first college of the future University of Wales. The cultural tone is further enhanced by the ever-growing National Library of Wales which stands like a giant strong box on a hill above the town, an outward and visible national symbol of Welsh culture.

We had a perfect view of this 'Aladdin's Cave of Welsh treasures' from our hosts' kitchen window. Richard Morgan was managing a charitable trust with special interest in Welsh projects, and he also lectured at the University. He proudly showed us the trust's *'piéce de resistance,'* a contemporary translation of The Bible into Welsh, which the trust had helped to finance.

'The last translation was in 1620 and only took four years to complete.' Our host reverently touched the ancient leather-bound volume. 'Our new one has taken dozens of eminent scholars over twenty years. So much for modern technology.'

There was only time for a visit to the laundrette and a promise that we should return to sample more of the cultural delights of Aberystwyth, before we set off for Borth and a short scheduled train ride to get us round the Dyvi estuary.

'It's only six miles to Borth and then we'll walk from Aberdovey to Tywyn where we'll be met. We should be OK for time to catch the one . . . (mumble) train at Borth.' Richard sounded relaxed so I didn't fuss about the times.

We had no coast path booklet to warn us of the rigours of the route. It was a late start from Aberystwyth with a very steep pull up onto the cliff by the Camera Obscura.

'Pity it's shut. We should have enjoyed that,' Richard said as we munched our mid-morning dose of carbohydrate.

The path soared and dived like a big dipper. Fit though we were, it was going to be hard work to catch the one-something train from Borth. From the top we had a good view of the straggling town. It was already after one o'clock. I wanted to ask Richard just what our chances were of catching the train, only he had bolted down the hill like a bat out of hell. I careered down after his flying figure, just hoping the station was our end of this long town.

UPPER BORTH - 'Phew - we'll make it.' I thought until I realised the station was in Lower Borth. I half-walked, half-ran down the long dingy high street, nearly knocking someone off a ladder.

'So sorry!' I puffed. 'Train to catch.'

The town was a one street affair with the railway running behind shops which were mostly boarded up or shut. I still had no idea how far I had to go. By now I was very hot and very angry.

'Grrr. . . He wouldn't do this to a dog.' My anger kept my speed going but by now my long-legged partner was out of sight. It was one thirty five when I saw the B.R. logo, turned the corner and collapsed onto the platform.

'Are you trying to kill me?' I spluttered when I had enough breath.

'We've got two minutes in hand,' Richard replied calmly. 'I thought if I went ahead I could delay the train for you.'

'Great. Thanks. If only I'd known the right time . . .'

The little branch line train appeared and drowned some rather rude words. I sat in furious silence as we moved easily across the beautiful Cors Fochno swampland, and then along the equally beautiful Dyfi estuary. No-one could be bad tempered for long in such surroundings. We changed trains at Machynlleth, had an argument about how to pronounce the name (Mahuntleth) and returned to the coast on the north side of the Dyvi.

The sheltered Dyvi estuary was a balm. The great tidal river runs between gently rising hills backed by the blue-green mountains of mid-Wales. The silence only broken by curlews and oyster catchers and the occasional lawnmower. The tide alternately exposes and covers the wide golden sands in a soft-focused light. Behind the desert-like beach, the click of golf-balls and the braying of middle-class voices accompanies the thudding waves. Tinny percussion comes from the clanking stays of incomers' yachts in the neat harbour. Aberdovey makes a perfect English ghetto for golfers and sailors from the Home Counties; another 'little England beyond Wales'.

During supper we discussed the Welsh resentment to incomers with our host.

'There's a lovely story for you about the early Welsh bishops which is a good thumb-nail sketch of the Welsh attitude to the English. When St. Augustine arrived in Canterbury, he summoned all the bishops nation-wide to see him. The Welsh bishops sought the advice of a wise hermit before they accepted. He advised them to undertake the journey, but only to stay if St. Augustine rose to greet them when they entered his presence. They made the long arduous journey, but when the saint didn't budge from his chair, they turned on their heels and retraced their weary but independent steps.'

Malcom paused and poured us another glass of wine.

'Even the local rulers here couldn't agree about who should be overlord of Wales after the Romans left. So they decided the rulers of the three principalities, Gwynedd, Dyfed and Powys, should each sit on their own chair on the beach, and Canute-like wait for the incoming tide. Whoever sat the longest would be overlord. Maelgwyn Gwynedd was a crafty character and had made his chair out of wax and feathers. It floated and he won the contest.'

'Gwynedd was obviously a clever little Welsh bugger!' I said to Richard as we approached Fairbourne. Here the little narrow-gauge railway had just started the season.

'CHA, CHA, CHA. CHHHHOOOOOoooo.' The shiny little Tommy the Tank engine, polished and smiling, smoking and hissing, drew neatly into the halt. HOOOONK! HOOONK! Children of all ages appeared and piled happily on board. Then it was off again, a chuffing diminuendo in a diminishing cloud of smoke.

Richard was looking dreamily at Barmouth bridge. He was down memory lane.

'We used to have holidays over there in Arthog.' He pointed up the Mawddach estuary.

'We stayed in a bungalow belonging to Mr. and Mrs Jones-Effans.' He lapsed momentarily into a recognisably Welsh accent.

'Mr Jones-Effans owned a few sheep and a trac*tor*. His misses took in lodgers and packed them in like sardines. I don't know where they slept, but I was in a cubby hole off the kitchen with

my sister. Sundays were bad, mind: Mrs. Jones-Effans cleaned in
chapel so her lodgers only got sarnies.'

We laughed.

Our boots clattered over the long wooden bridge that spans the
Mawddach estuary. The mainline diesel roared past us blowing
our hair in its wake.

'That reminds me of the time my father lost his new pork pie
hat.' Richard's mental clock was still on his first year in double
figures.

'It blew off in a puff of wind right here. My mother had just
bought it for him and she half-expected him to dive in after it. The
new hat floated gently away on the tide . . . My mother tore my
father off such a strip I was surprised the bridge stood up to it!'

A wizened little man with a thick Welsh accent accosted us
from his little booth.

'That'll be 30 pence each see . . . Ta. Haf a good journee.'

'I remember when it was one old penny. Still, I suppose if you
take inflation into account it's still not a lot.' Richard returned to
the present.

'HOOT! HOOT!' We looked up to see my father hooting and
waving from his van which was obstructing traffic in all directions.
We climbed aboard and were thankful to get out of the hurly burly
of downtown Barmouth.

Harlech's well-preserved castle looked bleak and inhospitable,
on a grey day. My mood was grey too as my dose of Celtic Revenge
had returned, now immune to the 'fix'. I wasn't even impressed by
Clough William-Ellis pastiche of Porto-Fino distantly viewed from
across the Dwyryd estuary. However, as we headed inland towards
Porthmadog we came across a shepherd and his dog working the
sheep. The shepherd's gaunt, lined, weather-beaten face was half-
hidden under a battered brown felt hat. His shabby clothes hung
off his gristly frame like a scarecrow. His economical movements
were quiet and purposeful. His dog, a black and white coiled spring,
watched and listened. . . The little band of massed sheep vocalised
in uneven counterpoint. One panicked and moved out of line. A
black and white rocket streaked across the grass to prevent woolly
discord. A shrill whistle, and the dog returned to his place. Shepherd
and dog, control and power, perfect harmony.

'Reminds me of the male voice choir. The bond between them
and the control.'

'Amazing.' Richard agreed climbing gingerly over a rickety style. 'Watch this one it'll tear your trousers. I think I'll offer my services repairing these styles, they're all rotten just here.'

'Better than repairing rotten teeth?'

My dentist nodded agreement.

A pit-stop near Porthmadoc provided me with some much-needed concrete mix for my runny tummy. We passed a large new building squatting in a muddy field by the roadside.

'That's the new Snowdonia National Park H.Q. It cost millions of pounds and has produced a lot of local ill-feeling. They used Spanish tiles and foreign bricks, *here* of all places where the slate quarries are world famous.' Richard sounded indignant.

'No wonder it looks so odd.'

'Hardly a good P.R. exercise. They leave lights on all the time too, yet can't afford to mend the stiles.'

Along by the railway line, the path into Criccieth was a mass of polythene sheeting, nylon rope, and plastic containers, brought in on the tides by the prevailing winds. Small caves in the rocks made natural over-filled litter bins We waded ankle deep through the debris.

'Ouch!' Ironically I had kicked a rusting old litter bin.

I sank onto some boulders under a 'DIM PARCIO / NO PARKING sign near the beach. Richard thought this deserved a photo, before going off to buy a couple of home made ices for which Criccieth is famous.

'No time for poor old Lloyd George I suppose?' I said stuffing my mouth with a delicious double-barrel of chocolate and vanilla.

'Not today Josephine. Pwllheli's still a fair way.'

Revived by my ice cream, I practised my Welsh pronunciation of 'P-Fweli?'

'It's more F-Whelli.'

'I think I'll just concentrate on walking. How many miles?'

The sun came out as we reached the long wide beach. Now we threw off our boots thinking that walking would be easier with our soles on the sand. After half a mile we had to pull them on again. Carrying a lot of weight, our feet relied on the cushioning effect of insoles. With our boots back on we speeded up at once.

It was a long, long beach, peppered with dogs and people. Pwllheli, a blurred mirage, appeared as a dot on the horizon. It became distinct painfully slowly. The outer harbour was filled with yachts. 'A larger version of Aberdovey,' I thought. Richard, anxious about the time, had gone on ahead to make a phone call to our host at the station, where we were supposed to rendez-vous. When I arrived he wasn't there, but had found another call box which created a certain amount of acrimony. Our host suggested we started walking and he would pick us up along the way. That news didn't cheer me too much either.

Roy was a 75-year old retired dentist from Wolverhampton. Like most dentists, he had a wealth of hobbies to keep him busy in his retirement. He used to fence, still enjoyed sailing and was a keen radio ham. Their rural home had distant views of the Snowdonia range across the bay.

'We're daft to go on living out here at our age,' Peggy, his energetic wife, confessed to me. Our health isn't brilliant, but I couldn't imagine living without this view.'

Later we spoke about the problems of incomers on the Llyn peninsula.

'Integration is difficult. There are a lot of us incomers here. We've tried to learn Welsh but it's no good. The Welsh members of our Rotary Club left. I think a lot of resentment still exists.'

When I lived in Liverpool all our friends seemed to go to Abersoch for their summer holidays and raved about it, so I was curious to see the place. Our guide book denounced it as:

'*The one real intrusion of the modern world into the timeless charm of the Llyn Peninsula . . . transformed from a quiet fishing village to a busy centre for power boat enthusiasts.*'

'Strange how the Lleyn peninsula is like an arm with thumbs down. A sort of natural feature signifying Welsh disapproval of the incomer. The thumbs down bit starts at Abersoch.'

For once I had been studying the map. We only had time to skirt the village, which was waiting reluctantly for its overpowering tide of incoming Mancurians and Liverpuddlians. The pleasure craft sat listlessly on the sandy banks of the river under a grey sky.

We had arranged to meet my godson and his parents half-way along a three mile stretch of straight sandy beach called Porth Nergwl. This translates to Hell's Mouth. Distances on a long beach are misleading. We walked and walked, peering myopically into the distance, and squinting through binoculars at any parties of three. When we finally met up, we had walked three quarters of the length of the beach, and they can only have covered half a mile, although they were sure they had reached the half way point.

We had a happy lunch with them on the warm sand, catching up on news of the real world, and they spent the next two days walking part of the way with us. It was a good interlude. My father in his motorized caravan, was shadowing us for a few days. Each evening we found some well-selected pubs to eat, drink and be merry in.

Meeting friends and family fused us temporarily to the real world. It was as though we were on holiday. Far from envying them when they returned home to their 'normal' existance, we felt elated, knowing that we still had many months of adventure before us.

From Port Meudy near Aberdaron we had a clear view of the hump-backed island of Bardsay just off the end of the Lleyn peninsula. It was from here that the constant stream of pilgrims would embark for the ultra holy island. This inhospitable whale-back of rock, some two miles off shore, was apparently a 'tranquil refuge for Christians, fleeing the chaos of mainland Britain', after the orderly Romans had departed. A church was founded there in the 3rd century.

'It ranked so high on the pilgrimage credit scale,' Richard informed me, 'that three pilgrimages to Bardsay were equal to one to Rome or the Holy Land. It was also *the* place to be buried if you were holy enough. There are so many skeletons over there, it's like an island of the dead.'

'I hope they made it to Heaven. It looks mighty inhospitable to me.' I shuddered and looked around at the cairn-strewn moor land, reminiscent of Carn Lledi at St. David's Head.

'Bardsay Sound is also famous for its tidal race and treacherous currents. I presume that canoeist knows what he's doing.' Richard pointed to a small figure far below, calmly paddling towards the rocky island.

Our awareness of the importance of the Lleyn Peninsula in the Age of Saints, grew as we walked. The pilgrims to Bardsay had their last mainland drink at a holy well at St. Mary's near the mountain of Mynydd Mawr. The tiny cove of Porth Meudwy where they embarked was deserted, with just a few fishing boats and tractors drawn up on the shingle. The little chapel at Pistyll, dedicated to St. Bueno, was a stopping place for pilgrims on their way to Bardsay. This simple stone chapel was described as:

'*A lonely little sanctuary by the sea . . . within whose nave the story of the centuries in silence sleeps.*' Adding a challenge to contemporary pilgrims, '*Canst thou pass by without kneeling here to bless and pray?*'

We stepped inside. It was cool, bare and sweetly smelling. Wild flowers decorated the stone sills and the bare floor was strewn with medicinal herbs. Its simplicity and the pungent smell of the herbs, gave it a potent resonance. There was no sign of the nearby monastery, inn or hospice where pilgrims would have had shelter and care. However, wild fruit bushes and hop vines still flourish by the remains of the ash grove, and Danesberry still grows in the churchyard. We learned that this plant was once reputed to possess power to assist in the transmigration of souls.

We came across St. Bueno again at Clynogg Fawr, a large church whose wealth had come from the hoards of pilgrims passing through in Middle Ages. St.Bueno had founded a monastery there in 616 A.D. The holy well was supposed to have curative powers, but only if the patient spent a long cold night on the saint's tomb which didn't seem a very curative exercise to us.

We certainly needed the protection of the saint on the main road to from Dinas Dinile (pronounced 'Dines Dinckly' my godson informed me). It was twisting and narrow in places, and very busy. There was no verge for the pedestrian, and round corners we had to shrink back into the bramble bushes to avoid being mown down.

On the Caernarfon road we found another ancient church sitting alone in a field near Llanfaglan. It was an interesting mix of farm-building and church with tombstones embossed with all sorts of mysterious emblems - clasped hands, a pair of wings with a long neck. I felt as mystified by this culture as an illiterate might have found the following eulogy for a Mary Ann Robbins of the County of Tipperary, the Kingdom of Ireland, who died in 1809 aged 47 after a tough life:

Our lovely mother,
Happy change for thee,
Better far than in this world to be;
Exposed to fear, to trouble, pain and grief,
Thy state how blessed and lasting thy relief.

We left my father in Dinas Dinelli on Good Friday and walked into Caenarfon where we had time to spend looking round this walled and castillated city. There was a general feeling of spring in the air, and we found a camping shop which sold us a pair of walking shorts each. Little did we know then how much use they would have.

Thanks to more friends, we managed to climb Snowden on Easter Saturday afternoon. We both love mountains, and our plan to climb one in England, Wales and Scotland was pure self-indulgence. We took the Miner's track with a stream of others. It felt a bit like a pilgrimage. The weather cleared to give us good views until we reached the cloud at 300 feet from the summit. The temperature plummeted in the cold wind, and we sat with a group of equally chattering teeth outside the concrete bunker that passed for a cafe. It was owned by the Snowden Railway, and was shut, although the train was chugging up and down the mountain.

'Someone could make a fortune if they revamped this place and made it warm and welcoming. Just think of all the people that will come up here this weekend, longing to part with their money.'

'Mmmmm. If we had some capital I wouldn't mind the job. Meanwhile, thank God for thermals,' I said as I handed Richard a piece of chocolate and hot drink from the thermos.

'If we're cold what must those people feel like?' Richard was looking at a group of Japanese tourists with light jackets, thin cotton trousers, no socks, and trainers.

Easter day heralded the start of Spring and an early Summer. The woods were burgeoning with spring flowers and drenched in birdsong and scents. Conway's ancient walls were a mass of wallflowers and valerium. There was a strong smell of new-mown grass, and the first game of the cricket season was in progress.

The only blot on the day had been a few miles near Penmaenmawr when we were forced to walk along the new A55 Expressway, a busy trunk road which carves a swathe of tarmac between the holiday resort of Penmaenmawr and its once popular beach. Historically it was a quarrying town and our current hostess Ann had been born and bred there.

'My father was a quarryman, skilled mind, he made the granite setts for paving by hand. He and his mates used to meet in their little shelters of a lunchtime and put the world to rights. Now there's very little quarrying and the beach is inaccessible. It's sad now.'

It was sad. A long line of Victorian houses punctuated at regular intervals by dissenting chapels and churches.

'I remember when they were all full,' Ann told us. 'When I was a child the Presbyterian ethic prevailed and frivolity on a Sunday was forbidden. Once one of my aunties came to stay wearing a black hat with an ostrich feather in it. The feather was burned.

Such adornments came under the sin of vanity. I found the quill in the embers next day. In the 18th century people were taken across to Anglesey in horse-drawn carts at low tide, and by ferry at high tide. The granite and aggregate was shipped away by boat Liverpool. It was a busy place and full of character.'

The hillside is still a mass of industrial scars and the tram tracks were clearly visible running vertically down the mountain.

We met our third marathon runner host in Conway. Roger lived in Prestatyn and had offered to walk the dreary 18-mile stretch with us. Luckily for me his wife Val came along too.

Roger set a pace that would have done credit to the London Marathon. I was thankful to have Val in the rearguard to keep me company. I remember little of the walk except the incessant roads, the rain and the cracking pace. Then of course there was Rhyl.

The Victorian sea front terraces looked seedy and run-down.

'They're mostly bedsits now.' Val sounded apologetic.

'You remember the horrific story of the baby who starved to death because both parents had overdosed on drugs?' I remembered it well. A gust of wind hit us as we rounded the corner. Now we were passing a garish fun-fair; a late 20th century cut and paste toy town.

'That was only finished last year,' Val said shaking her head. 'It was supposed to re-incarnate Rhyl, but it's been a big flop. Everyone thinks it was a waste of money.'

'It looks as though it fell from Mary Poppins' umbrella.' We paused to stretch our weary muscles and I kept an eye on toy town to see if Noddy or Big Ears might come round the corner.

Poor Val was not used to doing long-distance walks at any pace. She was coping brilliantly, but getting tired.

'The last couple of miles are always the worst,' I said with feeling. 'You know the end is in sight but you still have to get there.'

The approach to The Dee estuary was a motor way of sand. At the Point of Ayr there was a lighthouse and here Richard pointed across the estuary to the Seaforth Container Dock Terminal just north of Liverpool.

'We could see Liverpool itself if the Wirral Peninsula wasn't in the way.'

I gazed through the binoculars across the water.

'Wow! Look out Liver birds!'

I had spent most of my teenage years in Liverpool so the city held special significance for me. We had planned to spend two nights there in the very house where I grew up. While the Beatles were warming up in the Cavern, I was learning to waltz, fox-trot and tango in the Mecca Ballrooms, only streets away. I felt as excited as any ten year old. This visit we were going to enter Liverpool the right way, that is to *'ferry cross the Mersey'*; something I had never done in all those years.

Meanwhile we still had to walk up the west bank of the Dee where we came upon our first industry since South Wales. A colliery, steelworks, and, at Mostyn Quay, a surreal ferry sitting self-consciously at right angles to the river, surrounded by green meadows. Once a respectable Liverpool to Belfast ferry, the big white liner had been converted first into a hotel and then a cash-and-carry. Now, quietly rusting, it awaited its fate.

The phone rang that evening while we were eating. It was our friend John Hill from Tunbridge Wells ringing to say he and Sally would be at Chester station at ten past one the next day. Richard was happy for me to take the call, and under the impression that it was an eight mile walk, I said we'd meet their train. Richard was furious.

'We'll never make it by then. It's nearer twelve miles. Why did you do that?'

'You said it was eight miles, which should be quite possible in three and a half hours. If we meet at the station we can go to their hotel, wash and brush up and leave our packs. Anyway, if you feel that strongly ring him back.'

Richard hates phones. He didn't ring back. It was a gallop into Chester but we made it with no minutes to spare. Our wash and brush up was more than welcome, and we had a civilised afternoon, sightseeing without packs.

Chester's patchwork of history can be 'bird's eye viewed' from a walk around the still complete city walls. Romans, Tudors, Stewarts, Georgians and Victorians have all left their mark in an interesting collage of cultures. We relished the time to be real tourists.

That evening we had a delicious Italian meal with John and Sally and caught up with news. Tunbridge Wells, we learned, was still turning on its axis, and the family surviving without us. We shared news and views over pasta and chianti, and left for our beautiful Regency Youth Hostel in Hough Green, in plenty of time to walk the mile and a quarter before they closed at 10.30 p.m. Richard had asked me to phone them, and book ourselves in, earlier that day. Suddenly his pace quickened. I looked at my watch. It was five to ten.

'What's the rush?' I yelled to his back. 'There's no need to go off like a rocket!'

Suddenly I was cross. He obviously thought the hostel closed at 10 p.m. I caught him up at the reception.

'You do stay open until 10.30 don't you?' I asked pointedly.

'Sure and there's plenty of beds tonight. I'll get you your sheets. Breakfast for two was it?'

Richard nodded.

'We don't need that expensive breakfast. I've got enough provisions. Catering is my job remember?'

I was furious and thankful that we were put in separate dorms.

I had a sleepless night, partly because I was so cross, and partly because my stable mates did not suffer from communication problems.

'Git into that double sheet and put it over yer pellow,' a young Aussie instructed her mother in a whisper that could have been heard in the Sydney Opera House. Switch off the loit will yer and don't talk.' Her dazed mother complied. Later, we had an invasion of Dutch, who assumed that because nobody understood their language, nobody could hear it either.

Chapter Ten

*Objects are strange and unfamiliar because they were there
before and will be there after. So far as I remember,
childhood is solitude amidst
a confederacy of things and creatures which
have no name or purpose.
Names and purposes are thought up by us afterwards.*
Miroslav Holub

We left Chester along the Shropshire Union Canal with its old
warehouses and dry docks, neatly lined with brightly painted long
boats. Mrs Mallard swam proudly downstream followed by her
fluffy brood. The last little duckling was struggling to keep up,
batting through the water for all its tiny form was worth.

'Go for it,' I encouraged. 'You'll catch up. Don't give up. I
know what it feels like!'

Richard noticed I was busy recording and stopped to let me
catch up.

'Have you mentioned this acquaduct bridge?' he asked
harmlessly enough.

My anger from the previous night still seethed beneath the
surface and I lunged as if to strangle him, in mock battle.

'Yes, yes, yes. You don't trust me to do anything. If you don't
think I do it well enough why don't you do it?'

'You're mad. I'm always having to mop up your explosions.
You're too competitive to share a pavement with. Best thing to do
with that recorder is to throw it into the canal.'

Stunned, I dropped well behind to do some serious thinking.
How on earth were we going to be able to complete this walk if
we squabbled like this when everything was going well. My
confidence was undermined. My walking partner didn't trust my
ability to make a phone call, housekeep or record what we saw. I
was sick of just plodding behind like a dog, not being consulted. I
decided to give it until Blackpool and if things hadn't improved I
should leave him to finish it alone.

The day was full of sunshine and birdsong. We could almost see the fresh green leaves bursting from their brown buds. The sun was energising everything. The Wirral was a green oasis, separating the urban sprawls of Liverpool and Birkenhead from the steel and chemical plants of the north east coast of Wales.

We looked into the ancient sandstone church at Shotwick with its original oak numbered pews and three-tiered pulpit. It smelt of narcissi, broom and furniture polish. The peaceful little village had once been the port for Chester, before Parkgate took over in Georgian times. As the Dee silted up, Liverpool grew, and in the 19th century became one of the largest and most important ports in the world. Parkgate itself came as a surprise, retaining a faded black and white 18th century elegance. It had once been the home of Nelson's fleet, and it was here that Nelson met his mistress Emma Hamilton.

I sat on the long stone quay which now looks over a mournful stretch of marsh land where the Spartan grass has choked and silted up the estuary. It was hard to believe that only 200 years ago it was alive with packet boats and ships like Nelson's *Victory*.

'I've bought you an ice-cream,' a quiet voice said at my elbow. 'If you look through the binoculars you can see Mostyn Quay and the stranded Belfast ferry.'

'Mmmmm, delicious. Thanks,' I mumbled, my mouth full of chocolate and pecan.

The English spring loves to tease, and as we approached West Kirkby next day, the strong prevailing winds blew rain straight in our faces. By the time to reached Hoylake we were cold and wet. As we turned north east we left our green oasis and entered the desert of soulless streets, brick terraces and cemeteries. We stopped in a draughty bus shelter where I pulled on my discarded thermals. We tramped along grey pavements into Seacombe, to catch our ferry *'cross the Mersey'*.

Liverpool loomed out of the cold grey mist. A tidy outline of new skyscrapers had usurped the tangled web of cranes. I was relieved to recognise the familiar shapes of Pierhead, St. George's Hall and the great Anglican cathedral. The only docked ship on the river was the Mersey ferry.

Liverpool had metamorphosed. Gone was the dirt, the docks, the ships, the merchandise, the trams. Space has replaced clutter, historic buildings have been polished up and set in aspic; new ones built. The great Albert Dock has been refurbished for tourists as the city struggles to find a new identity in a changed world. Gilbert Scott's great sandstone cathedral, now complete after seventy years, stands as a monument to perseverance. Not to be outdone, the Catholic cathedral, known affectionately as 'Paddy's Wigwam' sits at the other end of Hope Street. The ghetto of Toxteth lies beneath the garnish; the old Co-op at Aigburth is now a wine bar, and the little Victorian terraced houses are now the preferred accommodation for post-graduates.

'Look at the Liver birds, they've still got their larver seaweed in their mouths - as long as they hang on to that, Liverpool will survive, or so the myth goes.' It was my turn to give Richard a little local knowledge.

'I can't see Julie Walters anywhere.'

Undeterred I continued.

'When we first came to Liverpool I remember half-bombed houses with peeling wallpaper that hadn't been pulled down. There were real slums then. The docks hummed with noise and smelt of coal and rotting vegetables. The west wing of the Anglican cathedral wasn't finished, and Paddy's Wigwam wasn't built. I took my driving test on those roads round the cathedral. They were perfect for hill starts.'

I fell silent, lost in memories as our ferry docked at Pierhead.

We were able to stay at 9b, Fulwood Park, and sleep in what had been my very own room. Gone were the paraffin stoves, the black lino and the bottle green black-out curtains, but the fabric of the house had changed little. Our cottage had been the coach house for the Victorian mansion next door. It was now owned by two retired medical consultants, both Liverpuddlians who were kind enough to share both their home and their city with us. The quiet park led down to the Mersey, where, what in our day had been a rubbish tip and crumbling cliffs, was now a smart three-mile long promenade from Otterspool to Pierhead.

We were proudly shown Liverpool's new clean face. The Albert Dock complex, reverberating to the Beatle's music, was now a maze of tourist shops, Granada T.V., smart apartments and a Tate Gallery. The newly painted St. George's Street with its Georgian houses and magnificent town hall. The shiny red brick Victorian mansions of Sefton Park were once homes for the wealthy shipping magnates. Even the daffodils in the park, where my mother and I used to walk our dog, seemed to have been polished.

As we crossed the wide Aigburth Road I reminiscenced,
'There were trams down this road and that wine bar was the Co-op. In those days the change was put into a little brass container and sent whizzing across the ceiling to the cashier. She was a po-faced old bag who sat behind an ornate till.'
'Now who's sounding her age?' Richard said.
Disregarding him, I pointed to a narrow street of small Victorian terraced houses. 'There'd always be women out scrubbing their doorsteps in those streets. They'd have their hair in a scarf, a wrap-around pinny, carpet slippers and a fag out of one corner of their mouth.'
I suddenly realised what a priggy little snob I sounded.
The park hadn't changed at all. The trees were bigger, the houses looked smarter, but it was just as if there hadn't been a thirty-year gap since I left.
We walked out of my time warp along the reclaimed land of Otterspool promenade to Pierhead and then out of the city through Bootle. These few miles had a nightmare quality. Bootle docks, built from 1824 to 1860 by Jesse Hartley, had made Liverpool great. Now, only rusty skeletons remain behind the great granite wall and castellated dock gates. Breakers yards, a few dry docks, empty spaces, deserted warehouses, boarded-up pubs, miles of railings, puddles and litter make a sad epitaph. The occasional lorry roared past, splashing us with dirty water. Beside its own depressing dock stood the H.& O. Wills warehouse, dated 1900. It was a megalithic red-brick edifice; a ghostly remnant of wealth, power and exploitation.
'I have recurrent nightmares about those sort of docks. That huge building reflected in that dark dank water . . .' Richard shuddered.
We were relieved to reach the shiny new container port of Seaforth. This anti-septic port handles as much cargo as Liverpool did in its heyday.
Both of us were glad to reach a visible sea again, at the Victorian suburb of Crosby, and leave industry behind. It was the last big city we should see for several months.

* * *

Leaving Formby we rejoiced in sun, sea and sand as far as Southport. Here we turned inland, on another foray down memory lane. Friends, who now live in the house my uncle designed for my parents in 1939, offered to put us up. At that time, my father was working for the Royal Ordinance Factory at Chorley. My brother was born in our 'guest room' in 1941.

Our rendez-vous point was Hesketh Bank, near Beccansall. Landscape, houses, tarmac and pavements were all flat and featureless. As we shambled along the dull roads, we missed the sea, hills and cliffs. I sank down on the step of a corner shop, among the fag ends and the litter, waiting to be collected. On the dot of 5 p.m. Ralph drove up in an immaculate steel grey Saab convertable with beige leather seats. Wal had a cheeky little cloche hat on to keep her long hair under control. We sank into total comfort, and accelerated into another world.

Our walk to Blackpool took us through Lytham St. Ann's which I described in my diary as:

Reeking of respectability. A composite of Hove, Angmering-on-Sea and Bournemouth. All promenades, rock gardens, polished brick houses and rhubarb and custard flower beds.

Lytham had a paucity of letter boxes. Remembering my soggy postcard at Dartmouth, I made a major effort to post cards before they disintegrated into pulp. There were no red boxes on the miles of promenade. I struck off across the busy road, towards the heart of the town, cursing under my breath. Traffic, crowds, shops, dogs, pedestrian crossings, lollipop ladies, but no letter boxes. A perfumed lady with dyed hair in a leopard-skin chiffon trouser suit, teetered out of a shiny red-brick block of flats.

'Excuse me please. Could you tell me where I can post a letter?'

Her eyes travelled from my tousled hair and weather beaten face, past my rucksack, settling momentarily on the piece of binder twine that was holding my trousers up. They continued their journey down my faded trousers, finishing with my cracked walking boots. There was a long pause.

'Turn left by the next traffic lights and it's a hundred yards down on your right.' Her nose shifted a degree or two upwards. She left in a trail of perfume and a clatter of stilleto heels.

Blackpool, playground of the north, stretches itself for seven gaudy miles. Pleasure here is a serious business. Piers, promenades, a mini Eiffel Tower, amusement arcades, horses and carts, piped music, tacky lights, candy floss and donkeys. You have *got* to enjoy yourself in Blackpool. If statistics are correct, people do.

What Blackpol lacks in aesthetics, it makes up for in numbers. More than six million people visit Blackpool annually, many more than once, making a staggering sixteen million. 375,000 bulbs light up the front each Autumn, which must make it the brightest, if not the brashest, of seaside resorts. The roller coaster in the 40-acre Pleasure Beach Amusement Park is known as 'The Big 'Un' taking its passengers round 360 degree loops, accompanied by 360 degree screams.

'I can't believe people acutally pay to do that.' Richard and I stood staring in amazment as the tiny trucks, rattling loudly as they hurled themselves down the near-vertical rails, whooshed up the next loop, teetered, and fell again, accompanied by a crescendo of thrilling terror.

Piers are an interesting phenomena. Originally built to provide deep-water landing for steamboats, they evolved into terra firma cruise-liners where pleasure-seekers of all ages and stages could enjoy a candy floss of popular culture with their feet on the deck. Amongst the brass bands, fortune-tellers, peep shows, saucy post-cards, deck chairs and fishing rods, those who venture onto the wooden boards, are castaways from the real world. Here you can snooze in a deckchair or indulge your fantasies; here it is your duty to be happy.

Meanwhile, back in the real world of the coastal walker, our feet were firmly on the ground, searching for a public loo that was open. We reckoned the drug trade must be brisk in out of season Blackpool, for they were all locked and barred.

'Nothing for it but to cross your legs,' Richard said.

The promenade seemed endless, especially with crossed legs, and we were late getting to our pit-stop in Bispham. Doreen and Peter gave us a wonderful welcome and calmly saw us through the next twenty four frenetic hours.

In this short time, we had to take on our camping equipment, decide what we did and didn't need, develop and mark up films, mend kit, wash most of our clothes, buy a new pair of boots, contact the family and write up a newsletter. Richard's sister, Sue, had bought our equipment up from Bristol, and was taking all our superfluous gear away. The turn round was under an hour. Friends

Eastbourne - January 1st, 1995.

Cliffs near Lulworth Cove.

South Devon Coast Path.

Smiling wetly in
Downderry.

Soar Mill Cove - South Devon.

Quarried cliffs
near Tintagel.

Bull Point - North Devon Coast Path.

Kellen Head near Port Quin.

Roughing it at Porthcawl.

End of Pembrokeshire Coast Path.

Criccieth, North Wales.

Well met! Shally and her father.

Richard, Gordon and Fred looking for a Skafell Pike!

Ailsa Craig from Ayrshire coast.

Ferry at Kilchoan.

Cyclist in Knoydart.

Skye and Raasay from Applecross Peninsula.

Richard at Redpoint Sands.

Old track round Applecross Peninsula.

Rough camping near Kenmore on Shieldaig Road.

Crossing a river in western Highlands.

Quinag - looking north.

Richard at Cape Wrath.

Lone piper on Orkneys.

Noup Head - Westray.

Richard and 'Joggle' traveller in Sutherland.

Richard leaving Fraserburgh.

Chain walk - Elie.

Shally with the sea on her right - Holderness.

Staithes on the Cleveland Way.

Sea defences on the east coast.

Birthday cake in Burnham-on-Crouch.

of ours from Brussels had arranged to take us out to lunch, and in the evening Doreen and Peter had walking friends round to meet us. We only managed to achieve it all due to excellent teamwork. Peter sewed my rucksack, Doreen washed our things, I wrote and made phone calls, Richard dealt with the photos, our friends took us to the outdoor shop to buy boots. By the end of the day we were in a daze.

For us, Blackpool was a watershed. From now on we bid farewell to the trappings of normality. No more friendly faces offering bubble baths and comfy beds, three-piece suites and elegant meals. From now on we would be on our own with one tiny tent, a small cooker, some unleaded petrol, two plastic plates and a lot more weight.

'It'll be good to be out on our own,' Richard had said several times lately.

I felt ready for the challenge too, yet when we set off on April 28th, with bulging packs now filled with our survival kit, we were full of anxieties.

'Don't look so worried,' Peter scolded gently, camera in hand.

I pinned on a grin. 'That's better.' Click. 'You'll be fine.'

I felt anything but fine. I was wearing new boots, and that always spells trouble for me. The extra weight made my pack nearly 40 lbs and Richards well over 50 lbs. Katie rang yesterday to say she was having recurrent health problems. She had met Mr Right but he was now sailing round the world. She had just changed jobs and might not be paid for her sick leave.

Meanwhile, back at the ranch, Jo was coping with Granny's boils and constipation. You can walk out and leave your job, your house, your plastic cards, your insurance policies, but not your family. Then there was us. How were we going to manage in an undiluted state? One man and his appendage? God knows I thought.

'Shut up!' said my alter ego. 'The sun's shining. You're completely free. You want to do this and it'll be OK. Live for the moment!'

* * *

The Fylde peninsula did not inspire. It was flat and lifeless. We crossed the River Wyre on the Shard Bridge. Back on the coast we saw hundreds of birds along the Pilling Marshes, pink-footed geese, lapwings, dunlins, redshanks and shelducks. Heat-hazy views of the Cumbrian hills, Heysham Power Station and Barrow-in-Furness, cheered us, but it was a long hot tramp into Cockerham. My feet were fighting my new boots and the extra weight we were carrying was increasingly noticeable.

Richard waxed lyrical as we walked along the peaceful towpath of the Lancaster Ship Canal.

'This is a pastoral Garden of Eden' he murmured.

The little path took us through fields and woods, under and over a series of old stone bridges. Bleats, birdsong and the occasional chug-ggr, chug-ggr of a long boat slipping easily under the bridges were the only sounds. Here, all nature was a garden.

'That's just like a Gainsborough painting. All we need now are Mr. and Mrs. Andrews.' The stone bridge ahead was topped with an elegant balustrade. The mature beech trees round it were just coming into leaf and some cattle stood decoratively under the trees. While we inhaled the sweet smell of bluebells we heard a faint roar.

'The M6,' said Richard. 'So much for Gainsborough.'

The canal bought us right into Lancaster. A bustling historic university town, where the old priory church and Norman castle straddle the hill with sweeping views. The harbour is in terminal decay since the river's navigable channel silted up. In the 18th century St. George's Quay was a busy port. Now the warehouses sit mouldering, listless and empty. Our attempts to learn more about this interesting town were thwarted at The Maritime Museum.

'Naw rooksacks can be left 'ere.' They told us firmly.

'Strange effect rucksacks have on people. Sometimes they're a key and sometimes a lock. We went on our way to Morecambe.

An hour or so later we passed a pub. Carrying the extra weight was thirsty work and I longed for a drink. Richard was out of earshot. A middle-aged man leaving the pub watched me walk past.

'Ees left yer ain't 'ee,' he jeered.

I felt like telling him to mind his own business.

Instead I took out my little whistle and blew it at least ten times. The retreating figure didn't alter his course one degree.

Morecambe struggles to keep going as an important seaside resort. Traditionnally catering for the mill workers that are no more, it now caters mainly for the 'traditional' elderly. The four-mile curving promenade along the edge of Morecombe Bay, backed by serried ranks of Victorian hotels, looked tired, in spite of a brave show of tulips under the clock tower. The brash Superdome and Marineland looked like daubs of rouge on a pale old face. The elderly sat quietly in shelters, or fly-like behind the warm plate-glass of the hotel window, gazing out to sea. A small group of old men in cloth caps and beige anoraks were racing their remote-controlled sailing boats across a pond. A few old ladies crawled along the promenade.

No tent yet. We were being put up at The Lothersdale Hotel by a Rotarian. The hotel bulged at the seams with O.A.P.'s on a special pre-season package. After supper we watched the dance floor fill up with over-seventies unashamedly enjoying themselves. Although young enough to be their children, we sloped off to bed, unable to compete.

Richard was patronising and sarcastic when I couldn't operate the shower. I flipped and threatened to leave him. We had a sleepless night. I woke with a headache, probably due to an overdose of cheap wine. My diary entry for Sunday, April 30th, starts: *Still together!*

We planned to camp that night, but were thwarted, as the campsite Richard had looked out near Arnside was no more than a run-down farm. A hopeful sign over a shed door invited enquiries.

'Yea, you can camp 'ere,' a large woman informed us.

'£2.00 each but if you want the toilet there'll be a £5 deposit.'

She leaned on the rickety door post and gave a hearty wheeze.

'If you want food you'll 'ave to go to Arnside. There's none 'ere.'

We walked on through the bluebell woods above the River Kent, which was bordered with red cliffs and golden sand. The evening sun warmed the scene and we had good views to Grange-over-Sands on the far side. This was the attractive end of Morecambe Bay. As far as I was concerned the rest of it was for the birds.

'We'll use the Youth Hostel at Arnside,' Richard said firmly.

A large map of Britain on the Youth Hostel wall caught my eye. I scanned it eagerly. Eastbourne was now a long way down. Oban, our half-way mark, was not so very far up the map. Every place we had walked through now meant something to me. I was seized by an overwhelming sense of achievement and, more surprisingly, possession. Somehow all those long miles were now my property, all those places exclusively personalised.

With the help of Youth Hostel tins and packets we had a good meal. Afterwards I opened the window of our family room and leant on the mullioned sill watching the sun set across the estuary. The past few days had been hard graft. Perhaps it was our row in Chester, my new boots, the flat landscape, the heat or the extra weight. Probably a mixture of all these. We still had a lot of road walking to do . . . The sun had disappeared over the horizon. An owl hooted mournfully in the trees below. I closed the window and told myself to take each day as it came and enjoy it.

The little train from Arnside was on time to take us on a seven minute journey over the water-and-sand to the Victorian town of Grange-over-Sands; a rail trip which saved us hours of walking. Grange means 'a granary' and dates from the days of the Augustinian monks of nearby Cartmel Priory. It was a genteel Victorian resort, gardens burgeoning with exotic plants. It faces south-east and is therefore sheltered from the prevailing winds. It seemed to be full of tea shops and bakeries.

'Now we're in Lancashire I think we should buy some eccles cakes. Have you ever had one?'

Richard hadn't and put up no resistance.

As we left the shop a lady in her seventies looked at me in amazement.

'Ooh! You are lucky carrying all that weight,' she exclaimed.

'Er. Yes. I suppose I am,' I replied. After a moments reflection I realised what she meant. I was lucky to be hale and hearty enough to carry 40 lbs. No doubt the lady had herself once been a walker. I stored that one away in my main directory, for future use, when the going got tough.

The little stone-housed tree-streamed village sat peacefully among the green undulating landscape. The air was full of birdsong and bleating and heavy with scents of spring. We noticed a racecourse near the little village and soon we heard the clip-clop of hooves. A stream of horses clattered past.

'Can I take your pack?' a friendly voice enquired above the clatter.

'I wish you could,' I replied. 'But I'd rather hang on to it. Thanks all the same.'

We realised that our packs now contained everything that matters to us - they were our home and our survival kit, too precious to part with.

Chapter Eleven

Parting is all we know if heaven
And all we know of hell.
Emily Dickinson

It was May 1st and the landscape was green and undulating. The woods were full of violets, primroses and bluebells and the little stone villages were softened with pink and white blossom. Sheep dotted the fields. We ate our frugal lunch beside a fast flowing river, alight with kingfishers, before taking the Cumbrian Coast path to Ulverston.

Ulverston has had a chequered history. Originally the property of the monks of Furness Abbey, it was a favourite target for raiders from Scotland under Robert Bruce, burned down twice, and fought over during the Civil War by both sides. In spite of these set backs, it prospered as a port in the 18th century. Its busy market square was known as 'the London of Furness.'

Our first camp site was situated in a quarry, sheltered from the wind, but rock hard. As I was blowing up my sleeping-mat, (a self-inflated one that supported bony areas much better than thin foam), Richard emerged from Reception wielding a mallet.

'Are you going to put me out of my misery?' I enquired.

'Not till you've cooked supper,' came the reply.

The cooker behaved, my al fresco cuisine was edible, and we both slept well. Morale notched up. We set off for Walney Island in good spirits.

We skirted the industrial heart of Barrow, but there was still a lot of pavement and road walking. Raising my eyes, I noticed a huge black and white poster. A naked pieta-like figure was being hustled out of a great crowd by a couple of embarrassed-looking policemen. The P.C.'s helmet was firmly clamped over where the loin cloth might have been. The caption read: *It's one to remember.* Slowly I realised that it was B.T.'s clever memory jog, to put a one after the zero with a regional code. The real world seemed far away.

We crossed the bridge onto Walney Island, a strange crab-claw shaped strip of land, twelve miles long, which shelters Barrow. To our left, sleek nuclear subs lined the docks, and to our right stood the massive new Devonshire Docks of Vickers Engineering. Ahead lay the brick sprawl of Vickerstown, an early 19th century Welwyn Garden City, built for the workers of Barrow.

'We'll have time to see Barrow properly tomorrow,' Richard announced. 'Our campsite is at the south end of this island.' With this he followed a signpost for the Council Refuse Tip.

Sea, sky and land seemed to merge into one amorphous mass along this appendage of land. Flat, marshy and windswept, the island appeared all infill sites, caravans and quicksand. The highest feature was the refuse tip. A haven for seabirds, perhaps, but a second class playground for humans. The island seemed very long indeed, but when we arrived the natives were friendly.

Our campsite had an inviting indoor pool and large bar and cost only £5.00. We had a little trouble lighting the cooker, due to the stiff breeze, but ate well and enjoyed a drink in the bar and the chance to sit on a chair. Sitting down was becoming something of a luxury. However, we were woken in the small hours by blood-curdling screams and screeches and I thought marauding Vikings or Robert Bruce must be on the warpath and our time was up. Richard was sleeping like a babe. I went out of the tent and listened carefully. Remembering that Walney Island is something of a bird sanctuary, I concluded that Civil War had broken out on the gull colony. The cacophony lasted for several sleepless hours.

Our campsite looked across Morecambe Bay to Piel Island and we learned more of this in the morning.

'That ruined castle belonged to the monks of Furness way back,' our campsite owner told us. 'They built a warehouse and fortress over there for goods traded from the abbey. Food, wine and stuff. I think there was all sorts of unholy contraband goings on.'

'Didn't Lambert Simnel have something to do with Piel Island?' Richard asked.

'That's right. In 1486 he attempted to seize the crown from Henry VII. It was the last invasion of England. It's never been forgotten, and when a new landlord takes over the pub on the island, he is always crowned King on a special chair in the old castle.'

We thanked her for her history lesson and wished we had time to see this little island with its romantic ruins and fascinating history.

'Remember Colonel Tate's invasion of Wales near Strumble Head, repulsed by the intrepid Jemima Nicholson?' I said. 'In Scotland we shall have Bonnie Prince Charlie, so that's one 'last' invasion in each country. I like this history on the hoof.'

Back in Barrow we had time to visit the Dockyard Museum which welcomed packs and walkers. We learned all about Barrow's rise to become largest steel-producing town in the world at the end of the nineteenth century.

'It certainly did its bit to help Britannia rule the waves. I suppose it still does with nuclear subs.'

'The trouble is, Barrow is just Vickers. All its eggs in one nuclear basket. One shift in Government policy, and the town would be finished,' Richard commented.

Although it was only early May, the temperatures soared, and by noon it was over 70 degrees. We set off for Askram-in-Furness in relaxed mood. It wasn't far, and we had time on our side. I was dreaming away, minding my own business, when suddenly I tripped on the pavement. The weight of the pack prevented me saving myself, and the pavement inexorably neared my face. I went down, SPLAT, like a felled tree.

'Shit, damn and blast!' I lifted my battered face and tried to right myself. The weight of the pack plus camera and binoculars pinned me to the pavement. I felt a cross between a junky, Worsell Gummage and a vampire.

It took Richard some time to release my appendages, enabling me to shamble to my feet. I retreated behind a wall to lick my wounds and assess any damage.

'I 'arn o'en ay 'outh,' I explained, dabbing the blood away.

Richard, used to this language from his patients, understood the problem.

'Try pushing it forward with your tongue,' he suggested.

My crowned front tooth had taken the brunt of the pavement and swerved backwards locking my mouth shut. After a few minutes of pushing, the crown re-aligned, but then gave up the ghost and fell off. I passed a tentative finger across the mini-mountain on my jaw.

'It's OK,' I pronounced. 'Nothing broken and my legs are fine. Let's get off this horrible road.'

Richard looked relieved and we made gentle progress to Askram where our campsite was in a field shared with cowpats, dandelions, a water tap and the luxury of a picnic table.

The farmer's wife inspected my smashed face with some concern.

'Would you like a doctor?' she asked.

'No thanks. I've got a dentist' I replied, trying to smile.

'You can call me stiff upper lip now if you like,' I said as we made a mile-long journey to the phone box. After the family, we rang the friend who was coming over to walk Skafell Pike with us in two days time.

'Sorry, Richard,' his wife said. 'Fred's not in yet. Could you ring back in an hour? You'll catch him then.'

'No, we can't.' Richard was unusually firm. 'Shally's had a fall, we've walked two miles to ring and we haven't had a shower yet.'

We agreed that we were in a different world.

On our way back, we passed a middle-aged man, sitting ankle deep in cow parsley on a seat by the road. Green fields stretched out behind him to the Cumbrian hills. He was playing soulful melodies on a fiddle, in tune with the roosting birds and the spring twilight.

Friends were joining us for the walk to Haverigg that day and I felt very self-concious about my bruised jaw and gappy grin. They were in fact a wonderful tonic, and we enjoyed their company and conversation as we walked through the lush green countryside, bursting with spring. In one field a ewe had just dropped her lamb and we watched fascinated as the little purple bag came to life. First it shuddered, and then a tiny head emerged. Helped by the ewe's strong licking, the little bundle rose shakily onto its stocking feet and attempted to find mum's milk. For us town dwellers, it was a hypnotic and emotional moment.

In spite of our congenial company I found the last few miles hard and wrote in my diary:

No longer feel on top of the walk. My left forefoot is painful much of the day and my new boots have given me blisters. Only able to eat slops at present. Lucky R is fine. For me each day is a worry.

As we progressed along the Cumbrian Coastal Way, our premature heat wave continued. Richard pointed towards the Cumbrian mountains.

'Skafell Pike's over there. We'll be going up tomorrow if you feel up to it.'

'Hold me back,' I replied. 'Walking up a mountain will be a pleasant change, especially without a pack. The only thing that bothers me is meeting Fred and Gordon with a gappy grin. Gaps are OK when you're six, but not so good at my age.'

'I'll try and fix it for you tonight at Ravenglass.'

There are some advantages in walking with an itinerant dentist, I thought.

Not far from Ravenglass, we met the River Esk, where there was no footbridge and the road route was five extra miles. There was, however, a rail bridge. Neither of us hesitated, but made a quick dash for it, clattering over the wooden boards along the steel rails hoping a train wouldn't end it all. 'Look out.' Richard shouted from the rear. 'Some of these boards are rotten!'

'Too bad.' I shouted, breaking into a trot. 'I'm not hanging about to see if they've got rising damp.'

Safely across the river, we were soon at the peaceful little campsite where the owners lent Richard a tube of glue, and gave me some prepared food to heat up for supper. When we had eaten, I reclined my head on the picnic table admiring the blue sky of this al fresco surgery, while Richard busied himself with tissues, nappy pins and glue. At last he seemed satisfied. The crown was reinstated and my 'ring of confidence' returned.

To reach Eskdale we took the narrow gauge railway from Ravenglass and met Fred and Gordon as arranged. It was a perfect day with brilliant visibility. From the summit of Skafell Pike every peak in the Lake District was eager to be admired. We could make out Wales; Dumfries and Galloway beckoned from the North West, and the Isle of Man rose out of the sea like a Japenese water colour. I forgot my aches and pains and revelled in the buzz that mountains always give me. Three days ago I had been flat on my face in Barrow, and today I was up a mountain. I felt very lucky. It was V.E. Day and what a way to celebrate.

* * *

It was Sunday, May 6th, and the bells of the 12th century priory church of St. Bees rang out joyfully as we headed for the coast again. Hand and hand on the beach, a young couple wet their boots in the Irish sea, embraced briefly, and set off for Robin's Bay at the start of the Coast to Coast Walk. We decided that our boots had had enough of sea water, and scrambled up onto the sandstone headland, delighted to be back on a cliff path where the sea birds were busy breeding. This stretch is well-known for puffins, but we had to make do with the black guillemot. This was, we read, their only breeding ground in England. The cliffs were colourful with pinks, bluebells and gorse and here we spotted our first razor bills.

Whitehaven was like a corpse. Only a limp sea filled the harbour which once must have been filled with boats exporting coal and iron. Nearby we passed a disused coal mine, sunk in the 18th century to a depth of 160 fathoms, making it the deepest pit in the world. Now it too has shut. It was hard to believe that in the 18th century Whitehaven was one of the major ports in Britain, important enough for the Scots-born American Commander John Paul Jones to attack it in 1778 during the American War of Independence. His attempt to destroy the merchant fleet failed, but he was a colourful character, and one whom we were to meet again in the next few weeks.

'Whitehaven's heart and soul must be over there in that new heritage centre, preserved behind glass,' I said. 'There's just a lifeless body out here, dressed overall in granite setts, lamp posts and hanging baskets.'

We were relieved to find that Maryport showed at least some signs of life, with a couple of cranes and cargo boats. Workington, too was still alive and exporting railway lines and coal in a small way.

It was altogether a rather sad stretch of coast, and we were glad to leave the industrial decline behind and head on towards Carlisle and the Scottish border

Allonby was in jubilant mood celebrating V.E. day with flags, bunting and balloons. Even our campsite was having a caravan street-type party with bunting, old songs, a gaggle of grannies and a clutch of grandchildren. We put up our tent to the strains of *'Pack up your troubles in your old kit bag, and smile, smile, smile.'*

'That's one for me to sing as I road walk.'

'Spare us please.'

'Don't worry, you won't hear it. You can't even hear my whistle when I blow it!'

From Allonby we had good views of the hills of Dumfries and Galloway across the Solway Firth. It was heartening to be able to see Scotland, but we had to cut inland to reach Glasson near Port Carlisle that evening.

'It'll be 21 miles of road walking,' Richard warned me.

The weather changed dramatically the moment we clapped eyes on Scotland. The wind got up and the temperature dropped. Snow was forecast north of the border.

The morning, as usual, was not a problem. We walked along beside some of Hadrian's wall and passed signposts to places like Silloth and Aspatria. The Romans had left their mark. The minor roads we used seldom gave us views either of the Solway Firth or the Cumbrian hills. It was dull and hard. By early afternoon I was finding the miles were going by very slowly indeed. I used everything I could muster from my cerebral broadcasting service to distract my brain from my aching body. I had taped some information about saltpans and the process of making salt. I gave it my full attention and felt words like sleach, kench and hap would be good for scrabble, if only I could remember them. 'Pattlin' the pans' was the expression for cleaning the giant saltpans of scratch and I wondered whether women did that unpleasant job.

By teatime I had exhausted my repertoire. I decided that, although I had enjoyed climbing Skafell Pike, it must have taken some of the stuffing out of me. My stupid fall in Barrow had also given my morale a knock. Whatever the reason, I ached everywhere and felt exhausted. It was cheering to see the brown sign with white tent and caravan on it, between Glasson and Port Carlisle, and even more cheering to read 'Bar Meals'. I really didn't feel like cooking if there was any alternative.

The reality was different. The huge site was mainly for static caravans, and an officious sign at the main entrance indicated that tents were further along the lane. How far I had no idea, for Richard was blazing a trail in the distance. The lane seemed endless; eventually there was a modest entrance and a house. Nothing however, to indicate Reception. Richard had disappeared and I imagined he had walked through the ranks of caravans to find somewhere we could pitch our tent. He was nowhere to be seen, so I collapsed onto a handy seat, silently fuming.

A small boy on a toy tractor 'Brrrummm brummm'd' beside me. 'Wot you doing?' he enquired.

'Waiting for my daddy,' I replied. At this moment Richard appeared out of the unmarked house and walked slowly towards us.

'Run him over,' I instructed the little boy, who seemed eager to comply.

'Where did you get to? Why didn't you wait for me?' I hissed.

Silence. He led, I followed. Eventually we came to a scruffy field with shower blocks which would have done credit to Auschwitz.

'Do they sell food?' I snapped.

'Yes. At Reception. There are no bar meals.'

'God almighty! Now I've got to go all that way back to buy food. If I'd known I'd have bought it there and then.'

I changed my boots for sandles, and hobbled back to buy provisions from an unenthusiastic overweight lady in carpet slippers, masticating her supper.

Swallows were happily nesting in the concrete wash blocks, dropping their shit onto the cracked basins. I thought Zyklon not water would come out of the shower head, and at that moment I didn't really care. The whole place was seedy and run down.

After a silent meal we crashed out, too tired to argue that night. The next day the storm burst as we were breaking camp.

'Why don't you ever tell me what your doing next? I didn't know that place back there was the reception. You knew. You had the map. For better or worse your walking with someone you know.'

'For worse. You're just stupid. It was obvious I'd gone in to see if we could camp here. I just wanted to make sure there were no problems. I feel responsible.'

'OK. I'm not a small child or an idiot - so just tell me what you're doing and why!'

'You're just an ignorant little bitch!'

'You bastard!'

Two small children playing nearby, stopped their game to watch a better one.

I went off to fill up the water bottle and decided that this was it.

'If that's how you feel you're on your own now. I'm going to catch a train home from Carlisle.'

'Great. That suits me fine.'

'You'll need the fuel bottle,' I said, taking it out of the side pocket of my rucksack.

Richard opened his pack and tried to find a space for the litre bottle. It refused to fit anywhere. He simply didn't have room.

As I watched I realised what I had said. I didn't have a home to go to. The very last thing in the world I wanted to do was give up. How could I face friends and family? I think I really wanted him to realise that I needed him to communicate more. We were supposed to be a team. I was slower and he did get anxious about our night stops. We would have to be patient with each others failings. While he was trying to get a quart into a pint pack, I caught his arm.

'Is this really what you want?' There was a long pause. The children were still watching intently.

'No. Of course not. If you go now you'll miss Scotland and that's the best bit.' Richard gave up struggling with the fuel bottle.

'It won't fit,' I said firmly, 'and you can't go without it. It seems I'm some use after all even if it's only as the fuel carrier.'

It was a silent walk into Carlisle. I realized that my frequent stops to put wool on my heels, adjust my pack or have a mini rest to ease aches and pains, must be frustrating for Richard. Once on the road, he liked to keep going.

'If you keep stopping, it breaks the rhythm,' he told me. No wonder people do this type of marathon on their own, I thought miserably. We were warned. That night neither of us slept, but at least we talked . . .

Richard decided to rejig our itinerary and make our next stop Gretna Green.

'Second marriage?' I suggested.

We were then able to spend a leisurely morning collecting our new bundle of maps from the Post Office and making some very important purchases. New underpants, a webbing belt to hold my body and soul together, and two head nets to keep the notorious Scottish midges at bay. There was even a spare hour to spend in the Tullie Centre Museum; a bargain at half-price before 11 a.m.

Here we learned about the terrible border disputes in the 17th century, the lawlessness in the so-called 'debateable lands' north of Carlisle, and the Jacobite Uprising in the mid-eighteenth century. Carlisle carries its history with it. Over the threshold of Marks and Spencer's the words 'Bonnie Prince Charlie stayed here 1745 - The Duke of Cumberland 1746' shows how involved this stategic border town had been in this uprising, and many others. Robert Louis Stevenson had a few words to say here which seemed apposite.

'England and Scotland. Here are two people almost identical in blood, language and religion. And yet, a few years of quarrelsome isolation has so separated their thoughts and ways, that not union, nor mutual dangers, nor steamers, nor railways, nor all the King's horses nor all the King's men seem able to obliterate the broad distinction.'

If not hand in hand, at least foot by foot, we crossed the miserable little River Sark into Scotland. That evening in our tent, we celebrated our joint arrival in a third foreign land; a land where we to spend the next three and a half months.

Chapter Twelve

Ye banks and braes o'bonny Doon,
How can ye bloom sae fresh and fair?
How can ye chant, ye little birds,
And I sae weary fu'o'care?
Robbie Burns

It was a bright cold day. From this north side of the Solway Firth we could see the blue-filtered Cumbrian mountains, the promontory of St. Bees, Allonby and Silloth. The great bulk of Criffel rose to our west, head and shoulders above the rugged Galloway hills.

'We could see Criffel from Allonby. We'll be walking right past it tomorrow.'

'I'd love to go up it. Just think of the views. Is it a Munro?'

'No. It's a Corbet which means it's only 2,500 feet. Munros are always over 3,000 feet.'

'I think,' Richard added, looking at me hard, 'we'd better just concentrate on getting our daily mileage done before we even contemplate doing anything extra.'

At an inauspicious place called Brow Well we came across Robbie Burns. This deserted little spa had been his Gethsemane. It was here in the July of 1796 that the ailing Bard came to take the sea water. He knew he was dying yet would daily wade up to his armpits in the cold water, returning to sit under a hawthorn tree and contemplate his nearing end.

A bright-eyed, bird-like old woman lived in the nearby cottages.

'This i' quite a' important pleece,' she twittered proudly. 'This i' the Brow Wheel. This is where Robert Burns, th' poet, came te cure all ills.' We can't have looked suitably impressed, for she added, 'It's quite a famous wee sport. E'en th' foreign folk come ye know.'

Robbie Burns has become both a cult figure and an icon. We felt like pilgrims who didn't really know their creed.

'Have you read any of his poems?' Richard shook his head.

'Nor've I. The best known ones like *Auld Lang Syne* have become part of our heritage too.'

We put this right in Dumfries, and bought a rucksack-size Burns Anthology.

Our route to Dumfries was all minor roads. After lunch, a car drew up beside me, and the driver wound down his window. His face invited me in. I shook my head. He raised his eyebrows, shrugged his shoulders and wound up the window. Not a word was spoken.

I felt I might keep a record of the number of lifts I refused on the trip. Refusal always gave a warm glow of satisfaction.

Dumfries was no more than a big village, cut in half by the River Nith, memorable for its old stone bridge, flowering cherries and dirth of grocery shops. We combed the centre for victuals without success.

'Ye'll have te get te Safeways. There's nae foodshops heer now.' Our cheerful informant pointed over the river and far away.

'Hell's Bell's. I've heard of doughnuting but this is ridiculous.' The supermarket was a good mile out of our way.

A mile-post on the old steeple in the town informed us that we were only 360 miles from home.

'Correction,' Richard said, 'in fact we've actually walked 1,800.'

'Well, we have taken the scenic route. We'd better find out how many miles it is to get some food.'

Shopping for the rucksack was a challenging experience. On the whole, except for an obsession for milk, Richard left me in charge of the catering. There were three things to remember - minimum weight and cost and maximum nutrition. I bought lots of dried pasta and rice, dried fruit, porridge for breakfast and bananas. Carrots were our only fresh veg. and I often bought salted peanuts and chocolate bars. Chocolate whips made excellent puds. Flying in the face of our self-imposed rules we would also carry a 'wee dram' with us. A half-bottle of scotch, we felt, oiled the system.

Before we left the town we managed a visit to the Burns Museum and learned a little more about the man whose poetry, songs, personal charms and sex appeal, were so universally admired. Bonnie Galloway was rich and fertile, bursting with blossom and new growth. The very landscape seemed to echo the vernacular outpourings of the self-confessed peasant. As we walked along the Solway Firth, in a rare glimpse of sun, I played some of the songs I had recorded in the museum. The haunting fiddle tunes and tenor voice singing *'Man to man the world o'er shall brethers be for all that . . .'* brought a lump to my throat. I was yet another spell-bound admirer of the ploughman poet.

The rain which had soaked us most of the day was now snow over the Cumbrian mountains. We could make out the whole coast of Cumbria and the southern side of the Solway Firth up to Carlisle. Southerness, our destination for the night, was the birthplace of the same John Paul Jones who in 1778 had sailed into Whitehaven intent on destroying the fleet. He was son of a Kirkbean gardener and goes down in history as America's first naval commander.

The old cottages that flanked the tiny street sat low and hunched against the wind. Once used to guide schooners from Dumfries on their way to the American colonies, the original 1748 lighthouse stands shakily at the end of this little phalanx of land.

The north end of the hamlet is all late 20th century golf course and caravan park, advertising: TAKE AWAY - SWIMMING POOLS - WELCOME!

'Just what I really need, a take-away swimming pool,' I muttered.

As the Reception, toilet block and shop were all closed, it was not much of a welcome. An odd-job man came to the rescue, but after supper we headed off to the Paul Jones Hotel to see if they could do better.

'So much for our 100-mile pints,' I said happily as we sat by a roaring fire. 'Scotland has it's own rules.'

'None at all in these border regions.'

'Cheers.'

I felt Robbie Burns would still recognise his 'Bonnie Galloway' which seems to have slept since the 18th century, aloof in its quiet south west backwater: broad sweeps of undulating pastures, whitewashed cottages, well-kept farms, black cows with white cummerbunds, fresh deciduous woods now ankle deep in wild flowers. Graceful rivers flowed softly through green fields below the gentle hills. The rocky coast reminded us of Cornwall. Dry stone walls bounded the fields, granite cliffs bright with sea pinks and gorse.

The short stretch of cliff path was a tonic, with views to the Isle of Man, the Cumbrian coast and the distant hills of Galloway. Sadly, paths were the exception rather than the rule. I continued to find roads brought on a wealth of aches and pains. I was in limping mode near Auchencairn when we passed a lovely old manse advertising Bed & Breakfast. Although it was only lunch time, we thought if we booked in, we could leave our packs and do the coastal path the easy way in the afternoon.

'There are no campsites in this area, anyway,' Richard reassured me.

A grand, very upright lady opened the door. She wore slightly ethnic clothes and her long grey hair was swept up in a cascading bun. There was nothing Scots about her accent.

'Do come in. We have a choice of two rooms, double bed or two singles. The room with the twin beds has the best view.'

The room, like the house, was large, rambling, and old fashioned. A delicious smell of cooking emanated from the kitchen.

'You can eat here or go to the pub in the village. I charge £8.00 and specialise in vegetarian cuisine.'

We sat at the huge window drinking in the view over the little bay listening to the strains of a Chopin waltz floating upstairs. Our landlady was a competent 'pianoforte' teacher of many years' standing. She had a disconcerting habit of talking with her back to us.

'That's probably because she'd have been looking at the music and not her pupils for all those years,' Richard suggested.

Kirkudbright (pronounced Kirkcoobree) is named after an early Christian church dedicated to St. Cuthbert of Northumbria. Described as 'one of the treasures of South West Scotland' it was a place no-one could just pass through. The little town lies on the banks of the lovely River Dee. It is mediaeval in layout, complete with 16th century castle, 17th century Tolbooth (where our friend Paul Jones was briefly imprisoned) and the perfectly restored 18th century Broughton House belonging to the artist E.A Hornell. The brightly painted old terraced houses were beautifully cared for, and the narrow 'closes' between them gave peeps up into the wooded hill or down to the river below.

'The Tolbooth 1629 . . . ' I read off a plaque. 'It looks a cross between a town hall and a prison.'

'It's an Art Centre now. Let's go in and find out more.' Richard suggested.

Kirkcudbright's charm comes, in part, from the colony of artists who settled there at the turn of the century. Much as Stanhope Forbes started an artist's colony in Newlyn, so E.A. Hornell founded a Scottish colony, known as 'The Glasgow Boys'. Students from the Glasgow School of Art were encouraged to visit the town and study this new trend, which, like the French Impressionists, rejected the romantic, sentimental and moralistic paintings in vogue at the time.

Our campsite, a few miles west of Kirkcudbright, was in an idyllic spot perched above the river. We gave it a walker's award for its well-appointed clean facilities for a mere £3.50. Campsites varied so much in price and value for money, and a good one run by friendly people made all the difference. Chatting to a fellow camper while washing, I found myself with a £10 note in my hand for our charities. People everywhere were fascinated by our long walk, and eager to give. If we had been able to do any serious collecting en route, we should have made a lot of money for our charities.

Small shops were few and far between, and always very expensive. The Post Mistress in Borgue told us her husband ran a smallholding and employed two men whose net wage was only £130 per week. Rural folk had to pay the same high prices for their food.

'Tatties are noo £10 a bag and you'll no get milk under 40p.'

For all this, Bonnie Galloway showed no outward and visible signs of depravation. We saw nothing but well-maintained homes, prosperous farms and healthy livestock.

If food in this region was expensive and scarce, strange kirks, Pictish crosses, cup and ring stones and Celtic saints were not. The present seemed suspended in the past. At the tiny hamlet of Kirkandrews, only the footings of the 12th century church remained among the old tombstones. One such, crudely ornamented with the skull and cross bones and hour glass, had the Latin maxims *tempis fugit* and *momento mori* inscribed on it. The young man was a 19-year-old Covenantor who died in 1748 for his beliefs.

It was cold and drizzling by the time we reached Gatehouse of Fleet and, when we found the campsite was closed, we were in no mood to do justice to the elegant little town. However, we were lucky to find an inexpensive and chaotic B & B run by a couple of artists and their three-year old tearaway twins. We shared the bathroom with their plastic ducks, the bedroom with their screams and the dining room with their parents' pictures. At breakfast we admired their paintings.

'There's not much call for these round here, but we have a London outlet,' they told us.

From the doorway, two identical pairs of eyes and a mop of fair curls smothered in plastic crash helmets gave us the once-over. The twins were sitting on plastic trikes like miniature outriders. Footsteps bearing breakfast arrived, and they scampered like frightened rabbits.

Memorable too, was the Amworth Hotel for its 179 varieties of malt whisky. Had we stayed in Gatehouse long enough, we might never have finished the walk.

Eighteenth century buildings were ubiquitous. Was there life here before it we wondered? Even our route was two hundred years old. The Military Road cut a gentle green swathe over the fells to Creetown. As we walked along, far removed from the 20th century, we could imagine the redcoats marching to the sound of fife and drum in search of Jacobite rebels . . .

> O what is that sound that so thrills the ear
> Down in the valley drumming, drumming?
> Only the scarlet soldiers, dear,
> The soldiers coming.

W.H Auden's poem cleverly brings out the fear of hunter and hunted.

Creetown, like Garlieston and Portwilliam, was a planned town. Political union between Scotland and England came in 1707 and Scottish landlords wasted no time in exploiting the lucrative English markets. They enclosed their lands to create large pastures to fatten the cattle and sheep for the stomachs of the prosperous English. This meant the livelihoods of the 'Bonnet Lairds' (self-sufficient Scottish small holders) were threatened. In the 1720's the Bonnet Lairds had had enough of being pushed about by the Establishment, and went on the rampage over the Western Stewartry and the Machars of Wigtownshire, tearing down the enclosures' 'dry stane dykes' in a gallant effort to maintain the status quo. Inevitably the rebellion was quoshed in 1725. The displaced rural population either joined the work force of the industrial revolution, or settled in planned villages built for them by the wealthy landowners.

We found the same story further north when we came across the Highland Clearances.

The weather ensured we saw little of Creetown. As we were sitting in a children's playground having a snack, large cold marbles sploshed into our cuppa soups. We had a wet walk into Newton Stewart along the A75, deafened and soaked by fast flowing cars.

It was so cold that night we had to wear woolly hats and were not surprised to see a frost-bitten world outside the tent.

'You know what they say - 'Nae cast a clout til May is out,' I muttered through chattering teeth as I poked my head outside the tent.

The sun shone intermittently between the squalls. It was the sort of weather which lit up the hills and brightened the lively River Cree. However, it means the walker has to waste much time pulling clothes on and off which doesn't improve his/her humour.

We were now on roads a lot of the time and averaging a good 16 miles per day. My body, like the Bonnet Lairds, was threatening revolt. I was thankful to stop for lunch.

Physical discomfort was temporarily subdued by a Martyrs' Monument near Wigtown. It was a bleak spot on the marshes by a silted up river. A simple stone pillar, rising from a couple of boulders, marked the spot where, in 1685 two women aged 18 and 53 died for their beliefs. They were Covenantor sympathisers, Presbyterians who honoured only Christ as head of their church. When Charles I, as head of the Presbyterian Church of Scotland, instituted his bishops north of the border, the Covenantors refused to submit. They believed that God's power superseded the power of Kings. This was seen as a threat to the 'divine rights' of Kings. A mercenary force called 'The Highland Host' was sent in and a terrible period of persecution followed, known as the 'Killing Time'.

The two women, were 'executed by drowning' at this spot. Tied to posts which were pushed into the soft mud by the river, watched by the villagers of Wigtown, they waited for the rising tide, refusing to recant in spite of the desperate pleas of the onlookers. The women slowly submerged beneath the murky waters, till only bubbles, and then nothing, was left.

I shivered and thought a secular society must be preferable. Wigtown kirkyard had the following lines written on a memorial for the younger woman:

Let earth and stone still witness bear,
Here lyse a virgin martyr here.
Murdered for owning Chryst supreme,
Head of His church and no more cryme . . .
Tied to a stayke, she suffered for Christ Jesus sayke.
The actors of this cruel cryme
Was Lac Strachan Winrum and Graham.
Neither young years nor yet old age,
Could stop the fury of their rage.

Aches and pains returned as we neared Garlieston. My legs and feet were being martyred in the cause of commitment. Many of the small roads in this region still kept their old milestones. Painted whiter than white they were easy to spot. I would time our walk between them trying to see what speed we were doing. Twenty minutes was, I reckoned, about three miles an hour. For some reason I now had to stop and rest at every milestone. Richard was patient and even walked behind me for the last few miles so I couldn't cop out. The logical side of my brain told me I was mad to go on, my alter ego told me I could do it, it was just a bad day.

We were recommended to try Number 17, Cowgate, for a possible bed and breakfast. The 18th century house sat squarely at the corner of the regular streets of this 'planned town'. There was no hopeful sign advertising B & B. We rang the bell and waited a long time. Eventually we heard a scuffing footfall, and an elderly man with a kind face opened the door. We asked politely if a room was available. There was a long pause and eventually the stuttering reply came in a public school accent.

'I do take in certain selected guests.'

Determined to be a selected guest, I told him about our walk.

He invited us to follow him. The poor man had obviously had a stroke and had great difficulty climbing the stairs to show us our room. Like him, the quality furnishings and decor were faded and worn. He told us that he lived there alone and managed without help. I admired his guts. Later, in the Queen's Arms, we learnt more about him.

'That'll be Michael Keeling, locally known as "The Rev"', the landlady told us. 'He advertises in some Christian magazine and sometimes 'boys' come to stay.' She paused a moment.

'He's gay of course. In a small town like this people are very prejudiced. But he's a good man for all that.' She fetched the tomato ketchup for us and continued. 'Last year he had a bad stroke. Took the cure at Lourds and came back much better'. She shrugged. 'He's got courage. I'll give him that.'

A bellow came from the bar and she disappeared.

We had noticed a rather scrappy sign with the words HOTEL FOR SALE. IF INTERESTED PLEASE SEE GRANT. in the sparsely furnished little bar. If Grant was the inebriate gentleman behind the bar we felt the hotel might be on the market a long time. His florid features looked prematurely aged, and a shaky hand would sneakily reach for his glass beneath the bar when he thought no-one was looking. His cheerful and energetic wife seemed to do everything yet still had time to chat. When she heard we what we were doing, she disappeared into the bar and reappeared with £2.50. We were loath to accept anything from a community that was economically on the margins.

'Talk about the widow's mite! It's always the same, those with the least give the most. Remember the male voice choir?' I said feeling very humble.

Back at The Rev's, Richard was pouring over maps.

'I'm going to re-jig our itinerary so your feet have some hope of completing the walk. We'll give The Rhins a miss, which means we can stay two nights at Burrowhead tomorrow, and have two easy days.'

He showed me on the map.

'We'll turn north at Stranraer and go up the Ayreshire coast to Ardrossen where we catch the ferry to Arran.'

I felt a mixture of relief and regret. Relief to ease up, but a growing awareness that I was keeping Richard back and making him cut corners for me. My fear of not being able to complete the walk was very real.

We got to know our landlord a little better at breakfast. In spite of his English accent he had been born and bred in Galloway, the son of a minister. He recalled his childhood delight of Covenantor tomb-hunting, where the forbidden word 'bloody' was legal tender. He had spent seven years teaching at Brighton College in the 1950's, had been ordained an Anglican priest in the 1960's and spent some years as a rector in Australia. At this stage he gave up being a parish priest (for whatever reason) and concentrated his efforts in helping the homeless first in Australia and then in London. The ten years leading up to his retirement in 1992 were spent helping the mentally ill and AIDS victims.

'I've a quiet upper room here, set aside as a chapel where I hold Holy Communion regularly. If you know of anyone seeking solace, or a spiritual retreat, do let them know.'

After a night's rest, his speech was much improved.

'I had a lovely day out yesterday on the Waverley. It's Britain's only surviving paddle steamer still carrying holidaymakers to the Clyde resorts.'

The Rev. managed to talk while cooking us an excellent Scottish breakfast, one eye on the clock waiting for a hospital car to take him into Newton Stewart for his physiotherapy.

As we left Cowgate, we saw the hospital car arrive. He waved us a cheery good-bye with a lop-sided smile. We felt admiration for him and gratitude.

'I wonder whether his improvement was due to Lourdes, physiotherapy or just guts?' I said.

'All three, I should think.'

I had slept like only the exhausted can, and felt ready for anything again next day. Well, anything except a 16 mile road walk, that is. Garlieston's neat rows of white and cream houses were a tribute to 18th century town planning. The 'Bonnet Lairds' didn't seem to have done too badly after all. The town boasted the narrowest bowling green in Scotland, so narrow it had been divided into two sections. We noticed how the town had come to life during a bowls match the evening before; the game was obviously a central part of the little community.

Lying behind the thickly wooded rim of Rigg Bay lay the crumbling stately Georgian mansion belonging to Lord Garlies. The present crumbling laird is now languishing in a warden-controlled apartment, while Galloway House has been sold to an Australian couple and their one daughter for a mere £250,000.

'They won't be short of space exactly. Still I could manage to live here alright. On a day like this it's hard to beat.' Richard agreed.

Burrow Head was a windswept promontory of land, topped with a sprawling campsite, which had taken over a dis-used army camp. Strong gusts of wind funnelled through the vast expanse of bare green set aside for tents.

'Aye, it's windy up heer,' the young receptionist said.

'Last yeer we had a tent over the cliff.' Her voice was without a trace of emotion. 'It'll be most sheltered by the bank theer.'

We staked our little tent down firmly and realised the army surplus toilet block wasn't even visible on the horizon. Sand swirled around the footings of dismantled buildings. The few static caravans appeared to be deserted. A dilapidated wooden building backed onto the shop, advertising a restaurant and bar. A lop-sided sign said CLOSED. Our only companion was a black-headed gull, who swaggered up and down outside our tent like a sergeant-at-arms, periodically letting out a raucous screech.

That evening we investigated the bar. The dismal-looking prefabricated door opened into another world. A latter-day Elvis, in sequinned waistcoat and tight black trousers, was singing to a crowd of Geordies, in a warm comfortable bar where the alcohol was flowing freely. The barmaid was in low-cut black lace dress. Elvis was something of a comedian as well as a very competent singer. The decibels of his electric guitar and the vibrato in his voice shook the heads on the Newcastle Brown in syncopated rhythms.

It was at this moment that I suddenly felt very alienated, aware that we were only transient voyeurs who didn't 'fit' anywhere. Self-imposed itinerant exiles.

On the rocky promontory near the Isle of Whithorn, among the grazing cattle and sheep, lie the ancient ruins a small 13th century chapel. For centuries pilgrims from all over Europe landed here when they came to visit the shrine of Bishop Ninian at Whithorn Priory, Scotland's earliest known Christian church. Saint Ninian started his mission at the end of the fourth century AD, beating the better known St. Columba to it by 150 years. It is ironic that these two humble men were responsible for bringing, not only Christianity, but its concomitant wealth and status borne in by the tides of God-fearing pilgrims who came to visit the shrine, until the Reformation destroyed the cult at the end of the 16th century. The site of this chapel on it's little green hill, perched above the dark rocks and white sands, felt like holy ground.

'We're supposed to be able to see five kingdoms from here,' Richard said screwing up his eyes and gazing at the horizon.

'I can see the Cumbrian hills . . . there's the Isle of Man, very clear, The Mull of Galloway, that's Scotland. Mmm. Ireland doesn't seem to be visible today. What's the fifth one?'

'That's easy. Look up - the Kingdom of Heaven is all around us!'

We were on the trail of the Celtic saints. St. Ninian's cave was on the shores of Luce Bay just a few miles from our campsite. The story goes that the saint would come here to be alone and meditate. It was certainly a lonely spot, carved out of the sandstone cliff at the end of a pebbly beach, and had a very spiritual feel about it. Rough crosses had been carved on the walls by pilgrims who visited the cave from the 8th century, and elaborately carved Pictish stones with Christian symbols were also found here. . As we approached, we saw a Nordic-looking latter-day pilgrim sitting quietly outside the cave. He turned out to be not only a priest, but an author, psychoanalyst and a member of the Christian Celtic Trust. He was taking a sabbatical to study Celtic Christianity for his next book. In no time at all we were discussing dreams, fears, death and resurrection as freely as if we were discussing the weather.

Turning inland to Whithorn through the woods at Physgill, we walked beside a gentle stream, waded through a scented blue carpet beneath lanky tree trunks, canopied with fresh green leaves. Birds sang their hearts out. Energized by all this burgeoning growth our spirits.

An archaeological dig was in progress in Whithorn, to discover more of the 1,500 years of history since Bishop Ninian built his first church there. When Ninian died, his church and shrine became a centre of pilgrimage. The Cult of St. Ninian was established and prospered until the Reformation put an end to all this. Pilgrimages were banned, and the fortunes of Whithorn declined. Now, it is just another sleepy little town in the quiet backwater of Galloway, attempting to dig its way back to prosperity. Today it is tourists not pilgrims who worship at a shrine of potted history.

We had been keeping our eyes peeled for cup and ring stones - ancient man-made indentations in special stones, for reasons we can only guess at. Our 'pilgrim' at St. Ninian's cave told us they were carved into rocks with ferrous metal in them. The hollow was then filled with little prayer stones which would ring when wind or small mammals disturbed them. When all the stones had been dissipated, the prayer would have been answered. Unless wind and small mammals were very busy, their prayers, I felt, would only have been answered in Heaven.

After much searching we eventually found some in a field near Monreith. The small hollow was scored with concentric circles, but otherwise rather unimpressive.

We ticked that one off the list and stumbled across the Maxwell family. A bronze otter poses on a lump of rock overlooking Monreith Bay in memory of Gavin Maxwell, author and naturalist. '*Where he lived and where he loved*' said the plaque. He spent his childhood in this area where his family owned the Monreith estate, later moving to Sandaig near the Kyle of Lochalsh, where he wrote his best-seller *Ring of Bright Water*. A Latin inscription below the otter is translated: *This place he loved as a boy and made famous as a man.*

Stranraer was a turning point. Once more our feet faced north. We lost all that was 'bonnie' about Galloway, and had mainly road walking along a fairly dull stretch of coast, often on major roads.

Our proposed campsite at Invermesson did not take tents. It was an inauspicious place with a few static caravans, a plethora of concrete bases, little grass and a beach that resembled a building site. However, the manager, Dr. Carson Dunlop, was no ordinary retired business man. In his late sixties, tall, with thin grey hair and suit to match, not only had he founded an international alternative therapy business, but had a host of disparate qualifications. Chiropratic and acupunturist extraordinaire, he had been awarded 'Cavalier Order of A.N.I.O.C.' by none other than the 'Accademia Tiberino Roma'. An ex-school master, he confessed to being addicted to learning. Apart from an orthodox PHD in Natural Science, he was a hypnotherapist, Grand Master British Guild of Drugless Practitioners and Beauty Therapist. He was also a mind-reader who knew about Richard's predeliction for milk for he left a litre of the precious liquid at our tent flap.

Ayreshire was memorable for the roads, fields of potatoes, villages sleeping through a permanant recession, Ailsa Craig, and the silhouetted peaks on the Isle of Arran. At Ballentrae we saw our first eider ducks. This was the most southerly point we were likely to find them, and we followed them right round these northern coasts to Northumberland. We watched the dapper drakes' plumage change from his courting black and white to a sombre brown, and the mottled brown ducks rearing their babies from fluffy brown balls to waterwise adolescents. They believe in safety in numbers, bobbing along in convoys or rafts. Their sloping beaks come straight off the forehead, and are very distinctive even to a novice like me. For us, they became a sort of logo for the north, and we were sorry to lose them.

There was no coastal path, so we were forced to route march along the A77. An unforgiving, monotonous grey ribbon where our foot falls were broken only by the 'whoosh' of cars, narrowly missing our left elbows. Occasional lorries roared past, leaving us staggering in a whirlwind of exhaust. There was often no kerb at all, and the grassy verge would be uneven, with drainage ditches at regular intervals which would break our rhythm. We made the best speed on the tarmac and would walk the narrow band inside the white line, sole following sole, jarring our feet, legs, back and head with dreary monotony.

At times like this I had to switch on my cerebral video, write this book in my head, or make up verse and worse just to pass the monotonous miles. It was more of a relief than ever to shed our loads and rest, even if it had to be beside the busy road.

'Do you want to stop here for lunch?' Richard's question was rhetorical.

He threw his pack down on the grassy bank, and was about to throw himself after it, when he hesitated and signalled me to stop in my tracks.

'Look! I almost sat on an adder's nest. I disturbed them, but they'll be back.' We moved away quietly and later returned to see the adder once more snoozing outside its hole.

'A good thing it was you,' I said. 'I'd have stuck my bum straight down on top of it. Still from now on I'll be sure to look first.'

Ailsa Craig was hypnotic; a mighty plug of granite which rises abruptly out of the Firth of Clyde like some prehistoric sea monster. It's sheer cliffs make an ideal breeding ground for gannets and other sea birds. We viewed it for several days through a cloud of seabirds, and later learned that at one time, tenants on the island used to pay their rents in gannet feathers.

'I think it looks like a nipple,' was Richard's comment.

I pondered this for a minute, found it rather worrying and wondered what Freud would make of it.

'Wow! Some nipple!'

Gradually we drew away from this maternal giant, and at Culzean, focused north to the beautiful blue peaks of the Isle of Arran.

'Our gateway to the Highlands,' I murmured longingly.

In the little village of Alloway and in Ayr itself, Scotland's national poet Robbie Burns is big business. As Whithorn was the cradle of Scottish Christianity, so Ayr was the cradle of the peasant poet. Charabancs of secular pilgrims from all over Europe pour into Alloway to snap the Auld Brig-O-Doon and worship at the low-slung cottage where Burns was born in 1759. They are invited to share the 'Tam O'Shanter Experience', visit Land O'Burns Centre, the Burns Monument and Gardens, the Alloway Kirk and purchase his biographies, poems and memorabilia. After all, Lord Byron himself had been fulsome in the Bard's praise:

What an antithetical mind! - tenderness, roughness - delicacy, coarseness - sentiment, sensuality - soaring and grovelling, dirt and deity - all mixed in that compound of inspired clay!

Shortage of both money and time meant we plodded gravely past these shrines and headed for the Scottish Baronial Youth Hostel.

'We've just clocked up 2,000 miles,' Richard announced as he wheeled his revolving 'fob watch' up the Firth of Clyde.

We left our packs and set off to plunder the local Safeway, piling our basket high with fresh fruit, meat and veg.

'One minute we moan about towns not having small food shops or over-charging if they do. The next we revel in a bonanza in the supermarket,' I said, my hand hovering over the chicken breasts.

'Mmm,' Richard grunted while gently placing bottle of red plonk in the loaded basked.

For all our extravagance, our bill at the check-out was little more than the more modest goods we usually bought.

Back at the Youth Hostel we had to share the good news with a friendly receptionist.

'Tharts grate.' He smiled. 'But you'll not be drinking alcohol heer I'm afraid. It's against th' rools.'

'The Calvinist ethic seems to have endured up here,' I said, carefully decanting the wine into our water bottle. We enjoyed a celebratory meal and then, with seven Irishmen and one New Zealander, we watched the All Blacks trounce the Irish.

Later, the Irish adjourned to the pub and Richard took his head out of the maps.

'We've only got 125 miles to Oban and half way.'

'That wretched road is so bad I think we'll go inland now and miss out Troon. There are no campsites there anyway. We'll still be on roads, but they'll be minor ones and I can see there are campsites inland.'

There was less traffic on the minor roads, but they were dull and monotonous. My right thigh and hip let me know how much they hated roads. I was limping as we turned into a campsite in the grounds of a disused monastery at Roddinghill between Kilmarnock and Kilwinning.

A few large caravans littered the grounds, a cracked empty swimming pool looked less than inviting, a billiard table now stood where the high alter had been, and the toilet block hadn't changed much since the monks left. The monastery was built in 1897, and had seen better days. The man on reception told us they didn't take tents but had watched our slow progress up the long drive.

'You seem a wee bit weary,' he said looking at me. I nodded as wearily as I could and he relented.

'OK. You can stay, but please put yer wee tent right down the heel.' He pointed to the middle distance.

Happy to be allowed to stay, even though we felt a bit like lepers, we soon had our tent pitched in our small corner at the bottom of the hill.

By this time we had our camping down to a fine art. Our tiny one-woman-one-man tent took less than five minutes to put up, and was water and wind-proof. It looked like a little green U.F.O. made for leprechauns, for there was only room inside to lie down or pray. The outer area gave us storage space for rucksacks and cooking utensils. My kitchen consisted of an unleaded petrol-driven cooker, which boiled liquids at lightning speed, but would sulk and go out if turned down to a simmering heat. Occasionally it would pretend it was a mini-volcano and erupt into a great glowing ball, but Richard soon showed it who was boss. It was in fact one of our most valuable pieces of equipment together with a set of ultra-light pans. My work-surface was a polythene bag and my window had a view which changed daily.

Once the tent was up, we had a home. Off came the boots and it was tea time. If our cooker was fuelled by unleaded petrol, my motor ran on tea. The tea ceremony was followed by crash-out time with feet suspended from the roof like a bat. Thus energised I could totter off for my ablutions. Washed and re-fuelled I was able to cook the supper. While that was brewing, we had happy hour. Our bedrolls were reclining couches as well as beds, and we got used to eating like Romans. We found our sleeping bag, rolls tucked under the armpit, were a considerable help in stabilising the food-bearing arm, thus preventing slurping. Coffee and chocolate would follow soup, main course and pud. Richard would then wash up while I wrote my diary. Neither of us carried books, but Richard always bought a newspaper if he could, which kept us in touch with the real world. By 9 p.m were ready for sleep. I am sure that these supine 13-hour stretches gave our bodies a chance to recover, and meant that neither of us ever had one single morning when we didn't feel able to get back on our feet and attempt do the prescribed number of miles.

After days of dry weather we had a wet walk into Kilmarnock. Along by the river, we watched a mother dipper feeding her young brood. Four huge red mouths screamed vociferously from a small rock. Mother worked overtime, tirelessly diving for food, which was air-lifted straight back to her hungry babes.

Watching the dipper's aquarobics, my own feet began to feel wet. To my horror, my new Blackpool boots let in the water. I squelched the last few miles, knowing that I would have to buy another pair with all the concomitant discomfort. Kilmarnock had one small camping shop with very few suitable boots to choose from. After much agitated dithering, I bought a heavy seamed pair, just because the leather was soft enough not to fight my feet. My sympertex-lined suede ones went straight back to the manufacturer, together with sweat and smell and a 'yours disgusted, Tunbridge Wells' note. I must have looked as annoyed as I felt, for the manager gave me a new pair of socks (having just smelt my old ones) and Richard suggested an All Day Breakfast at Safeway.

Fortified with orange juice, coffee, fried egg, bacon, waffles, sausage, tomato, baked beans and two pieces of buttered toast and jam, I felt ready for the road again. We were getting tired of undulating cow-dotted pastures, inauspicious villages, and campsites that didn't take tents. It was a relief to reach Stevenston, Saltcoats and Ardrossen, the trinity of dreary towns, for Arran was now only a short ferry ride away, and the Highlands beckoned.

We had just enough shopping hours to have much-needed hair-cuts, get several films developed, and collect our parcel of maps from the Post Office. After a longer session over the maps than usual, Richard announced that our itinerary had slipped a day, and, as we weren't on the Date Line, we should have to catch an early ferry to Brodick, and walk across Arran to Lochranza. Originally he had intended an extra day on Arran and had visions of climbing Goat Fell.

'Aren't you glad we haven't got to continue up the Clyde to Glasgow?' Richard said as we looked over to the misty blue mountains of Arran.

'From now on we're going to have tiny roads or none at all, and the best scenery in Britain.'

'I know and I can't wait.' From Maryport in Cumbria we had walked 300 miles on roads. Aches and pains for me had become the norm. Doubts in my ability to continue the onslaught were surfacing daily.

We boarded the Caledonian MacBrayne ferry, feeling as excited as the mob of primary school kids skipping and singing on their school outing. The boat was late leaving, because the crew kindly waited for two latecomers. We were setting off overseas to a very different land.

Chapter Thirteen

My heart's in the Highlands
My heart is nae here.
My heart's in the Highlands a-chasing the deer.
Robbie Burns

Scotland's western seaboard awaited us. A ragged stretch of islands, mountains, water and sky. Although we had to walk along the road from Brodick to Lochranzer, the fells on our left, and the sea (for once on our right) kept our spirits high. The rocky coast was full of interest. Seals and submarines, eider duck, cormorants, herons, sandpipers, shell duck and mergansers were all going about their business. Summer was well on the way. Bluebells still visible under the burgeoning bracken, spiky foxgloves and bright ponticums gave splashes of colour, elder flower and may scented the damp air. The tops of the high peaks were thinly veiled in mist, and cold streams gurgled and spluttered down the steep slopes. Bright green fields were dotted with goats, donkeys and sheep.

At Lochranza, the sun was setting behind the twin-towered ruined castle which hangs over the sea loch. One or two boats sat decoratively on the streamed sand of this tree and gorse-ringed harbour where the mountains are rooted in the sea. Beyond lay the long finger of Kintyre, almost an island, just a short ferry journey away.

We were woken before dawn by a strange rhythmical tearing noise. It got louder and louder.

'Funny things people do in their tents,' I whispered. 'What d'you think's going on?'

'Dunno. It's coming from your side. Have a look.'

I unzipped the tent, (impossible to do quietly), and came eyeball to eyeball with a red stag carrying a good set of antlers. The noise had stopped.

I waited while the dignified creature walked a few paces further away, put its magnificent head down and started cropping the incredibly short grass. The rhythmical noise recommenced.

'S'cuse me,' I whispered, like Alice, feeling very much in Wonderland, 'could you do that a bit more quietly? Some of us are trying to sleep.' A soft snort came from velvety nostrils.

I retreated and dozed off, dreaming of Mad Hatters with antlers and dormice with big teeth.

The Caledonian MacBrayne ferry was waiting at the little jetty next morning, its metal apron resting on the slab of concrete and no other visible moorings. We chugged sedately over to great port of Cloanaig, just a jetty amongst the rocks and shingle, one little house and a ruined castle.

A signpost on the tiny road read 'Campbeltown 28. Tarbert 110.'

'A light-fingered little Scottish bugger has been at that one. Kintyre's long, but not that long,' Richard grinned.

'Come on. We need to shop in Tarbert and tonight we'll have to rough camp.'

At Tarbert we had to stock up for the next few days, as there would be no shops at all. Even if Kintyre isn't an island, it is certainly as remote as one. As we walked along towards West Loch Tarbert Richard told me the story of Magnus Bareleg of Norway.

'The little isthmus, which prevents Kintyre being an island, was used by Magnus Bareleg of Norway in 1098 to get a toe-hold on the mainland of Scotland. King Edgar must have been very fearful of this brawny Viking, for he gave him permission to take any land that he could sail round. Magnus immediately ordered his hefty fellow marauders to pick up their long boat, with Magnus at the helm, and drag it from East to West Loch Tarbert, so claiming Kintyre for the Norse.'

When I looked at the map, I thought the long thin peninsula of Kintyre looked like the arm of a rag doll, cradling the Isle of Arran.

We found a perfect spot to camp by the river. From the farm and large house opposite, we realised it was privately owned. I found a cheerful farm manager and asked permission to camp.

'Och aye! I'll let ye. The laird wouldn't ha mind. He'd no' let campers near his land.' The big Scot rolled his eyes to heaven. 'Still, he's up there noo.'

'That's very kind of you. Is it OK to drink the river water?'

'I would na do thaat.'

'Why not? Are there dead sheep in it?'

He laughed, wrinkling his nose. 'Worse than thaat. 'Sewage from the big hoos. Use the tap in the yard, that'll no harm ye.'

Glad of his advice, we quickly made ourselves at home. Watching the Caledonian MacBrain ferry sliding gently along West Loch Tarbert on its way to service the islands of Jura and Islay, we realized they were the lifeblood of these islands. If the ferries went, the islands would die.

The lowering sun lit the hills of Kintyre on the far side of the loch, and glowed behind the mature beeches which fringed the estate. I was dreaming away at my kitchen window, without a care in the world, when we were besieged by a cloud of uninvited guests. They found their way into our hair, down our necks, up our sleeves into the food, the drink, the tent. We dug out our Korean midge nets which prevented facial attacks, and settled down to enjoy supper. I quickly decided that Korean midge net doesn't taste particularly good. Lifting the net gingerly, I had a slurp of midge soup, then, keeping the cup inside the Korean defence lines, I gulped it down and rapidly yanked the drawstring tight. Every midge in West Tarbart wanted my soup too. I glanced at Richard and found he was having the same problems. We beat an ignominious retreat, and finished our meal in comparative comfort, zipped into the netted walls of our nylon castle. A small cloud of the front ranks had come in with us, but fortunately they were concentrating so hard on getting out again, that they lost their appetite for any accessible bits of our flesh.

'Thank goodness they're phototropic,' Richard murmured sleepily from the depths of his sleeping bag.

'Mmmm. So much for the al fresco. They did warn us . . . ' Free from our winged Lilliputians we slept soundly.

We had been invited to spend our 28th wedding anniversary on June 3rd, in a friend's cottage at Kilmichael of Inverlussa, a tiny hamlet near Loch Sween. Our walk up Knapdale was damp and midgy, what the Scots call 'dreich'. When the mist lifted it unveiled the long low rocky island of Gigha lying like a giant basking crocodile, and the majestic Paps of Jura The imposing ruins of Sween Castle were now swathed in static caravans, glittering loudly even in the poor light.

My weight loss meant that my pack no longer fitted properly. There was a growing gap in the small of my back and a low cloud seemed to have settled on my shoulders. I stopped by an overgrown gate, rummaged in my rucksack, stuffed a polythene bag with my smalls and tied it to the pack with binder twine picked up off the road. This was fine until the low cloud began to precipitate. Wet underpants were unthinkable. We now realised the vital importance of clean socks, pants and a hankie. Armed with these, we could face anything; without them, we lost confidence.

'I now know why an army needs clean socks to win a war,' I said, as Richard helped me rejigg my pack yet again. Then I had an idea.

'I know. Shoulder pads! I'll ask the Inner Wheel ladies if they can send me a few.'

No sooner said than done. By the time we reached Oban, I had a foam wedge squeezed into a pair of flesh-coloured tights, slung across the back of my pack like a limp artificial limb. Richard had padded my rucksack straps with foam, secured with red insulating tape. I felt I might blow a fuse at any moment, but at least my pack now fitted and my underpants were no longer at risk from the Scottish weather.

It was late by the time we reached Kilmichael, and we had walked at least three miles more than estimated. Now we had to collect the key of our cottage from a lady called Annie. The village consisted of six stone houses scattered round the Kirk. At this point Richard decided to sit down, while I went in search of keys. I knocked on the first door I came to. A well built lady in pinny and carpet slippers answered.

'If it's Annie ye want she's off on a wee holiday. She layfed at seex this mornin'. My name's Daisy Bell.'

She saw my face fall and noticed me eyeing the green, thinking we could pitch our tent there. No way was I walking one step further.

'Och now, will ye take a cup o' tae?'

'I'd love one but I've got a husband down there somewhere. We were hoping to stay in the Morrison's cottage.' My voice trailed off.

Her weather-beaten face brightened.

'I think there's someone up theer. It'll be him mebbe. I'll show you. I've a Yellow Pages to give him.'

I went down the hill to tell Richard the news and together we walked up to a cottage.

'There now,' Daisy said soothingly. 'There'll be someone a' home.' With this she thrust the Yellow Pages into my unsuspecting arms and disappeared.

My surprise and delight at seeing John standing outside his open door beaming at us was too much. Mentally I still thought we'd have to spend the night on the village green. In my confusion I handed him the Yellow Pages and my big boot stepped unceremoniously on his stocking feet.

After this things got better. Lots better. Gallons of hot water, followed by lashings of food and even more alcohol, saw us sitting round a roaring fire ruing the march of time in the Highlands in general, and Inverlussa in particular. We crashed out in the small hours, awash with malt whisky and fatigue.

I dreamed an army of midges wearing clogs had descended onto my right temple and were busy 'square bashing'. I was on a ship in a rough sea. I opened one eye and closed it rapidly. It seemed to be behind a barbed wire fence. Outside there was an amplified dawn chorus. Richard's noisy breathing added the percussion. I moaned and tried to sleep.

Sometime later I smelt bacon and eggs. The birds and the breathing had stopped. My stomach heaved and a small voice inside my head told me I should be up and dressed ready for the 19 miles to Ardfern. I told it to shut up. All I could do was concentrate on the square bashing in my head and keep my stomach where it belonged.

'How you doing?' A nauseatingly cheerful voice came from the doorway. 'I'm off now. John's offered to bring you across to Ardfern tonight. Hope you're feeling better soon. Byee!'

By midday I had recovered enough to get up and out. John had gone fishing. After a week of unsettled weather, a freshly laundered sparkling world lay at my feet. From the hill behind the village I could see a filigree of land and water strips, studied with mountains and islands. Jura, Scarba, Luing, Shuna and the mountains of Mull. The air was crystal clear. The only sounds were bird song and cascading water. The village itself was softened by mature deciduous trees and brightened by rhodedendrums, now in bloom. Buzzards wheeled lazily in the thermals. I filled my lungs with intoxicating purity, and pronounced myself cured.

My few hours of restful solitude, enabled me to catch up on washing and cleaning up our portable larder. John appeared for lunch, and I didn't refuse his offer to take me out on Loch Sween in his dory. We roared through the stillness bumping over the wavelets to Tayvallich.

'Only takes five minutes by boat, fifteen in a car,' John shouted proudly. As we drove over to Arduane to meet Richard I felt well enough to hate myself for not being able to do a day's walk in scenery and conditions that would be hard to beat anywhere. Richard had enjoyed every step of his nineteen rucksack-free miles.

'Never mind,' I said cheerfully. Just think we've got clean pants and clean J-cloths. My body's had a rest and I've travelled just as far as you with the help of an outboard motor. And, I've seen my first golden eagle.'

It was happy hour, but I was strong-minded.

'Not for me thanks,' said Richard.

Oban was half way. We had been away six months and walked 2,150 miles. We had survived gales and rain, domestic discord, deadly roads, broken teeth and twenty four nights camping. We had settled down to a routine both on and off the road. We would start out together in the morning, and walk together until coffee break. This was a time when we would discuss anything or everything, people, places, politics or merely where we going to buy our next pint of milk. Later in the day I would drop behind in my own little world. All I had to do then was to put one foot in front of the other and keep Richard's back in sight. Communication had improved since our debacle at Carlisle. We were both excited about reaching the Highlands. In a few days we should be facing the most testing stretch. Six days in the wilderness of Knoydart, where there are no shops, no roads, and we thought, nobody.

After a short walk through a Gaelic dictionary, I decided that in future, we must *hoddle* and *spang* with our *knoost* and have none of the *hodge grummel!*

We were often asked what we thought about in those solitary pedestrian hours. I would switch on my cerebral video, compose doggerel, use my recorder, recite any poetry or prose I could remember, or write in my head. Richard, on the other hand, would 'read' the landscape like a three-dimensional map, totally absorbed in what he was passing through. This enabled him to anticipate. He missed little, be it ancient civilisations, flora and fauna, or the way. I consoled myself that if you can't be an intelligent walker, the next best thing was to be with one. Richard's knowledge certainly enriched my walk.

Just as Richard was entirely responsible for the route and mileages, I was responsible for the photography, recordings and communication generally. I would find the B & B, tackle the campsite receptionist and do all the shopping and cooking. In this way we worked as a team. Camping was easy. Once we had found a suitable site, we washed, cooked, ate and slept. Our tent was our home. Because it was so tiny we would have a 50% rule; i.e. each kept to his or her half as far as possible. It was a bit like being seabirds on a tiny ledge in an overcrowded colony; our own space on the ledge was very important.

We were both fit and well, even though Richard was continuing to lose weight. Usually he avoided scales, but now, obsessed by his shrinking frame, leaped onto them with alacrity whenever chance presented itself. In Ardrossen he weighed eleven and a half stone, a stone and a half less than his pre-walk weight. My weight seemed to have stabilised around eight stone, a stone less than I had been at Eastbourne. I knew I should have to put up with my various aches and pains, which were always worse on the roads. However, the sight of my aortic veins standing out from my abdomen like blue roots, was somewhat disconcerting, especially as they didn't disappear after rest. I assumed this was from the pressure of the waist strap on my pack. Our shrinking frames caused problems with our rucksacks. Our waist belts were pulled in to the limit, and even with padding, my hip bones were becoming chaffed, a problem that became more acute in warm weather. A thick layer of sheep's wool taped on them worked wonders.

* * *

Leaving the cosy hospitality of Oban, we set off across the Firth of Lorne to Craignure on a large, luxuriously appointed, Caledonian Macbrayne ferry. Patches of sun and deep clouds swept across land and sea in a fresh wind, throwing mountains and islands into sharp-focused relief. The captain's safety instructions were in both English and Gaelic.

Propping myself by the rail for a better view of Duart Castle as we slipped into the Sound of Mull, I felt we were now deep into our third 'foreign land'. The great massifs of Ben Mor and Ben Buie rose majestically to port and the island had a wild windswept look.

'Mull's a very strange shape,' Richard was studying a large map of the islands on the ferry wall.

'There's nearly as much water as land.'

The many deeply penetrating sea lochs shred the land mass into watery strips.

We camped at Salen, on a perfect patch of grass by the River Aros, which we shared with the midges and a herd of cows. The Sound of Mull was a deep indigo blue, alive with wind and white horses, while racing clouds chased shadows across the mountain tops. Our campsite near Tobermory was cold comfort, offering only a loo and cold water. More seriously our cooker went on strike. Unable to fix it with margarine and a corkscrew, Richard sounded glum.

'If I can't mend it, we'll have to get another one. If they don't sell them in Tobermory we'll be in trouble. We're in the wilds for the next ten days or so, with no shops at all.'

I tried to be optimistic, but Richard spent a sleepless night, rising at 6 a.m to attack the cooker with furrowed brow. No keyhole surgery this time. He pulled the cooker apart, blew, spat and smoothed the rubber intestines, put it together again, pumped extra hard and lit a match. There was a healthy roar, and the red ball of fire turned obediently to blue jets of flame. We celebrated with hot coffee.

The colourful houses of Tobermory sat snugly round the harbour, cradled by hills. From here we could look across to Morvern, Loch Sonart and Ardnurmurchan (Point of the Great Ocean) which sticks out 23 miles further west into the Atlantic than Land's End. Our little car ferry rose and fell gently over the waves as it took us over the strip of water to Kilchoan. Two frightfully middle class middle-aged English couples, complete with Volvo estate, kept their noses buried in a fistful of Sunday papers. One man never took his eyes off the pages of The Financial Times. The sound of Mull, Ben Nhor, Loch Sonart, Coll and Tiree were obliterated by the Nikkei, the Dow Jones, the FTSE and the Han-Seng.

We alighted at Kilchoan, a tiny landing stage on one of Scotland's wildest peninsulas. Alighted is perhaps, the wrong word. We were weighed down with provisions. I wrote in my diary:

We have enough food to see us through the next two to three days of rough camping. The tendency is to overstock for fear there will be no shops. Food is an essential energiser and morale booster but, when shopping, I have to think three times whether we really need it or not.

From the lighthouse at Ardnurmurchan Point we had our first views of the silhouetted mountains on the islands of Muck, Eigg and Rhum. It was a lonely spot. We sat in the shelter of the old walled gardens by the most westerly lighthouse on mainland Britain designed by Alan Stevenson in 1846. An information board told us that the men who built it suffered from scurvy. Perhaps it was after this that the walled vegetable gardens were built to ensure the workforce were fed the correct vitamins. As with most lighthouses, it was no longer manned.

A hesitant sun came out and we threaded our way up the western side of this wild and barren peninsula, past the empty white sands of Sanna, and inland down into the core of an old volcano. Here we found a place to camp by a stream which warned us to 'respect' the water which supplied the nearby hamlet.

Even in fine weather, it was an eerie spot. The two-mile area of peaty moorland made up the base of the volcano, which was ringed by a lip of uncompromising hills. After days in wide open spaces by the sea, the area had a claustrophobic feel. As we squelched across the boggy ground back to the coast, I felt the hills were as unyielding as prison bars. A ruined isolated farm stood alone in this God-forsaken place, a testament to more prosperous times. The silence was awesome.

Even this bleak landscape had its share of flora and fauna. We saw a jack snipe, skylarks and martins, tiny golden sovereigns, bog cotton, bilberries, orchids, heather, bracken and some elderly bluebells. We even came across a weary group of narcissi.

'D'you realise we have been seeing spring flowers since the south coast of Cornwall?' Richard observed. 'Travelling like this from south to north certainly elongates the spring.'

It was good to be back on the coast. At Ockle I knocked on a door of a boarded-in caravan to ask if I could buy some bread. A large lady with an English accent answered.

'Come in. Tea, coffee, or would you prefer a 'wee dram'?' she said cheerfully, while she rummaged in her huge freezer and re-appeared with a bloomer from Safeway.

Her husband was out, she was bored and we were entertained for half an hour with local gossip.

'We live in Stafford and come up here every summer. The locals don't like it mind you. They call us white settlers in these parts. Take our neighbours now. They let their property go to rack and ruin and now their being given fat grants to do it up for a holiday home and let it for £600 a week. When it's been let five years, it's theirs. We've had to pay every penny of this place ourselves because we're incomers.'

She handed us each a mug of tea and some chocolate biscuits.

'What do you do about shopping?' I asked, thinking of Safeway bread.

'There's a small shop in Kilchoan, but we usually take the ferry to Tobermoray. Once a month we drive to Fort William and stock up there.'

As we left Ockle our little road petered out. It was strangely quiet and empty. On the tops of the misty boulder-strewn fells, we met a wall of silence so intense it almost hurt. We blundered through this with heavy footfalls. Descending back into the real world of sound was almost a relief. A burn gurgled noisily near a level patch of grass by a ruined croft. We pitched camp, lulled to sleep by the sound of wind and rain, the bleat of sheep and the baying of a stag.

We woke to clearer skies and a mass of juicy black slugs who had been examining our larder for longer than I cared to think about.

'Slug cereal for breakfast!' I called to Richard, throwing half a dozen of their glistening black forms as far as I could. 'I wonder what they do taste like?'

'I hope we shall never have to find out.'

He gave our boots a good clean, and we set off in the direction of Moidart and the wilderness of Knoydart.

'We'll be able to stock up in Arisaig. Hopefully we'll find a campsite tonight to clean up a bit before we get in there,' Richard said happily.

That night I wrote the following excerpt in my diary:

This is our fifth night camping rough. Living like this is a strange existence. We are either vertical or horizontal and rarely, if ever bored. Our time camping passes pleasantly. Chores take a while, and even with nothing to read or do, we are not searching for things to occupy our time. We eat well and sleep well. Everything we eat tastes good and nothing gets left on the plate. We might feel encouraged to do more washing of ourselves if the burn water wasn't so icy. We've stopped using purification tablets as they make the water taste like undiluted chlorine. Pure burn water tastes so good. A wee dram is something to look forward to at the end of the day. The temperature outside is very cool, even by Scottish summer standards, but the tent is snug enough and we are not cold at night. No midges last night or this morning due to the wind. Tomorrow we should reach Glenuig.

A strong breeze blew coldly in our faces as we descended the hill into Glenuig. Our walk had taken us past Loch Sheil, and on into Moidart, crossing the gentle tree-lined river at Kinlochmoidart, where cows grazed the lush grass and the banks were bright with rhodedendrums. In a meadow nearby we saw the seven beeches commemorating 'The Seven Men of Moidart'; Bonnie Prince Charlie's seven loyal supporters, the only army he bought with him from France. A cairn at the head of the loch, erected by the '46 Society, marks the place where Charles sailed back to ignominious exile in 1746. Two hundred and fifty years later the myth lives on.

Glenuig, on the shores of the Sound of Arisaig, had a few scattered houses and an Inn. We had found no suitable place to pitch our tent and it was nearly 6 p.m.

'Let's go in,' Richard urged. I needed no encouragement.

The inn was warm and welcoming. A big fire blazed in the hearth, an attractive blonde smiled from behind the bar and delicious-smelling food was being served.

Richard ordered two beers and asked if they had a room for us.

'We've a wee cabin next door. I'll just check it's free and faytch the key.' She disappeared returning with a key in her hand. 'That's just £10 each.'

We felt jubilant. A hot shower, followed by food, drink and sleep and we'd be in heaven. There was however, a small snag. The shower only ran cold. The comfortable spacious cabin was then reduced to £7.00. A well-cooked robust meal and several malt whiskies later, we wandered down on to the beach to watch the sun set behind the jagged peaks of Rhum, with the flat island of Eigg lying infront of it like a great sea wall. Several black-headed sheep lay on the rock-strewn sand. The shattered carcass of an old working boat lay rotting amongst the seaweed. Several boats were moored on the ebbing tide. A blushing sea shone in a monochromed landscape. The notes of a harp drifted across the stillness . . . We stood spellbound, paying silent homage to the Highlands.

Bright sunlight woke us early. Having been told breakfast was served from 8 a.m. we were up and packed, ready for an early breakfast and a brisk start.

The hotel, rocking with life and laughter the night before, looked deserted. The front entrance was closed and no-one answered our loud knocks. At 9 a.m. I decided to ring from the nearby call box. No reply. I then walked across the road to the little Post

Office and stores. A small van outside was delivering vegetables. The post mistress was young and helpful.

'Don't worry,' she soothed. 'This often happens. I'll give Peter a wee ring. He'll no' be long.'

While she was ringing, the delivery man beamed knowingly at me.

'It's usual,' he said. 'Only last winter I came up to the Inn for Gaelic lessons. When I arrived there was a couple in the dining room still waitin' for breakfast.'

The post mistress returned.

'Theer's no reply, but I've layft the phone ringing - that should wake him up. You'd best knock on his partner's cabin door!'

I did. Someone got out of bed and shuffled across the room to the door. It opened a crack. A young blonde waitress looked at me through bleary eyes.

'Throw stones up to his window,' she suggested sleepily, and withdrew.

By this time Richard was brewing tea on our doorstep.

The hotel was still quiet as the grave, and together we tossed a hail of stones up onto the window in sheer desperation.

At that moment the front door opened and a handsome man of 30-something beamed at us and invited us into the dining room. There was no word of apology. As far as he was concerned it might have been 8 o'clock.

He may not have been a lark, but he certainly was a charmer. We were his only customers that morning. We had a large, quickly prepared three-course breakfast and talked about fishing and long-distance walks.

Arisaig is no more than a line of houses and a general stores, yet the views across the Sound of Arisaig to the broken jigsaw of islands, Rhum, Eigg and Skye, slowed our progress. The jagged silhouettes of these mountainous islands, never failed to thrill, guiding us northwards for many memorable days. Stout rowan trees along the road, dripped juicy orange berries, silver birches and broad oaks grew from mossy beds, and rhodedendrums bloomed vigorously. Here was a chink in the rugged armour of the Highlands.

It was an effort to drag our eyes away from nature and concentrate on nurturing our stomachs for the next few days. The general store sold everything. By the time I staggered out I don't think there was much left. Provisioning for six days was the easy part; then we had to pack it all into our already full rucksacks, and then carry it. We spent an energetic half hour on a seat beside a phone box, throwing out packaging and ramming powdered milk, dried fruit, muesli, smoked sausages, cheese, yoghurts and bananas into the packs until they nearly burst their seams. The sliced loaf rode jauntily on the outside, eventually replaced by our bag of litter.

Heave ho time! We sat on the edge of the bench, and eased the packs gently onto our shoulders. The extra weight hit us as we leaned forward and straightened our knees.

'Did we really need all this?' Richard asked, easing his shoulder straps of their 60 lb burden.

'You'll be glad of it tonight,' I replied pulling in my waist strap defiantly. 'Anyway it'll weigh less every day.' The full 43 lbs registered and I added, 'I think we'll have second helpings tonight.'

The little village of Morar was the last of civilisation for us for the next few days. A brave new road to Mallaig, bypasses the attractive hotel and row of cottages perched above golden sands. From here, there are good views across the Sound of Sleat to the islands of Rhum, Eigg, and Skye. Cut off from its life-blood of tourists the little place was dying. The shop and Post Office had closed, the one pub was so quiet we had to dig someone out to serve us, and the hotel looked in need of attention. In spite of this, monumental masons from the Council were busy tarting up the corpse. A smart new pavement was being laid, the new 'antique' lamp posts were adorned with hanging baskets, and new litter bins mushroomed on the pavement. In the distance came the roar of cars speeding their way on to Mallaig. We turned our back on the traffic and headed off into the wilderness.

Chapter Fourteen

Earth's crammed with heaven,
And every common bush afire with God;
But, only he who sees, takes off his shoes.
E. Barrett-Browning

Laden with overfilled rucksacks, beer and pioneering spirit, we left the tiny road for a track along the shores of Loch Morar. It was a perfect evening. Not a breath of wind and the steep hills rising from the loch looked as velvet-soft as a deer's antlers, grey-green in the evening sunshine. To the west, the silhouette of Rhum's sharp peaks across the loch, blushed pink.

'Hello!'

'Lovely evening.'

A grey-haired couple passed the time of day with us on their way back to Morar.

A mile or so from the road, we found just enough flat land to pitch the tent. A nearby burn gurgled down the hills into the loch. We could see nothing but still water, steeply rising hills and distant peaks.

'Hi!' Puff, puff.

'Hi!'

A lone jogger ran along the steep rocky path outside our home.

After supper, Richard washed our few dishes in the burn, and lit a fire to destroy all the rest of our rubbish. We were determined to leave only our footsteps in this magic wilderness. He then lit a cigar - 'to keep the midges away' and pulled out his one luxury, a sketch pad. The midges had risen and were hungry. I retreated and wrote my diary lying supine.

'Gut everning. Zat looks nice.'

A couple of young Germans with big boots and small rucksacks passed by.

Richard gave up the unequal struggle and joined me inside.

'Is this really the wilderness of Knoydart?' I asked. We've seen more people in the last few hours than we have for days.

'That's the trouble with a wilderness. They draw people like a magnet.'

'Like us?' I said with a grin, snuggling into my down sleeping bag. The nights were so light now it was hard to sleep.

'Tomorrow will be tough. I want to get to the head of Loch Nevis where there's a bothy. Most of the way there'll be no path at all. We'd better get some sleep.'

'G'night.'

'BBBrrrrrrrrrrr . . .'

It was as dark as it was ever likely to be. The engine of an outboard motor echoed in the stillness, shattering the silence.

'Bloody motorboats . . .'

A small path led us across North Morar to Tarbet on the shores of Loch Nevis. This long strip of water is the last sea loch before the wilderness of Knoydart. It lies deep in a cradle of ancient mountains, accessible only by boat or on foot. Instinctively we knew we had shaken off the motor car. The air was clean and pure. The sparkling blue water filled with the delicate forms of aurelia jelly-fish, opening and shutting themselves like parasols, in silent progress amongst a fringe of brown seaweed. We felt like heavy-footed intruders and respectfully lowered our voices. Although narrow in places, this loch was not oppressive. To the west it widened in a broad sweep of bay at Inverie, and in the distance we could see the Cuillins of Skye. The loch narrowed at its head to the north and east; here the great peaks of Garbh Choich Mhor and Sgurr na Ciche rose like a mighty altar in this outdoor cathedral.

Tarbet was just two houses and a church beside a little shingle beach. Someone on the far side of the bay, was examining the intruders with a pair of binoculars. A little motor boat lay silently on the clear water, and a couple of open boats were pulled up on the shingle. There was barely a ripple on the blue loch. Nothing stirred. We rested on the close-cropped grass, absorbing the sunlight, the silence, the scent of elder flower, sheep and seaweed. Quietly relaxing there, we began to feel in harmony with these awesome surroundings.

The sound of shots echoed round the hills, deepening the silence as they died away. It was our cue to move.

'Come on! We want to get to Sourlies before dark and we've got six very hard miles and no path.'

Richard was on his feet, hitching his huge rucksack from a supporting thigh and hip, and so onto his back in three deft moves.

'I'm coming,' I said stretching slowly, one part of me wishing we could stay just here, the other part eager for the challenge.

Suddenly, a tremendous roar shook the virgin silence and folded the ether in waves of ear-splitting sound. The valley rocked, as a large metal insect screeched low above the loch and disappeared into the hills at the head of the valley, followed by fading blows, echoing and echoing.

We moved on in stunned silence. The first few miles of bog, heather and stony headlands didn't seem too bad. One or two remote houses stood by the loch shore, and we passed the ruins of many more crofts. Progress was slow, and got slower, as we traversed the steep terrain and negotiated headland after steep headland, squelching through bogs or knee-deep in heather. At one point we were scrambling across a sheer drop of rock, to avoid going right over the top. With our heavy packs it was physically hard and had we not been very fit we could never have done it. Round each headland, I hoped to see the bothy at the head of the loch, and time and again I was disappointed.

Eventually we reached the end of the world. It was just after 5 p.m. The little bothy is tucked under the hills on the north side of the loch, surrounded by a watery flat area, before the ground rises gently to the foothills of the great mountains beyond. The day's walk had taken us seven and a half hours. As the weather was good, we decided to camp and not use the bothy, and, helped by a not-so-wee dram, we managed to cook and eat before crashing out.

Just as we were settling down to sleep, we heard a strange distinct churring sound, which came close to the tent, and then receded, coming and going for over twenty minutes. Looking out into the nocturnal twilight, we could see no sign of anything that might be making the sound, just loch and sky and mountains. The noise persisted, and I tried to record it but without success. It was an eerie persistent sound which was to recur on several more nights in this area.

We were up early and brewing tea, when a fit man in his thirties, carrying only a day sack strode up to our tent.

'Hello. Where are you off to?' He asked.

We told him briefly.

'I'm Steve from Sussex. Staying at Inverie with some friends. As the weather's good, I thought I'd try and climb Sgurr na Ciche. I left at 4 a.m.'

He sounded as though he was going for a walk in the park.

'Well you're just in time for tea,' I said handing him a cup.

We chatted about the Nine Crofters at Inverie, dispossessed by Lord Brocken in 1948. Steve had been reading a book called *The Last Land Grab*.

As we talked, two figures emerged from the bothy, striding towards the great peaks of Sgurr na Ciche and Garbh Cgiucg Mhor. The leading figure was in kilt and tammy shanter, followed by a retainer carrying two fishing rods.

'Do you see what I see?' I asked the other two, just in case I was dreaming.

They nodded, staring hard at the retreating forms. I just wished we'd stayed at the bothy last night.

As we crossed the spongy land, we noticed a curious blue flower on a long stalk with four leaves at the bottom which our Sussex fireman informed us was the carnivorous butterwort.

'They eat midges,' he told us.

'I'm glad something does,' I said, anointing myself with insect repellent.

A rusty swing bridge saved us getting wet in the river and then we began to climb the first of two big passes into Barresdale.

Pausing for a puff stop, we looked across the loch and could see how steep our traverse to Sourlies had been.

'We didn't do too badly did we?' I said with satisfaction, more to myself than Richard.

'Don't get too cocky. We've got to climb Everest this morning and K2 this afternoon,' was the reply.

It was a long steep climb greatly helped by a dry zigzagging path. From the top we could see a great sweep of valley rolling away before us down to Inverie, with the Loch Nevis and the Cuillins in the distance. On the valley floor, a great cross topped a grassy hillock, the memorial to the Brocken family. We thought it should be for the dispossessed crofters.

Before we reached our second pass, we saw a pair of red-throated divers on a lochan, so near that their neat grey and white striped head and necks, red eyes and red throats were clearly visible without binoculars. They dived as soon as they were aware of our presence, reappearing on the far side of the little loch.

'That's what I was hoping to see. Now, if we can see some black-throated divers, I'll be very happy.' Richard was purring.

The second pass was easier than the first, and we descended to Barresdale where a mass of bright tents mushroomed round the bothy. Bossy notices telling us to pitch our tent only at the campsite came as a shock; we were just getting used to the freedom of camping anywhere we chose. A loud vibrating sound from the generator shook the air as we neared the river, where a host of brightly-coloured human insects moved round their coloured tents. Most were young Munro-baggers, who looked as though they had stepped from the pages of a Field and Trek Catalogue.

'So much for a wilderness,' I said, returning from a visit to the bothy-come-mountain-rescue hut. 'I'm glad we don't have to sleep in there.'

The hut, no doubt a haven in bad weather, was noisy, dirty, overcrowded and smelly. We had become used to our own space, clean burn water, and the use of the great outdoors for all our ablutions.

We walked up to Barresdale Bay to escape the noise of the generator, and watch the sun set. A herd of deer were cropping the grass beside the blushing loch and glowing mountains. Tomorrow we would walk up Loch Hourn, the most remote and mystical tentacle of water we should encounter.

Of the four lochs, Morar, Nevis, Hourn, and Duich, which lie in parallel in this remote part of the west coast, Loch Hourn is the most implacable. Profoundly still, each mountain, tree, rock and shadow was echoed in its glassy surface. Like Loch Nevis, it has no road round it, although cars can reach Kinlochourn at the head of the loch. At this end the water narrows to a dog leg, the mountains rise to 2,000 feet on either side, and the result is a feeling of claustrophobic unease enhanced by the eerie silence. Shroud-like clouds wreathed the mountain tops, and the water darkened in the fading light.

'Imagine this in really bad weather. It must be fearsome.' I shuddered.

'It has a reputation for being one of the wildest places in the British Isles. The loch is incredibly deep,' Richard was watching camouflaged ringed plover down on a shingle beach.

The climb up on the north east side of the loch, to the corries backing the Glenshiel Forest, was steep. The rocky path was hard on the feet. The weather was now 'dreich' and a line of pylons were an unwelcome intrusion into 'our' wilderness. Then, looming out of the mist came a slim man pushing/carrying an even slimmer bike, dressed in black lycra trousers and day-glow jacket. This wilderness was a challenge for him and his bike.

'I've always wanted to cycle this stretch. It means I can make a round trip from Shiel Bridge via Arnisdale and Kinlochourn, a nice 84 mile circuit. We're up here to celebrate our 25th wedding anniversary. The wife's not with me today, but yesterday we cycled from Kishorn to Sheildaig over the Applecross pass in a head wind. Get sick of tarmac don't you?'

We congratulated him and his wife. They must be Mr and Mrs Superfit.

'I'd better be off. I've only done 24 miles so far. Have a good trip!'

I looked at my watch. It was 4.30 p.m.

'Good thing they have long evenings up here. He won't be back in time for supper.'

A mile short of Arnisdale, Richard decided to stop. It was raining steadily, and he had found a possible camp site by a roaring torrent under some trees. Before we slept he recorded the following, supine in a sleeping bag:

We're inside our tent because its cold and pouring with rain. The midge count is about a million per cubic foot. Our supper, which I managed to burn and deposit about a quarter of an inch of soot, congealed rice and blackened tar over the bottom of two saucepans, was even so, very acceptable. We have a difference of opinion about the number of miles we do each day depending on how we perform. On good days mileage shrinks, on bad days it expands. Today we walked about 14 hard miles. We lost a film with 36 exposures of these last few days which has lowered morale as they have been the highlight of our trip so far. However, apart from having very few dry clothes left and feeling disgustingly dirty, we have survived well.

After a disturbed night, listening to the rain, the roaring stream and a barrage of twigs and creepy-crawlies falling from the tree, I cooked some porridge for breakfast, combed the midges out of my hair, and set off for Arnisdale and civilisation once more. I felt elated and recorded the following:

Life in the Scottish Highlands is a fight. You fight for everything. You fight for breath going up the hills, you fight to get there at the end of a long day, you fight the midges, the rain, the wind. You fight to keep yourself from degenerating into something horribly sordid.

Why do it at all?

When the weather lifts, when you are going round each corner, you are just magnetised by the beauty of the place, it lures you on, you know it's there even if you can't see it. When you can see it, it's so magnificent, it's like stepping from purgatory to paradise.

There is satisfaction in fighting and winning. If you're in the tent, you've managed to get there, you've cooked yourself a hot meal, you're stomachs' full and you've had a wee dram, that also brings a sense of satisfaction.

The unspoiled nature of the place, means you are the alien here with nature, and you have to treat it with respect.

As we emerged from the wilderness and met the first tarmac road for four days, a roughly written sign in the gorse said - NO CARS BEYOND THIS POINT. Beneath the sign lay five bags of coal.

The low-slung, stone-built cottages in Arnisdale had gardens bursting with brightly-coloured lupins, poppies and broom. Some were holiday lets. Out of one of these stepped a lady with brown legs, shorts, velvet mules, huge earrings and grey hair swept up in a bun. In her hand was a scarlet lead, and on the end of this was small black cat, complete with collar and bell.

'Come on Cleo. Silly little thing. Come this way!' The huge earrings nodded encouragement as kissing noises were made through pursed lips. Cleo meowed her anger. The thick make-up frowned and jerked the scarlet lead. Cleo refused to budge.

'Morning,' we said brightly, having difficulty controlling our facial muscles.

We were back in the land of cars and tourists.

With difficulty we found our way down to Camusfearna by the river Sandaig and the island of the same name. Here Gavin Maxwell had lived with his otters and written his best-seller, *Ring of Bright Water*. There are no signs to tell you where to go, just a simple plaque on a stone where the author's home had been, and a little memorial by the river where Edal was buried, inscribed with the simple words: *Whatever joys she gave to you, give back to Nature.* A single white croft, tucked in below the hill, looked seawards. Swathes of white sand lit up the little rocky island. The Ring of Bright Water remained intact.

It was raining again by the time we reached Glenelg. Cold, wet and tired we found the Inn. Having scorned civilisation, we now longed for a hot bath and food that didn't look like sick and taste like sawdust.

The bar was simply furnished with a couple of warm rugs thrown on the stone flags, and a huge log fire blazing in the inglenook. Behind the bar stood Jamie, six foot of Highland charm complete with kilt and sporran.

'Sorry lassie, we're full just now.' I stood, speechless with disappointment, while my Gortex dripped gently on the flagstones. It was like being turned away from the Pearly Gates.

'We can do you a meal though,' Jamie added brightly.

'I think we need a bath first. We've been camping rough for nearly a week.'

He fixed us up with a B & B down the road, and we promised to return when clean.

In the summer, Jamie's Inn catered almost exclusively for Americans. He offered them the perfect Scottish experience, good food, good whisky, simple but comfortable surroundings, and as much walking, climbing, shooting and fishing as was required. The Americans formed their own party and came en bloc complete with tour organiser. At supper they swarmed round us,

'Listen Dave. D'ya hear this? These two are walkin' all round the coast of Britain for charity. 4,300 miles. Gee. Isn't that really something!'

They plied us with questions while we ravenously demolished some bar food in the form of chilli con carne. Jamie, meanwhile was taking orders for the dining room.

'I can recommend the salmon, or the venison. And what will you have for starters?'

'Now we've had our starters, I could do with a main course,' I whispered to Richard.

The Americans floated off into the dining room in a cloud of perfume and aftershave. We asked for the bill.

'It's all taken care of. Sorry we've no deserts, but if you'd like a drop of coffee go through the bar, it'll be the second door on the left.'

Nervously we opened a door marked PRIVATE and found ourselves in a stage set. Striped yellow wallpaper, apricot curtains, antique grandfather clock, oil portraits of the ancestors, a stag's head and some comfortable sofas. Glossy books on Scottish walks were carefully arranged on the coffee table. A log fire was laid in the grate with an invitation to light it. Coffee was ready on an antique occasional table.

'Wow. How's this for civilisation?' I sat down carefully, feeling very strange.

'Coffee for Madam?' Richard's love of caffeine had overcome his natural inhibitions.

'Jamie's got it about right hasn't he?'

'Mmmm,' I was busy savouring an after-dinner mint. 'Civilisation's not so bad after all.'

Refreshed after a good night's sleep, Richard reckoned we were fit enough to take the scenic route to Sheil Bridge along the shores of Loch Alsh and then Loch Duich.

'We could go along the Ratagan Pass - that's the old military road made famous because Johnson and Boswell walked along there in 1773 and took the ferry to Kylerhea on Skye. I think we'll see more if we really do keep to the coast though.'

The little road out of Glenelg passed Bernera Barracks. Built in 1722, and garrisoned until 1790. The imposing ruins were a reminder of the strategic importance of this area in the 18th century. Now it stands, peaceful and deserted, near the Kyle Rhea where the Sound of Sleet narrows to a bottle neck and Skye looks near enough to touch. Rounding the corner we could see the new controversial bridge over to Skye, not yet completed.

Here, we left the road on a well-marked wide track to Ardentoul and Tontaig.

It was clearly marked as a footpath. Richard looked pleased.

'This looks promising. They don't usually have footpaths in Scotland. You're supposed to be able to walk anywhere.'

Our walker's motorway soon dwindled into a very tiny rough track, through woods where we bent double under silver birches, and through bogs where we squelched up to our shins. We emerged at Ardentoul on Loch Alsh, where we paused for lunch on a beach, thinking we had done the worst of it. Then the ground sloped steeply away from the loch and we lost our path altogether. Richard looked anxious.

'We must find the path,' he said firmly, leaping across a raging torrent on none too secure rocks.

I hesitated. Crossing fast-running water was a problem for me. The more you looked at it, the more sure you were of getting wet.

'I can't do it with my pack on,' I panicked.

Richard took his off and came across to collect mine.

'Can't we just go down to the loch and walk along by the water?' I prevaricated.

'Come on,' he encouraged. 'Don't think about it, just go.'

I did. Once committed there was no going back. I concentrated hard on the rocks, keeping my eyes off the water rushing frenetically past. There were several nasty wobbles but I kept dry, reaching he opposite bank with pride intact.

A few minutes later we reached a business-like six foot deer fence.

'I'm sure the path's this way.' Richard was nodding at the fence. Now it was his turn to panic. Having lost his bearings, he was not enjoying the sensation.

For me this was the norm, so it was easy to keep calm.

'We can get through here if you like. Look there's a large hole. If we push our packs through we can follow.'

Safely through the fence, and a lot of scrambling later, we came across a vestige of path with clearly defined cycle tyre tracks. We were in thick conifer woods on a rock-strewn slope of about 45 degrees.

'It must be our friend from Knoydart again. It's incredible how anyone could get a bike through here.'

It was an extraordinary path. At times we had to climb the steep moss and needle-covered hillside, scramble over rocks and streams, and duck under the spreading firs. Coniferous woods have an eerie sterile silence about them. No birds sang At times the path grew wider. Then we were on a soft needle-covered tunnel, under a dove-tailed canopy of branches suffused with green glowing light. Here, our footfalls made no sound. At last the trees fell back and we entered a clearing. The ruins of an ancient Broch perched on the hill-top with peeps through the trees to Loch Duich, the Seven Sisters of Kintail, and Eilean Donan Castle. We brewed tea on the well-preserved remains of this Iron-Age stronghold and felt on top of the world.

'We came. We saw. We conquered,' I said, momentarily euphoric, before hunger sent me searching my pack for our one last banana and a Mars bar.

'It's not all bad to have to work hard to get somewhere. I think it makes us much more a part of the landscape. We've struggled hard for six hours and we've got through it. That's good.' Richard might have been a latter day Iron Age chieftain surveying his domain.

'You're right. But it's now 4.30 p.m. and you said we've got another nine miles to Shiel Bridge. You also said we *had* to get there come what may.'

We left the hillside and took the tiny road along the lochside to Shiel Bridge. From this south west side we had perfect views of the Seven Sisters of Kintail rising majestically before us. That uninterrupted view into the Kintail Forest kept us going. The Youth Hostel at Ratagen said FULL, so we plodded on. We had over a mile to go, it was getting late and we had been walking for nearly ten hours. At that moment a car drew up beside me

'Would you like a lift?' The driver enquired.

My head said yes, my heart said no - the rest of me was confused. Richard was well ahead.

'Thank you. Er . . . I don't know how much further we have to go. I'll ask my husband - he's ahead. We're, er, on a sponsored walk you see.'

'Och weil I'll no give you a lift then!' He drove off in a cloud of exhaust.

Chapter Fifteen

Land of Heart's Desire
Where beauty has no ebb, decay no flood.
But joy is wisdom, Time and endless song.
W.B. Yeats

The Kyle of Lochalsh bustled with ferries, coaches and cars. We were told that when the Skye Bridge got the go-ahead, Caledonian MacBrayne doubled their ferry crossings and improved their services. It was like shutting the stable door after the horse had bolted.

We felt sad that the bridge had been allowed at all. Travelling on a ferry dislocates the journey, making passengers more aware of their surroundings outside the warm womb of the car or coach. Eilean Ban, the 'White Island', between the Kyle of Lochalsh and the Isle of Skye, was Gavin Maxwell's last home. There are plans to turn it into an otter sanctuary. Ironically, the island, unchanged for centuries, is now cut in half by the new Skye Bridge and lorries and coaches thunder past the cottage where Maxwell once watched his otters.

From Loch Kishorn we had our first views of the mighty corries of the Applecross range of mountains. The light shone softly on the giant scoops between the great shadowy buttresses. They were an awesome sight.

We spent a memorable night in Kishorn with friends. Percy and Gillian live in tiny whitewashed cottage in a latter-day Garden of Eden, full of scents and colour. They both had green fingers, and had landscaped and planted every inch of the fifteen acres. They were the most energetic and lively septuagenarians we had ever met. Gillian was kind and motherly, her mobility slightly impaired by arthritic knees. Percy's vibrant personality shone beneath his lean weather-beaten face, and his tall imposing figure belied his years.

'Gillian does the flowers and I do the veg and the orchard.' We were standing in Percy's walled vegetable garden, where the neat rows were bursting with life and energy like their owner.

'The secret's in the seaweed,' Percy told us. 'We pile it on every year and hey presto!'

'D'you eat it too?' I asked, thinking it was just what I needed to complete the next 2,000 miles.

When Percy and Gill weren't gardening, they were walking, canoeing, cycling or entertaining.

A friend from the south was staying in a cottage on their land and came over to supper. Being something of an actor, with a great love of literature, he read us some poetry after the meal. A pot-pourri of humour, wit and pathos, which we lapped up thirstily. Physically tired, well fed and in good company we purred with contentment as '*love bade us welcome.*'

Later Percy told us a little of his life history. As a young clergyman, he found himself as a missionary in the Far East at the outbreak of the Second World War and managed to get on a boat to America. They were torpedoed. Percy found himself in a life boat with a strange assortment of his fellow human-beings of all ages, cultures and creeds. Being a man of considerable faith and courage, he sat quietly observing his fellow-men during the bedlam of the next few days. After a while, the weeping, wailing and gnashing of teeth died down, and out of the chaos came a natural order of survival. The life boat, with its disparate but now homogenous cargo, was rescued. When Percy returned to England after the war he started a commune/retreat for people who needed time out. The project flourished under his charismatic leadership for many years.

We felt very small and insignificant as we crawled up the steep and tortuous road through the forbidding buttresses of the Applecross Massif. This old drover's road is however, more challenging for cars. Known to tourists as The Scenic Route, the original Gaelic name, *'Bealach na Ba'*, means the Pass of the Cattle. It shoots up a series of spectacular hairpin bends to a height of 2,053 feet ending in a rock-strewn moonscape which looks across to the Cuillins of Skye with the long low island of Raasay basking before it. Until the new coast road to Shieldaig was built in 1976, the Applecross Peninsula was one of the most remote parishes in mainland Britain. It was June 21st, midsummer's day, and the sun came out as we descended to Applecross, a camp site shared with red deer, sheep and a few vociferous human beings.

A cheery post-mistress in Applecross' well-stocked stores was helpful. We were due to collect our next parcel of maps and provisions from the post mistress at Diabeg. As it would be Sunday we needed to ask if she'd mind us calling in.

'Och no problem. I'll just ask Dennis the Post. I think it's a Mrs. Mackenzie up there. Her daughter-in-law's the community nurse round these parts.'

Next day she handed us Mrs. Mackenzie's phone number. 'There's nothing high tech about the tartan telegraph, but it works well up here.'

The sandy shore of the bay swirled cinnamon and cream against the blue Inner Sound and the more distant silhouette of Skye's great peaks. We had clear views of the Inner Hebrides basking like primeval monsters in the blue water. A hot June sun beat down on the tarmac of the new road. The old road, now a romantic overgrown track, punctuated by milestones, was a fading memorial to the crofting communities of the last century.

'I remember using this old road before that was ever built,' Richard jerked his head disdainfully in the direction of the empty tarmac ribbon. Below us we could see the remains of the old crofting settlements with their neat strips of poor quality land.

'A hundred years ago this place would have been alive. Now they're just ghosts of the past.'

We stood, oozing nostalgia, on that trickle of hard-core in the heather, amongst the telegraph poles embalmed in their tombs of peat.

The delicious miles passed quickly by and the great mountains of the Torridon Forest soon appeared across the loch. Their bulky shapes, so familiar to us, welcomed us like old friends.

Liathach, Beinn Alligin, Beinn Damph looked dark and brooding, while the quartz of Beinn Eighe's broad back sparkled like sugar crystals. The sandstone of these Torridon mountains is a humbling 750 million years old, about the oldest rocks on the face of the planet.

Shieldaig's lonely strand of slate-roofed whitewashed houses lay peacefully across the water. In such surroundings there were no complaints. We felt perfectly at one with each other and the very beautiful world around us.

'Whatever are they doing to Sheildaig?' Richard demanded as we drew near. The little village was littered with heavy plant machinery. They were making a new front as the old sea wall was crumbling.

'I discovered Shieldaig, thirty seven years ago when I came up here on my own. It was just a romantic strand of whitewashed cottages by the lochside. Now they've dug it up, polished it and dragged it into the 20th century.'

'D'you think they'll put hanging baskets and, perish the thought, poopscoops?'

'Probably.' Richard was having another dose of nostalgia. 'One thing's for sure it'll never be the same place again.'

We camped in Torridon under the massive bulk of Liathach, a mountain we had always wanted to climb. It was tempting to rise early and climb it before setting off for Diabeg.

'I think we'd better not attempt it. There'll be no road from Diabeg to Red Point and it's quite tough walking.'

'Mmm. I'm sure you're right but it's so tempting in these perfect conditions.'

Tents mushroomed round us in the Torridon campsite, just a field beside the Youth Hostel. It was fun watching other people after so long on our own. The evening was warm, and the midges decided it was supper time. Richard lit a fire, hoping to deter them. We anointed ourselves with repellent and ate outside. Nearby a lady in shorts and T-shirt disappeared inside her tent and reappeared a few minutes later looking as though she was going for a walk on the moon. A sunhat was pulled down over her midge net, her shell suit coller was pulled up and her hands hidden in mittens. Socks and boots protected her lower third. All eyes were on her as she attempted to eat.

It was a scorching day. We pulled on our new shorts and looked at one another in horror, then burst out laughing. The sight of two pairs of thin white hairy match sticks, which didn't look as though they could possibly propel us another 2,000 miles was too much. Even the highland cattle looked embarrassed.

The sun was melting the tar on the steep road of the Pass of the Winds which snakes above Upper Loch Torridon for nine steamy miles to Diabeg. It was a wild and lonely road threading through a barren rocky landscape. At the top the ground drops dramatically to peaty lochs with sea views and rocky islands to the west. Lower Diabeg's lush green pastures and blooming gardens contrast with the wild rocky hillside on the far side of the bay. For once there was no wind. Only the sound of bees and the scents of summer.

The tiny village of Diabeg is a cul-de-sac. There is no shop, no pub and anyone wanting the post office needs to be good at orienteering. A scruffy hand-written sign reads Post Office. A quarter of a mile along this little track, we found a portacabin, sitting like a large tardis on the sheep-cropped grass at the end of nowhere. Mrs. MacKenzie's little white cottage snuggled beneath some trees in the lee of the hill.

'Come on in and take some tae. You'll be tired in this heat, and it's a way yet to Craig.'

Her hair was a little whiter and her shoulders a little more bowed, but otherwise Mrs. MacKenzie had changed little since we stayed in the village four years ago.

After tea she opened up the 'tardis' and presented us with a large jiffy bag containing our new maps, a host of luxury items and dehydrated foods from the real world.

'This is like Christmas,' I said as deodorants, insect repellent, glucose tablets, lipsyl, foot cream and films fell from my jiffy 'stocking' onto the granite rock below the portacabin. Our used maps went back in the bag and entrusted to the MacKenzie postal service.

The road had ended. We set off across the rocks and heather to Craig, once a thriving little community of fifteen houses, now just a Youth Hostel set in a barren rocky landscape, four miles from the nearest road. At the top of the hill a notice said CRAIG - 15 MINUTES.

'They do it here in minutes rather than miles. I wonder what Scottish minutes are like?'

Richard was ahead, finding out.

It was a perfect evening. We found an idyllic place to camp beside the clear blue waters of the loch. My kitchen window had the best view yet, with Skye, Raasay and Rona across the water, with the Outer Hebrides, and Redpoint Sands all clearly visible. The smooth grey rocks shone through the clear water of the loch, draped in seaweed and studdied with limpets. A lone cormorant spread his great wings and flapped gently across the still water. The shrill cry of an oyster-catcher broke the silence. The sun refused to set, and the night glowed until dawn.

For once we didn't hurry to get off in the morning. We both needed time to pause, ruminate and relax. It was a hot cloudless day and this tranquil paradise was the perfect place.

The previous evening, Richard had lit a camp fire, and the young Dutch warden came down from the Youth Hostel for a chat. He was concerned about the detrimental effects of the ubiquitous fish farms on the western seaboard, and on the decline of the wild salmon.

'They net salmon at Redpoint,' he said angrily. 'You'll see the nets tomorrow. No wonder numbers are declining. Also the chemicals used to prevent diseases on fish farms impoverishes the water. It's bad. The result is there soon won't be any shell fish or salmon. I have been coming here for eight summers. Each year there are less fish and more dead seals. I think the fishermen shoot the seals because they eat their fish.' The earnest young man was genuinely upset.

'It's true about the seals,' I said. 'There's a dead one here just up the beach. The irony is, that pollution from industry originally caused decline in fish stocks, then salmon farms were put up here to save the economy of the Highlands, and now they in turn are polluting these waters.'

'And that's not all of it,' Richard replied slowly. 'The salmon are very inefficient at converting their fish-farm diet of dried herring and sand eels. A huge amount of this goes to waste. The big worry is that sand eels are a vital food for almost any creature in the sea larger than they are. Fishing for them in large numbers is like cutting off your nose to spite your face.'

'Well, you're not putting me off eating salmon while they still exist,' I said, squashing a large horsefly on my left shin. 'It's just a shame we're all such profligate vandals. D'you want sardine or horsefly in your sandwiches?'

Richard was busy working out our weather conditions on the walk so far.

'It's amazing. Since we left Eastbourne we have had 49 wet days, 68 half and half, and 79 sunny. Not bad?'

'Just keep that up. You're doing well.'

We had been able to see Redpoint's long stretch of golden sands from the far side of Loch Torridon. On the cliffs here, we could clearly see the salmon fishing nets like a great arrow in the clear blue water. After a scorching four miles across the rocky switch back path, we were ready to throw off our boots and most of our clothes, and plunge our sweaty bodies into the cold water. We shared the huge beach with a naked lady and a large Portuguese man-of-war. As we lay drying our limbs like a pair of cormorants, a couple of young men appeared on the rough path manhandling mountain bikes. Fit and strong though they were, they must have underestimated the path. They were drenched in sweat and looked all in. Without a word, they dropped their bikes and headed for the water.

I rolled onto my stomach to let the backs of my legs go as pink as the fronts.

'I've an idea. How about we just stay here all afternoon?'

'The only problem is we don't have a mobile phone. We are staying in a real house tonight - remember - beds and baths and things. We've arranged to meet at 5p.m. and that means starting now!'

'Shame,' I said, struggling up from the warm sand and reluctantly shouldering my pack. 'Still, a bath is very tempting.'

As we left, we saw the fishing nets slung on wooden poles just off the beach, drying in the sun.

We were taken to meet Hans, a big strong Dutchman who ran a large family-run Victorian hotel in Gairloch, overlooking the mountain-ringed loch. He worked flat out for half the year, travelled and self-indulged the other half. Dressed in kilt and sporran, he looked like an advertisement for porridge oats. His fluent English had an interesting tinge of Dutch and Scottish in it.

'Congratulations. That's a wonderful thing you are doing - I envy you.' He pressed a note into my hand for our charities.

'I too love Scotland and walking. Two years ago I thought my time was up. I had to have an operation in Inverness. I took a rucksack and walked through the mountains to Inverness hospital - alone with nature. I just told my wife if I didn't arrive in four days she was to call the rescue services! That was really living.'

We too felt we were really living as we stood at the lighthouse of Rubha Reidh. This stands aloof at the end of the peninsula; the landscape here is very Hebridean, wild and barren with few houses dotted at random among the buttercups. The views of Skye and the Outer Hebrides were soft focused in the heat-haze. From here we had our first glimpse of the mountains of Assynt. Soon we should be in Sutherland; wild, uncompromising and elemental. I felt a surge of excitement and disbelief. Cape Wrath and the top of the map were less than two weeks away.

At Loch Ewe the Torridon range of mountains were still visible. In a way I never wanted to lose their familiar silhouettes. The heat wave continued. Our hairy white appendages turned painfully from red to brown. Red and black Aussie football caps, given to us by a friend in Blackpool, were invaluable. The peak kept the sun out of our eyes, and a neat pull-down 'blind' at the back, kept the sun off our necks. We looked as if we had absconded from the French Legion.

Richard pointed down onto the loch where a naval ship bristling with high-tech equipment was moored to the jetty.

'That's the NATO refuelling station. The North Atlantic convoy ships assembled during the last war right here in Loch Ewe. My Uncle Norman was commander of one of the convoy destroyers, escorting ships to Russia. You can imagine how dangerous those crossings must have been. Uncle Norman was every inch a commander, tall and strong with a personality to match. After one particularly stressful crossing, he and his crew were granted 48 hours leave. They didn't want to spend this cooped up in Loch Ewe. A little jaunt to Glasgow was more to their taste. Knowing this would be good for morale, Norman slipped anchor, and took the ship down to Glasgow in the dead of night. For speed he threaded the boat through the Sounds of Sleet, damaging the hull in the process. Had it been peace-time, he would have been court marshalled. As it was, he got away with it, and his crew had their night out in Glasgow.'

'Wow. What a nerve! I never had relatives that did exciting things like that.' I looked at Richard with admiration. 'You've got your love of the sea from him, but not his recklessness.'

Richard would rather be burned at the stake than park on a yellow line.

Poolewe Caravan Club Camping Site was in a lovely position overlooking the loch. Now it was bursting at the seams with large caravans, whose owners felt the entire contents of their conservatories and patios needed to go on holiday with them. The place was littered with tables, chairs, sunbeds, parasols, plastic plants and barbecues. An ice-cream van jingled nearby and the chippy drew up just outside our tent. Meanwhile, watched by many pairs of eyes, I was attempting to make our throw-everything-in-a-saucepan-and-hope-for-the-best supper. Unaccustomed as I was to an audience, I jogged the cooker. Our supper slurped all over the grass. I scooped it back hoping no one was looking, wishing the fish and chip van would go away.

'It's dejeuner sur l'herbe aux fines herbes' I told Richard when he returned from the shower.

'It's amazing what you can eat when you are hungry,' he said with his mouth full.

The eyes were on duty the next day when we broke camp. An elderly couple, in pastel track suits and trainers, were staring in disbelief, as we went through our usual process of packing up. The contents of two rucksacks can look daunting when spread around, and shrinking our home and contents was something of an art. The tent was rolled up last, and the whole process took about fifteen concentrated minutes. When we finally shouldered the packs and looked back at the empty plot, the lady said,

'Well I never . . . However did you manage to get all that packed away?' She looked at Richard admiringly.

'An fancy carrying all that . . .Ooh you are wonderful!'

Richard's head swelled visibly, and he set off at a with a spring in his step.

The sun beamed down on us as we walked round Gruinard Bay and on to Ullapool. Here we were due to meet my father, with his five star back up systems. Summer flowers were now at their best, and the meadows and verges blazed with buttercups, orchids, foxgloves wild thyme and dog roses. The bracken grew daily and the yellow flags stood to attention ready to unfurl.

Shops were few and far between, and Richard was sure we could stock up in Dundonnel. Six miles before we reached the village the sign, Dundonnel Stores, pointed down a cul-de-sac.

'Very Irish,' I said and volunteered to go and get the shopping. I still felt bad about the twenty two miles I had missed at Inverlussa.

The shop, a house with a small extension, was nearly a mile down the tiny road. In the little back room shelves groaned with everything from toilet paper to tea cosies. The community nurse was delivering medicines. I felt it was an updated Llareggub in Dylan Thomas' *Under Milkwood*.

Veils of cloud hid the mountain tops round Little Loch Broom. An Teallach, 'the forge' was particularly unwilling to expose her summit, but as evening drew on, the veils melted and the naked loch glowed in the evening light. Just outside Dundonnel, sheltering under the big shoulder of An Teallach, we found a perfect campsite behind the Old Smiddy. The forge was now a mountain hut, very well appointed inside with fitted kitchen, bunk beds and a wood burning stove. We enjoyed the luxury of a simple wooden plank seat, propped against the outside wall. Not so long ago, this would have been used by the blacksmith's customers, when the interior would have echoed with hammer-blows and hooves, while sparks would have flown from the forge.

The poor soil and barren lochside changed to fertile pastures and mature trees, as we walked through the Dundonnel Estates. A lazy river flowed through lush green fields. We climbed over the steep hill and down to the shores of Loch Broom. Here the sprawling 'metropolis' of Ullapool faced us. We shared the tiny ferry with a dog, a wheelbarrow and some vegetables.

In Ullapool we met up with my father who shadowed us for the next ten days, taking our packs while we walked, and feeding us when we arrived at our destination. It was wonderful to be free of the heavy packs and we both found the miles easier and more pleasurable.

The road to the Summer Isles was another scottish footpath, this time round the base of the great mountain of Ben Mor Coigach. At times it was a scramble. Our admiration for John Merrill, the Guiness Book of Records walker who covered every inch of the real coast, grew, as we grasped the full significance of what he had achieved. We had good views of the castellated silhouette of Stac Pollidah and its smoother neighbour Inverpolly. As we rounded the shoulder of Ben Mor Coigach the barren Summer Isles lay below us, a group of pre-historic monsters, basking in a silent sea.

'The largest island is Tenera More where Fraser Darling had his Island Farm - you can see the quay and the ruined farm from here,' Richard pointed it out. 'I walked all over the island with my parents in 1959 and there was no sign of anyone living there then. Now I believe there are eleven families on it.'

We both had a soft spot for Fraser Darling. A pioneer of the ecological movement in Scotland, he left the comforts of salaried life in Edinburgh and subsistence-farmed at Tenera More with his family for three and a half years. The experience, he says, was a 'shriving' one. Nature, he felt, was the sacred elemental stuff of which we were made, yet in our mad-centred world, it is debased on a grand scale.

Acheltibouie's little crofts range along the strand, eyeball to eyeball with the rocky shores of the Summer Isles. As we approached the village, the sound of bagpipes mingled with the bleat of sheep. Suddenly we found ourselves in the midst of a Highland Gathering. Aberdeen butties, MacEwen's beer and the Ullapool Junior Pipe Band made for a heady mixture. The youngsters formed a ring on the grassy strand behind the beach. Neatly turned out in white shirts, dark kilts, white socks and little black shoes, topped overall with a tasselled cap, they tapped their feet off and blew their hearts out. The strains of Scotland the Brave against a backdrop of sea, mountains and islands brought a lump to the throat that even Mr McEwen could not wash away. It was hard to believe our eyes and ears.

We still had eleven miles to go to Achnahaird where my father was waiting. We were so late he was concerned for our safety. Tea, on a comfortable seat with feet up, was a real luxury. We had the added pleasure of a panoramic view of the familiar mountains of Assynt, Stac Pollidah, Ben Mor Coigach, Suilvan, Cannisp, Quinag. A litany of names, their giant forms lay like sleeping beasts rising from the flat land across Enard Bay, implacable and mysterious in the dimming light.

A couple, with a canoe and wind-surfer on the roof of their car, camped near us that night. We met them on our walk the next day. They were outward-bound teachers, strong and weather-beaten. It didn't bother them that there had been no showers at the campsite.

'I used nature's shower,' Jim said grinning.

It hadn't rained and I looked puzzled.

'Look up there,' he pointed to a rocky outcrop off the road where a shoot of water streamed off a sheer drop into the river beneath. 'Bloody cold, but it was great!'

'That makes me feel soft,' Richard murmured. 'It reminds me of a Junior leaders C.C.F. Camp in Wales one Easter holidays. It rained every day for a week. By then we were all so fed up with twenty mile forced marches, wet feet and wet food, that the thought of another day of a similar routine brought us to the brink of mutiny. Knowing that our officers were swilling beer in a warm pub, while we sweated blood with heavy packs on the wet hills, was too much. Our campsite that night was by a large river. Too tired on arrival to do anything but eat and sleep, in the morning we were ready to stand our ground. One of our officers was a six foot monosyllabic Neanderthal who played rugby for the Harlequins. He was also a classics scholar and did the Times crossword in twenty minutes every morning before breakfast. He mustered us early in the morning, and ordered us all to strip off and swim in the river before breakfast. It was surprise attack; such was the charisma of this guy that we obeyed. After that it was just a question of survival!'

'I wouldn't have,' was all I could say, relishing the warm sun, flower-filled meadows and sandy beaches.

Suddenly there it was, on a lochan on our way to Inverkirkaig, so near in we didn't even need to use binoculars. Velvet head, pinstriped neck and chest, black bib, coal black body with barred black-and-white wings, finely sprinkled with white droplets. The rare black-throated diver was the apogee of sartorial elegance bobbing gently near the shore. Three herons flew softly over the lonely water. A curlew's piping call sounded distressed.

'Come on. We must leave her in peace. That curlew's nesting.'

Reluctantly the clumsy intruders tore themselves away. A little further on we heard an insistent high piping call. Richard stopped.

'Look on the moorland there. That's a golden plover. It must have young nearby or it would run off.'

The bird's intricate gold-flecked back and black, white-rimmed chest was a memorable sight. Having watched our fill we crept quietly away and the sad piping ceased.

Chapter Sixteen

I returned to a long strand
the hammered shod of a bay,
and found only the secular
powers of the Atlantic thundering.
Seamus Heaney

At Inverkirkaig, we left Wester Ross for Sutherland, where peaty soil barely covers the ancient rocks of a skeletal landscape. Pockmarked with lochans, giant rock pools dressed in green and gold waterlilies, fringed with yellow flags; it is the most marginal and ancient part of our kingdom by the sea. Inland, the primeval mountains of Assynt loom over the flat earth, towering above the watery landscape. Wind ruffles the circling eagles, and the curlews cry mournfully across the glens. Fertile fingers of land penetrate up the river valleys; little oasises in an elemental desert. This inhospitable watery wasteland, stirred our souls and humbled our tiny progress.

Richard and I were walking side by side down the narrow road, threading our way between the lochs, gazing silently about us.

'Does it make you feel small?' I queried, wondering if Richard was experiencing the same strange excitement.

There was no reply, but I didn't need one. Richard's face had the same look of concentrated joy that I have seen when he is on a boat.

At Stoer we were in real crofting country. The croft is not the house, but the land which goes with it. Traditionally, this land has been farmed using low-tech methods by self-sufficient farmers. Historically, these environmentally-friendly systems have been scorned by the policies of so-called 'progressive thinkers'. The 18th century brought a growing demand for meat, and the infamous black-faced Cheviot sheep were introduced to the Highlands. The landowners found sheep were more commercially attractive than expendable tenants; the notorious Highland Clearances followed. It wasn't until the first Crofting Act of 1886 that crofters were given security of land tenure. Ironically the wheel has now turned full circle. Crofters are being given every financial incentive to stay and farm their land, for traditional methods help to safeguard the natural environment. There second name, we were told was 'Grant'.

Stoer village hall advertised '*A Lull in Time. Changes in the Highlands in 150 years*'. They also advertised teas. We fell through the door, fortified ourselves with drop scones and lashings of tea and then steeped ourselves in local history. The decline in crofting, the Highland Clearances, and the stern Calvinist ethic of the Free Presbyterian Church. It was all there.

'Did you notice,' said Richard as we walked towards Stoer Lighthouse, 'that 19th century separatist, the Reverend Gordon, thought the Church of Scotland incumbent was so soft that he upped and emigrated to New Zealand and many of his followers went with him? I suppose living up here was so harsh in those days, that without a strict code of ethics and healthy respect for Hell fire, the people couldn't have coped.'

'The Wee Free Church is still going today. I've noticed a few up here. The buildings are very basic. I wonder what the Rev. Gordon would have thought of our liberal society?'

My question was answered by the loud growl of a generator in the distance, and we noticed crowds of people gathered round some sheep-filled pens out in the middle of nowhere. It was Stoer's annual sheep shearing. A small crowd had gathered to watch while two men, in check shirts and dungarees, removed the fleeces at lightening speed. The look of ecstasy on each sheep's face as it shed its woolly coat, reminded me of Richard's expression as we walked the Highlands.

More and more we felt an integral part of this ancient landscape. The walker can see and smell and hear everything around him. In a car these senses are muted or obliterated altogether. The old roads wend their way deferentially round the rock-strewn hilly landscape.

The new roads blast their way through the ancient Lewisian gneiss and crystallite rocks, exposing rich veins which tower above the inconsiderate swathes of tarmac; traumatised cross-sections of time.

An English couple we met in Findhorn proudly boasted:

'We've done the Highlands too. 340 miles in one day on those new roads. Great aren't they?'

Most of the cars and motorised vans up in the extreme north were rented, or had Dutch, German or Italian number plates.

'It's very short-sighted. Fast roads take tourists quickly to the top of the map and equally quickly out again. They won't linger and spend money,' Richard commented.

Certainly Sutherlands is not to everyone's taste. My father described our night at Culkein as 'the most desolate place on earth.' A couple of crofts and a few holiday homes were the only signs of habitation. A few sheep grazed the poor soil. Skies were grey and a freshening wind gusted over the loch. We put up our tent on a small patch of grass by the little beach, and were lulled to sleep by the lapping waves and rocking tent.

We lingered and spent money on a B & B, at Unapool near Kylsesku, in order to climb our Scottish mountain. My father gave us a lift to the base of Quinag in his van. We were pottering along, minding our own business, when a French car pulled sharply in front of us forcing us to stop.

'You 'ave ze step down,' he said in broken English.

My father shouted out of the window in broken French, 'Mursi bowcoo. Je vous remursi Monsieur!'

Somewhat insulted, Monsieur scratched his head. 'Mon Dieu!' He tried again.

'Ze step of ze van eez on ze road. Eet eez dahnjerus.'

My father didn't move, but his reply was even louder,

'Vous etes tres gentee Monsieur. Mursi bowcoo!'

Monsieur took out a handkerchief and wiped his brow. Then, with very clear hand signals, he proceeded to mime the problem. He should have taken a bow, instead he shrugged his shoulders and raised his eyes to heaven muttering darkly about 'les étrangers'. With this he drove off.

Quinag, at just under 3,000 feet, misses being a Munro, but makes up for this with three great spurs stretching out above the watery rockscape of Assynt, giving spectacular views towards all points of the compass. The weather had been unsettled. A roaring wind made forward propulsion a major effort, at times nearly impossible. However, it was worth every ounce of effort to be king and queen of that particular castle. Between clouds, which streamed past like smoke, we could see the Point of Stoer and Eddrachillis Bay to the west, Lochinver, Suilven, Canisp and even the Summer Isles to the south, Ben Mor Assynt to the east, and Kylesku, Scourie, and, somewhere beyond, Cape Wrath. We were high in every sense. Standing on some of the oldest rock in the world, we were almost at the top of the map. At the end of the east ridge, the mountain fell away; we sat dangling our feet over the edge, heady with that intoxicating feeling of humility and power, anxiety and achievement that makes climbing mountains such a desirable pastime.

On our way down we met a young man who had been stationed up in Assynt for two years and eulogised about the region.

'It's a great place to live. There's lots to do, interesting people and all this!' He shouted across the wind, indicating the landscape far below.

'Look at that lochan down there - it's a wind vortex.'

We watched as a dark cloud seemed to dive into the little loch, ruffling its surface, visible beneath the furled water. A hypnotic whirlpool. I shivered involuntarily.

As we walked down the road away from the mountain, I thought that the north east face of Sail Garbh, appeared from below like an old testament prophet, gouged between natural pillars of rock.

* * *

The barren stretch from Scourie to Kinlochbervie was so skeletal, it was hard to imagine that anyone could have eeked out a living there. The pink crystalline rocks bulge through threadbare landscape, barely covered by the peaty soil. A few sheep graze, and the great skua preys on the lochans. Foinaven is the last high mountain in this north west corner. At Skerricha, we looked across the loch to John Ridgeway's Adventure School at Ardmore, where both Jo and Richard had spent masochistic holidays. Jo, at fourteen, grew from girl to woman in a fortnight. She had survived a night in a plastic bag on 'survival island', climbed Arkle, absailed off cliffs, shinned up the mast of a 40 foot boat, and run a mile every morning before breakfast with blisters the size of a 10 p coin. When she got home she slept for a week.

Richard pointed to a schooner moored in the bay. 'That's Ridgeway's *English Rose 4*, the boat he sailed round the world in. I just went to St. Kilda in her and wish I could do it again.' He nodded across the loch. 'This is where you either get a boat, or walk all round the loch. Ridgeway's place is about as remote as you could find.'

He really is laird of rocks, water, sea and sky, I thought, gazing across the loch to his house sheltering under the hill, in one of the most desolate parts of the British Isles.

The name, Oldshoremore, not only rolls easily off the tongue, it also tells us much about the place. It provided the first sheltered landing on the west coast, and was where King Hakon began his invasion of Scotland in 1263. Bare rolling moor, makes up the hinterland. Being on foot, we saw sheep dog trials taking place a half mile off the road; a rural scene easily missed in a car.

Shiegra was our last camp near a road for two days. From here we would be in the 100 mile square miles of peat-bog and heather, scrub and rock, known as the Parbh. This is the only way to reach Cape Wrath from the West coast.

Shiegra, set back from its little bay, is just a few houses and crofts. Drifts of white bog cotton lay like summer snow on the rolling empty landscape. The hamlets now had a Hebridean look, and we could once more see the rim of the horizon from the cliff tops. Cows replaced sheep in the flower-filled meadows of these 'machairs' or dune grasslands, enriched by the shells which had blown onto them. Translucent waves curled softly onto Shiegra's golden sands and the huge moulded contours of the ancient crystalline rocks caught fire in the evening sun. Amongst the greyness, the smooth rocks glowed pink and orange, as though lit from within. From here we could see Ben Stack and Stoer Point beyond, and the fluted sandstone cliffs of Handa Island. Graceful terns, screeched aggressively, dive-bombing incomers as they guarded their young. A curious seal bobbed up and down; black guillemots and fulmars were busy nesting on the cliffs. The only concession to 'incomers' on this meadow by the sea, was a cold water tap.

That evening, July 8th, I managed to send a post card to the girls which read as follows:

Just clocked up 2,500 miles! Wonderful scenery, fishing villages, cliffs, sandy beaches, sunshine. So looking forward to seeing you in

Edinburgh. I badly need a new pair of feet and a new body! Loads of love Mum. P.S. I have a new body. Dad.

We arranged to meet my father in Durness, and once more shouldering our heavy packs, set off for Sandwood Bay and Cape Wrath.

'And where will ye be off to?' A white-haired lady enquired as we walked through downtown Shiegra. When we told her, a wistful look came into her blue eyes.

'Och d'ye know, I've never been to Sandwood Bay, yet I've lived heer all me life. When I was young and fit, I was too busy. Life was hard up here in those days. I'll no' be able to walk there now for I've a heart condition. Och weil, enjoy yerselves!'

We would like to have taken her with us.

Richard was incredulous. 'That's so sad,' he said, shaking his head.

'Does it make you feel guilty?' I asked, lengthening my stride to keep up with him.

'Just lucky,' he replied, shifting his cap uneasily on his head.

Sandwood Bay's pink sands, edged by steep sandstone cliffs, stretch long and wide, shelving gently up to form great dunes. To the south a lone stack stands sentinel. To the north the headland of Cape Wrath lay benign as a basking whale. The word Wrath has nothing to do with anger, but simply means 'turning point.'

'D'you remember the last time we were here? It was pouring with rain and blowing a gale. We couldn't see the Cape.' I didn't need reminding. We had both envisaged the same desperate conditions this time round.

'Someone up there's looking after us,' I said, stretching out happily in the warm sand.

From Sandwood to the Cape there was no track, and we had a hard eight miles battling with peat hags and unending hills. In spite of the physical exertion we felt excited to be close in this primeval wilderness. What the Parbh lacks in people it makes up for in insects and ancient plants.

'Look where you're treading!' Richard shouted back to me. 'We're walking over sundew plants.' Sure enough, among the spagnum moss, delicate coral-coloured tentacles spelt death for any of the millions of tiny insects who might settle on them. We walked over thousands of these. I was glad I wasn't a small winged insect.

Ahead Cape Wrath drew us on, while behind lay the great mountains of Sutherland, and to the west we could see the outline of Lewis. Beyond this only the wide horizon. With a mile and a half to go, we found ourselves at the top of a hill which shelved steeply down into a tiny green valley through which flowed a small stream.

'It's made for us,' I said.

We pitched the tent, brewed some tea, and finished the last lap without our rucksacks. At 6 p.m. on July 9th, we reached the lighthouse at the Cape. I had an overwhelming impulse to rush inside, tell the lighthouse keeper what we had achieved, and hope he'd break open a bottle.

'I don't think he'd be too pleased to see you. Let's climb up to the top, then we can look east,' Richard said coolly. Perched above the lighthouse like a pair of proud eagles, we gazed east to Clo Mor, some of the highest cliffs in Britain.

I grabbed Richard's hands.

'We've done it for God's sake. We've done it! We've walked the whole bloody way!' We kissed briefly, and then looked knowingly into each others eyes through a pool of silent tears.

A few miles down the coast, lay the jewel in the Parbh crown: Kearvaig. This lesser known sandy bay, which nestles back from the towering cliffs, also hides itself from the little lighthouse road. Having been tipped off, we set off eagerly down an inauspicious track across the wild moor land, on MOD firing ranges. In less than half a mile we rounded a bend and saw a Garden of Eden.

The wide sweep of white virgin sand dazzles the eyes. Deep blue seas gently lift their transparent skirts, settling into lacy pools, hemmed by long lines of watchful gulls. Towering sandstone cliffs stand guard like ancient sentinels, spilling natural arches, caves and stacks, into the clear water. The anxious echoing cries of puffins, razor bills, guillemots and fulmars, disturb the silent heat. Uncanny clarity of vision; bright light that hurts the emptiness. Only two pairs of footprints mark the warm sand to the clear water's edge. Adam and Eve . . . in paradisum.

We were not alone in Paradise. Over the rocky moorland, on the far side of the bay, came a young man with staff and dog. Like us, he threw off his clothes and performed the same ritual cleansing ceremony while his dog barked anxiously from the shore line. We crept away leaving him space in Eden.

A simple bothy stood in the meadows just back from the beach. We entered a sparsely-furnished room with a large open fireplace.

On the table lay a visitors book and a slice of fruit cake. The only wooden armchair had the words 'King of Kearvaig' roughly carved on the top strut. The entries were recent.

'*Marooned at Kearvaig due to World War Three. Will try and hitch a lift from a military land rover. Tried wishing my way out by sitting in Cyril's magic chair*'. Signed Karen the Dane.

Bernard the Bike wrote the following:

'*Cycled from Hampshire in England. It's a real pleasure to stay somewhere like this in the 1990's. Meant to look round beach, go for a paddle and cycle home slowly. I stayed another night - bet I'm not the first to do this. P.S. Sheep's dung makes a wonderful fuel, beats peat any day!*

'Well we've missed the birthday party yesterday, but how thoughtful to leave us a slice of cake,' I said, carefully dividing the spoils.

The little tarmac road threads across the moorland to the Kyle of Durness where a ferry at Keoldale takes passengers across the water to Durness and 'civilisation'. Seals lazed and played happily on the wide ribbed sand banks, while the low tide skulked darkly in deep channels, rich blue and gold in the afternoon sun. A mini-bus groaning with hot sweaty tourists passed us. We felt smug.

Outside the Durness Supermarket we met Simon the Peace and his dog Bindhu. He was the only other mortal we had seen that magic morning. With several days growth on his chin and carrying a long staff, he looked like a latter-day John the Baptist. On his back he had an old canvas rucksack which weighed little more than a day sack. It contained a bivvi bag, anorak and a change of clothes. He looked fit and tanned. His faithful collie was very thin but had a good coat and bright eyes.

'Where are you from?' We asked.

'I'm on a peace pilgrimage,' he answered simply. 'I left London on January 30th and walked down to Cornwall and up through Wales. Cape Wrath was my destination. Now I shall walk back through the mountains to Inverness and on down the east coast back to Canterbury. I'm collecting for the Ghandi Trust.'

Our questions tumbled out.

'What was your worst moment? How do you manage without a tent? What do you do about food?'

Simon was, it seemed, travelling hopefully. Not only did he have no tent, he had no maps, virtually no food for himself or his dog, and very little money. He got by on faith, hope and charity.

Sometimes, when there was no bed, he and Bindhu had to keep walking. Incessant midge attacks also kept them on the move. Once he was nearly boarded into an empty house where he was sheltering. We offered him the chance to look at our maps.

'No thanks. I'm alright. I've a contact here who'll help me,' he replied.

Next day my father reported that he had asked him if he could look at a map. Not having any ordinance survey maps, Simon tried Mr. Mackay at the shop. Nothing doing. We often wondered how he had fared. His courage/naiveté filled us with awe.

'Surely that's the real way to do it. Think of the stories he'll have to tell. We're only playing at it, clinging as we do to the trappings of normality,' I said.

'I admire him, but I couldn't do it that way. Your father thought he was a scrounger, but then so are we. Our scrounging is just as meticulously planned.'

'Right on both counts,' I agreed. 'You wouldn't ask for help even if our tent burnt down!'

After the fertile meadows and soft sandy bays of Durness, Loch Eriboll bites deep into the impoverished landscape, sheltered by steep hills. Craig na Faoilinn, and the higher mountains, rose above the head of the loch. A sad string of houses, many in ruins, ranged along the lochside at a place called Leide, recalling the desperate plight of the displaced Highlanders in the last two centuries. Evicted from their homes on the more fertile areas, they were given miserable amounts of poor land in order that they might learn to fish rather than farm. Many were forced to emigrate.

'The loch was known as Loch 'Orrible in the second world war, like Loch Ewe it was used to assemble the North Atlantic and Russian convoys. That island in the middle there was used for target practice for bombers, before they destroyed the German battleship Turpitz,' my informant told me. 'And German U-boats surrendered here at the end of the Second World War.'

'It's hard to imagine that now. This place is so quiet.'

We lunched on the rocks by a beautiful river, which cascaded down the mountain in a series of mini-waterfalls and deep clear pools. It reminded us of the Cevennes. We swam and lay out on the warm rocks to dry.

Without our packs, the miles sped past. As we rounded the head of the loch and walked down the other side towards our meeting place at Ardneakie, we found ourselves in rich fertile pastures, fringed with mature deciduous trees, a striking contrast from the gneiss and quartzite at Leide.

'This little stretch is on limestone, that's why it's so different. See how the river beds are dry here. I expect those storehouses over there are limekilns.'

We passed the imposing gates of a beautiful 18th century house, and a mile or so further on the landscape reverted to the poor-soiled moorland; looking back it was a green oasis.

'I expect the laird of that place threw the tenants off to dumps like Laide, built the house and made a fortune.' I felt full of righteous indignation.

We camped by the roadside above the little hammerhead island of Ardneackie. My father was delighted to have found a remnant of old road to park his van level. This meant he wouldn't upset his fridge and there'd be ice in the drinks. Meanwhile Richard and I had kicked away enough sheep's dung to make a good fire, and pitch the tent. Suddenly the silence was shattered by a four-wheel drive car roaring down the road with horn blaring. An elegant lady with long fair hair, designer clothes and impeccable English, shot out of the car.

'You are not allowed to camp here. This land belongs to the Eribol estates and it's private. You'll have to go back to Durness. There's a campsite there.'

While I was still silently opening and shutting my mouth, my father walked calmly towards the tirade hand outstretched.

'Good evening. I'm so sorry if we are on your land but there are no notices to indicate that it is private. My daughter and son-in-law. . .' He broke off to wave a gracious arm in our direction, 'Are on a sponsored walk right round the coast of Britain. They have already walked 3,000 miles. We spent last night in the camp site at Durness. It's an 18 mile walk.'

There was no wind left in her sails. They shook hands. She scolded us gently.

'You should have asked at the house. There's a notice on the gate. I hope all goes well for the rest of your walk.'

With this she beat a slow retreat, but the car engine revved annoyance.

'Phew! We narrowly missed eviction. The thought of going back to Leide is worse than death.'

Our empathy with the tenants of Sutherland grew.

'Your father managed that very well.' Richard had got his voice back.

'He's been running the gauntlet with lairds and landlords all over Britain and Europe for as long as I can remember. He's well practised.'

The grey ribboning tarmac stretched long and straight through the scraggy moorland vegetation on the bleak plateau above the Kyle of Tongue. The lonely peaks of Ben Hope and Ben Loyal were wreathed in cloud. The only sounds were the intermittent gentle patter of rain on gortex, the bleat of sheep and the occasional cry of curlew or sandpiper.

The mist lifted as we walked down the long slope of moorland, leading down to the causeway and bridge which took us into Tongue. Streaks of blue lightened the wide stretch of water and sand. Beyond, lay a softer landscape of lush green and gold meadows and gently rising wooded hills. Fist-sized orchids blazed purple from the verges, white-washed bright-gardened cottages looked inviting. A ruined castle perched on a hillock above the estuary looked out to mountains and sea. The screech of terns grew as we approached the causeway. Among the smooth round pebbles, fluffy balls with eager open beaks, were perfectly camouflaged. Angry parents flew at our faces, white-feathered fans with forked tails, hovering with blood-curdling cries.

'They look magnificent when they're angry - no wonder they're called sea swallows.' I tried to photograph them, but without a tripod it was impossible. We left them in peace to watch dunlins and ringed plovers feeding as the tide dropped.

Our campsite in a meadow near the castle, had uninterrupted views of Ben Hope and Ben Loyal. The facilities were simple but clean, and we relished our 20p shower. My father parked his van near some French people, as our young German neighbours were deep in alcoholic celebrations. He established an 'entente cordiale' and could be heard practicing his French. In the morning he wanted to fill his water tank. Disregarding the young Germans who were washing up at the only tap, he backed his van precariously down the slope, produced a hose which didn't fit the tap. Undeterred, he put a funnel into one end and tried again. The French neighbour watched incredulously as he attempted to get the water to flow uphill. Sadly will power was not enough.

The Frenchman shook his head. 'Eet eez not possible. Not even for zee English!'

In good weather, we would wash our smalls and hang them out to dry on our packs. The only problem was we'd forget they were there. In Tongue Post Office I turned sharply on my heels, and my undies swung merrily against the man in the queue behind me. I shall never forget the look on his face. I just hoped he wasn't the Frenchman who had watched my father pushing water uphill.

The salmon-filled River Naver runs down to Bettyhill. We camped above the river and watched the great salmon jumping like silver rainbows, rippling the still water with a loud 'plop' which echoed along the valley. The midges were particularly bad here, and we were glad of my father's van where we could sit and eat unmolested. Later we visited the Strathnaver Museum and learned more about the horrors of the Sutherland Clearances. We took time out to visit Achanlochy, near Skelpic, once a traditional village of turf/heather-roofed blackhouses, now just a few bracken-covered ruins. In the early 19th century it was a village of 1,200 souls from the parish of Farr, who were brutally evicted and their houses burnt down infront of their very eyes. Ironically, nearly two hundred years later, it is not the people that are being cleared away, but the bracken, so tourists have a better view of the few remaining stones.

By the time we reached Melvich, we had bid farewell and thanks, both to my father and to the mountains. We were both looking forward to our few days on the Orkneys. A chance to catch our breath and be real tourists.

Orkney Interlude

Chapter Seventeen

Monday I found a boot -
Rust and salt leather
I gave it back to the sea, to dance in.
George Mackay Brown - *The Beachcomber*

Our large P & O ferry from Scrabster was dwarfed by the towering sandstone cliffs of Hoy. At over a thousand feet they are the highest in the British Isles with the Old Man of Hoy standing proud like a megalithic totem pole. The island was named by the Vikings, Hoy simply means 'high island'. From the deck we looked down on a mass of black guillemots, razor bills, puffins, fulmars and gannets all bobbing and diving in the choppy waves. It was the height of the breeding season.

The Orcadians are fiercely independent people. It is no accident that they call their largest island 'the Mainland'. Their roots are more Scandinavian than Scottish as 1,200 years ago Norwegians settled where Stromness is today, and called it Hamnavoe meaning 'Haven Bay'.

Rounding the sheer cliffs at St. John's Head into the calm waters of the sound, we retreated in time. Tucked neatly under the hill, hugging the shoreline, the grey-roofed stone houses of Stromness clustered round a church spire. A few dark trees softened the stones of this Nordic-looking port and bare windswept hinterland. In the old harbour, empty but for a few fishing boats, lay a majestic three-masted schooner, square-rigged with top gallants, flags flying proudly from the soaring masts. The graceful curves of her huge white hull and colourful figurehead were reflected in the still water like some great mythological bird.

T.V. cameras and videos rolled, the Sally Army exercised their lungs, and the paved main street of the little town blazed with bunting.

'Looks like a re-run of the Onedin Line,' I said, pinching myself to make sure I was awake.

'They knew you were coming,' Richard replied.

Later, we discovered it was a Norwegian Sail Training Ship (built in 1910), in Stromness, for the town's annual carnival-type Shopping Week.

We camped on the Ness, a tongue of land a mile from the harbour. The mountains of Hoy rose across the sound like giant waves. The widening blue thread of water opens into Scapa Flow, a deep pool, ringed by islands and causeways. Here the Germans scuttled their fleet in 1919, and the *Royal Oak* was torpedoed in 1939.

Between long periods of calm, bursts of marine activity would bring 'Haven Bay' to life. From our tent we could watch and hear the water traffic plying across the sound. Chugging fishing smacks, decks crammed with orange rope, lobster pots and coloured balls; silent dinghies gliding across quiet waters; noisy motor boats crammed with cargoes of bright skinny divers; huge throbbing car ferries, jewels at dusk, cutting the glassy water into smooth ruffles, their mournful hoots echoing loudly across the silence.

Our own peace was shattered by a party of English public school boys, who decided to convert the campsite into the playing fields of Eton. They pitched their tents round a large area of grass which they appropriated as their own. The click of balls, accompanied by the 'OK Ya's', and the braying inanities of pubescent schoolboys, was only matched by their masters. Two men in their late thirties, lolled beside their minibus, fleshy white legs emerging incongruously from bright Bermuda shorts, their radio competing with the throbs and hoots from passing ferries. Their charges would quieten down by midnight, but the masters talked long into the small hours, in voices that could be heard at the back of any school assembly.

We escaped to the pub, where the Norwegian schooner had discharged its youthful cosmopolitan cargo. The tall weather-beaten skipper, his blond hair and beard just streaked with grey, kept close to the bar with a couple of men his own age, while at a bulging table, lads and lassies communicated in a rich mixture of language, singing and physical contact, their voices rising as the liquid in their glasses fell.

Along the paved 'road' of the main street, every house had its own little jetty. From the deep set windows of the old Pier Arts Centre we looked out at the clear blue water, rowing boats pulled up onto the shingle, moored fishing boats, mottled brown eider ducks blending perfectly with the stones below them. A scene that hadn't changed for centuries. Inside the three hundred year old building, the gallery was filled with an incredible collection of St. Ives School artists, Hepworth's, Ben Nicholson, Patrick Heron and Alfred Wallis. The gallery's own pier was, at that moment, alive with small children happily making their own Alfred Wallis impressions in chalk on the weathered flagstones.

'It's the light.' We were walking round the Ness where the sea channel narrows, and the hills and sandstone cliffs of Hoy felt close enough to touch. The lowering sun warmed the bald cliffs and still water.

'It's so clear, just like St. Ives.'

Richard was right. The huge skies, clear light and feeling of space was perfect for artists.

It was promenade time for the waterbirds. Redshank, oyster catchers and sandpipers. Mother eider ducks with growing young, were conscientiously teaching them how to fend for themselves, while the dads were imbibing sea water at the Fish Inn. Seals were out and about, slumped like couch potatoes on the rocks, watching the world go by out of half an eye. Above the high piping of the birds the soulful notes of a lone piper echoed in the evening air. I expected to find a Bonnie Scot in kilt and sporran, but instead we found a young lady with long blonde hair and jeans, knee deep in cow parsley. We stood listening spellbound to the skirling sounds, perfect against the backdrop of mountains and still deep water. As the final notes of *Speed Bonny Boat* died away, we applauded.

'Gee thanks,' she said. 'I was just tryin' to find a quiet spot where I could practice. Now I learn there's a golf course up there and a campsite round the corner! Thanks anyway you guys.'

Skara Brae was more than a well-preserved Neolithic village; it was a revelation. Set back from a white sandy beach, the stone houses had been buried in the sand for 5,000 years, and were in remarkably good order. Looking down at the stone furniture, a three-piece suite, beds, dressers, a tank for fish bait and the grinding stones, we realised that these people were not uncivilised barbarians, but a self-sufficient fishing community, like us, without the technology. We felt at this interface, we could stretch back and touch the people who had once lived here.

The feeling of respect for our ancestors grew at the 4,000 year old tomb of Maes Howe described as 'One of the finest pieces of prehistoric engineering in Western Europe'. On the shortest day of the year, the setting sun shines down the tunnel and into the tomb, suffusing it with orange light, always presuming there is sun on that day. Bent double along the tunnel, heads on knees, we were thankful to reach the great chamber and re-align our bent backs. Our guide, a round rosy-cheeked lady with a long dark plait snaking down her back, had a Scandinavian sing-song voice. She told us the main part of the building was older than the Pyramids, and the largest stones weighed around 30 tonnes. The Vikings had apparently made use of the tomb and carved the walls with strange marks known as Runes. There was nothing eloquent in these messages, for, when eventually deciphered, they were no more than graffiti from Viking bounty hunters, furious at not finding any treasure. To make matters worse, they were imprisoned in the chamber. No wonder they carved their frustrations on the ancient walls.

'Magnus Bareleg,' I whispered to Richard.

My whisper echoed alarmingly and I had some black looks from the little crowd of tourists. Visions of *'Bareleg is cool'* and *'Redhead is a wanker,'* written in Norn, the ancient language of the Viking settlers, mentally replaced the simple vertical lines that looked like barley stalks.

At that moment a fairly stout lady came along the passage on hands and knees, followed by her partner, marginally more erect.

When there was enough headroom to stand up, the lady's flexed frame shuddered noisily into reverse. Looking hard at her little audience, she gasped the immortal words,

'This is positively my last tomb!'

The fields and verges of the Orkney Mainland were a vigorous medley of colourful wildflowers, orchids, yarrow, meadow sweet, marguerite, clover and buttercups. A wide-open landscape of meadows, water, sky and distant hills, where scattered stone cottages looked like tortoises under their heavy paved roofs. Wherever there was water there were boats, clinker-built working boats, modern fishing boats, sailing boats and the new Ro-Ro ferries which service the islands daily.

Our contact on South Ronaldsay apologised that she couldn't put us up for the five days of our stay, but offered us a croft in Westray instead.

'We're repairing it,' She told me on the phone. 'I think there's enough floor in the bedroom for the bed to stand on, and the kitchen and bathroom do work.'

'By the way,' she added, 'there are bikes in the shed. Help yourselves. The key's at the Pierowall Hotel and I recommend their fish and chips.'

We were thrilled. Neither of us knew where Westray was, but we soon found out and jumped on a Ro-Ro ferry from Kirkwall, on the Orkney Mainland, to Rapness on Westray. Kirkwall harbour was teeming with roll-on roll-off ferries laden with everything from hay bales and tractors to calves and groceries. The Orkney Islands are like the pieces of a shattered plate and ferries service the pieces, loosely binding them together. A few tourist cars sat between the tractors and freight lorries, as our ferry slipped into the Wide Firth, deftly navigating the wicked skerries between the low islands of Eglisay and Eday, past Rousay and into the Westray Firth. At Rapness, an integrated transport system in the shape of a small minibus, managed to squeeze us in somehow, buried beneath rucksacks and bodies, and deposit us at the Pierowall Hotel. This unpretentious grey building was the nerve centre of Westray. It was run by a middle-aged lady with blue eyes, tightly permed hair and a pink tabard. When we mentioned our contact's name, her stern features relaxed and she produced a key.

'It's just beyond the turn on this side of the bay. It's no' far.'

The vernacular little croft, under its red tile roof, had changed little since it was built in the last century. Squatting by the road, arms skyward, its two windows at the front missed nothing. The two at the back looked seawards to a garden of rocks and seaweed, alive with eider ducks, ringed plover and jelly fish. We squeezed our way in past the bags of cement, and found a comfortable bed on a dais of slate, amidst sand and builders' debris. The shower, loo, gas cooker and fridge were all in working order. All the furniture had been piled up in the living room round a huge harmonium, an airer draped in working clothes, nodded above the moquette settee, where there was just room to sit. A small folding table and chair stood infront of the window.

'Sheer luxury,' I said happily, as I cooked supper using all the saucepans I could find. 'Four jets of gas and they all turn down when I tell them to.'

It started to rain. Warm and dry, we smugly wondered how the school boys were faring in the wet. I sat by the window and wrote a newsletter. Suddenly the room darkened. I looked up to see the window filled with the most enormous bull. It was some time before I could concentrate on my writing; for one thing there was only a tiny road and a low stone wall between us, and for another its giant procreative apparatus was on full display.

'Spaghetti bullonaise for supper?'

We found the shed unlocked, and unearthed the bikes from under piles of wood and rubble. They were old and rusty, but they worked. We pedalled off up the hill to Noup Head in a fresh breeze and clearing skies to see the famous seabird colonies along a five miles stretch of old red sandstone cliffs. The Noup Head Nature Reserve is one of the largest seabird colonies in the British Isles with 130,000 birds present in the summer months.

The sheer cliffs were a mass of ledges, high rise housing for fulmars, kittiwakes, guillemots, puffins and razor bills. The non-breeding puffins were in the penthouse suites, looking drunk and clumsy as they wobbled in to land, red legs dangling beneath them like unfurled flags.

We lay on our stomachs watching the churning sea thudding against the natural pillars of cliff seventy metres below, throwing fountains of spume high into the air. It was like Heathrow in the rush hour. Kittiwakes and fulmars stacked the thermals, while guillemots and razorbills, dapper and obsequious, strutted like stewards in the departure lounges. The flight paths were silent, yet the air was filled with screeches, screams and rasping cries as the anxious birds guarded their territory and their young.

The grey cliff-tops were gold with lichen and softened with sea pinks. I rolled onto my back and watched the birds skimming within feet of my face. The young kittiwakes, distinguished by the dark bands on their wings, were learning to fly, while the poor mother fulmars continued to feed their powder-puff young. From time to time the large predatory skuas and great black back gulls darkened the sky overhead; opportunists, watching the unguarded young and vulnerable, patiently waiting their chance. On the green sward terns were vociferously dive-bombing intruders and seeing off any great skuas who dared to alight, too close for comfort.

We could have feasted our eyes for ever. The birds seemed oblivious of our presence, unafraid unless we came too close to nesting sites. We were alone, at the end of the world, in a great bowl of space and light, surrounded by seabirds, cliffs and long low islands.

Reluctantly we left the scene and headed our bikes down the long hill. As my rusty machine gathered speed, I realised there were no brakes, metal touched metal and the sparks flew. The screech of our two bikes outdid a whole colony of Arctic terns. The muscles in my hands went into spasm, hanging on for dear life to two prongs of useless metal. The bikes relentlessly gathered speed down the long steep hill, eventually halted by much shoe leather and a convenient ditch.

'Wow. That has to be our most dangerous moment to date,' I gasped, extricating myself from wheels, chains and nettles. 'Still, it was worth it. Why didn't we bike round Britain? It's a lot quicker and easier.'

A short while later we were sitting in front of a coal fire in the Pierowall Hotel, listening to the news in Gaelic and eating the best fish and chips in Britain. Back at the croft, Richard had found Radio Three and a newspaper. He was in seventh heaven.

Westray was a happy-go-lucky place. We felt at home where there were more rucksacks than suitcases, and more bikes than cars. The post office was tucked behind a small garage and the postman was in overalls as if he had just emerged from the bonnet of a car. I handed him my postcards.

'Sorry lassie, you've missed the plane. There's one flight out daily, but I'll see these catch the ferry.' He gave a big smile. Nothing was too much trouble.

We wandered round the ruins of a large mediaeval kirk with well-preserved tombstones. The name Isbister's were as common here as Jones in Wales.

'It was a James Isbister who was the first war casualty up here. He was killed in 1940 by shrapnel from a German bomber off-loading on his way home. The poor guy was just minding his own business at home,' Richard told me.

On the large deserted beach waiting for the ferry, Richard, watching me cut my toe nails, warmed to his storytelling.

'A few survivors of the Armada sailed north after their defeat, hoping to escape back to Spain the long way round. Some ships arrived on Shetland, where they were welcomed. However, as winter approached, the Shetlanders, concerned about sharing their meagre food supplies with hungry foreigners, threw their Mediterranean guests over the cliff.'

'Nice one. That story'll do Shetland's tourist industry good.'

'Ah but, the inhabitants of Westray not only welcomed their shipwrecked Spaniards, they married and produced descendants who were renowned for seafaring skills and smuggling.'

Not to be outdone by Stromness Shopping Week, Kirkwall had its pipe band in full throttle on Saturday morning. There is nothing quite like the highland dress to quicken the heart, and a crowd had gathered in the high street to watch the massed bands of Kirkwall town, kilts swinging, bagpipes skirling black and white feet tapping, drums beating. Several of the men had swarthy complexions and dark hair which I thought looked suspiciously Spanish.

The little island of Papa Westray has only seventy inhabitants, and all the commerce on the island is run on a co-operative system. There is an integrated transport system, meeting ferries and taking tourists wherever they liked. There was no charge, just an offerings box.

'What'll ye be wanting to see then?' Our hefty young Glaswegian driver asked politely.

'Beltane.'

'Och that's no problem. I'll meet ye later and take ye te the North Hill te see the seals an' birds. Watch out for breeding terns.'

He was as good as his word. On North Hill he insisted on opening a gate and driving us across a field, depositing us just feet from the beach. I quite expected to see prohibition signs for walkers.

Papa Westray has the earliest standing house in Northern Europe, a plaque which read *Last Great Auk shot here in 1813*, the shortest scheduled airline service in the world (two minutes from Westray), and the smallest golf club. A round wooden summer house in a field, mown and fertilised by rabbits and sheep, had the words GOLF CLUB inscribed above it.

Wars seemed a far cry from the peace of these far-flung islands, yet they have played a very important part in Orcadian history. This century alone, Scapa Flow has played a major part in the dramas of two World Wars. We felt we couldn't leave without visiting the Churchill Causeways and the Italian Chapel. A couple of bikes and a hard pedal later, we were admiring what has been described as 'one of the most remarkable feats of engineering of the 20th century'. Four giant causeways link Orkney Mainland with the islands of Lamb Holm, Glimps Holm, Burray and South Ronaldsay, thus protecting the valuable anchorage at Scapa Flow. It was a windswept bleak spot, and for the soldiers stationed up here in the second World War, the bleak windswept islands must have been purgatory. Their feelings are explicitly summed up in the immortal doggerel of Captain Hamish Blair and Alex Burnie.

Everything's so bloody dear,
It's one and ten for bloody beer.
And is it good? No bloody fear
In bloody Orkney.

Best bloody place is bloody bed
With bloody ice on bloody head,

The Sea on our Left

You might as well be bloody dead,
On bloody Orkney.

On the little island of Lamb Holm stands the only visible remnant of Camp 60, the prisoner of war camp where hundreds of Italians were housed while they worked on the Churchill Barriers. Now simply known as The Italian Chapel, it was made from two Nissan huts by Italian P.O.W.'s who must have been horribly homesick on these dark, windswept Northern Isles, so different from their Mediterranean homeland. Under the guidance of artist and sculpture Domenico Chiocchetti, they created an ornate little chapel out of bits of barbed wire, left-over cement, scraps of metal and bully beef cans. Not only did the challenge raise the men's morale and renewed their faith, it also formed a lasting link with the Orcadian peoples. A very beautiful and moving phoenix has risen from these ashes, We spent a prayerful moment in front of the mural of Mother and Child, behind the delicate rood screen which was fashioned from war time scrap metal.

South Ronaldsay was a softer island. Undulating green fields, fat cattle, woolly sheep, free range fowl and grazing goats gave a feel of peace and plenty. Yet the couple we stayed with had a sad tale to tell. They had been implicated in the Ritual Child Abuse Scandal of 1991, when their two sons then aged 11 and 15 were taken into care for five weeks. The emotional trauma of these horrific events, has never healed. The children involved had no rights under the law, and the protagonists are fighting to have the law changed. They also want an apology and their names cleared. They fight on, but the stigma persists. Busy with teaching, farming family and church, they still had time to look after us. We shall never forget their kindness.

Chapter Eighteen

And first I brought the sea to bear
Upon the dead weight of the land,
And the waves flourished at my prayer,
The rivers spawned their sand.
Geoffrey Hill

Sitting on the deck, like the couple of emigrating Highlanders, we pitched and rolled our way across The Pentland Firth, past the forbidding cliffs of Duncansby Head. As the little ferry took us to our own mainland, we both had a feeling of impending anti-climax. We were on our way home, it was supposed to be 'downhill all the way', yet we felt the best was now behind us.

These unwelcome feelings disappeared with our queazy stomachs, as we entered the harbour at John O'Groats. Standing on the quay was Mike, a dentist friend who had trained with Richard, and had flown all the way from Wiltshire to meet us.

'Mike, what a wonderful surprise!' I wasn't sure whether I was hugging him or his bottles of champagne, but the bubbly went down a treat out of plastic mugs on the top of Duncansby Head.

'I think we'd better do something about that gap,' Mike's professional eye was watching me struggling with a sandwich in the pub that evening.

'Say cheese. Lovely. That looks like a B.2. I'll send the impression material to Nairn, and you should have your smile back in Aberdeen.'

'Thanks Mike. You're a star!' I gave him a parting hug and he was as good as his word.

The A9 stretched bleakly into the flatness of Caithness. The tar was melting as the temperatures soared into the 80's. The traffic was light, and there was a sense of comaraderie between travellers at this end of Britain. Everyone waved and smiled at us. We watched cyclists doing the JOGLE (John O'Groats to Land's End) and wished each other well. A stout lady leaning on her gatepost shouted gleefully.

'Och ye've got a gud way to go yet!'

She might, I thought, have offered us a drink of water. We were becoming increasingly aware of the value of drinking water. Not only had we lost the mountains and the midges, but we had also lost the delicious tumbling burns of the West Highlands. Water in Caithness doesn't flow cleanly over boulders, it oozes slowly from the murky peat, emerging as unappetising black sludge. As the tarmac miles plodded past, our mouths became dry and parched. Our clothes stuck to us and the packs felt like lead. Suddenly a large concrete building loomed ahead like a mirage. As we approached, a sign on the locked gates read 'Caithness Spring Water'. Mentally I was slaking my thirst on cool refreshing bottled water and throwing it all over my sweaty body. A Safeway container truck roared past leaving me wrapped in warm exhaust and rudely curtailing my hallucination. Then we stopped by the roadside and shared a few sips of lukewarm water from our diminishing supplies.

We pitched our tent south of Old Wick Castle and found the burn undrinkable. The nearest house was half a mile away. I thought we had enough in our water bottles to see us through, but, in my eagerness to conserve the precious liquid I knocked the cooker; hot tea scalded my wrists. Richard, not one for asking for anything, was bird watching from a nearby geo, so I took a bottle and two pans and headed off into the sunset. The farm was deserted, but luckily a brand-new tap outside the back door filled my containers. I made a slow hazardous journey back, through the bogs and ditches, slurping as little as possible. Exhausted, but triumphant, I re-brewed tea, awarded myself a girl guide badge and we drank our fill.

Drifts of white marguerites and blue vetch softened the cliff tops along this stretch where we had to thread our way round eerie convoluted geos. These are giant chasms in the sandstone cliffs, broken into rocky perforated islands which guard narrow channels. The ravines echoed with the raucous screech of seabirds. The insistent 'cark, cark' of the predatory black-backed gulls, added a sinister note as they flew above the corpses of young kittiwakes floating gently on the swell below. Young fulmars sat calmly on their nests watching their companions swirling past, too young yet to fly, but toilet-trained with military precision; a short waddle to the edge of the cliff, rear ends seaward, a rapid shoot and back to the mess for tea.

It was hot and sticky and there was no path at all. Richard waited for me to catch up.

'I think we'd better head back to the A9. We've got to meet our man from the Sunday Express in Dunbeath, and we don't want to be too deadbeat.'

'Fine by me. We'll need a wash and brush up before the photo session. Lead on MacDuff.'

The sun was scorching, and our neck blinds had been pulled down for several hours. I stopped to have a pee behind a convenient barn, and when I emerged fastening my belt, I found Richard talking to our roving reporter.

'We need you at Dunbeath at 4 p.m. The photographer's concerned about the hazy light and the sooner you can make it the better.'

Ollie had blue eyes and a charming smile. He shook hands warmly.

'See you soon,' he said and drove off.

'Huh. So much for a wash and brush up. There won't be time, will there?' I was feeling cross.

'I expect the photographer just wants to get off early.' We were getting a little more cynical about the press.

Compliant as ever, we reached the hotel on the dot of 4 p.m. There was no time to wash. We were hot, tired, sweaty and dirty. I was toothless and there wasn't a moment for Richard to stick my crown back for the photo call.

The photographer was all charm as I proffered him my sticky hand.

'It'll be authentic, anyway,' I lisped, pulling my broken comb through matted locks and jambing my Foreign Legion cap back on.

The photos took an hour, the interview another hour. Ollie seemed genuinely interested in our odyssey; he was diplomatic and courteous. We sat on a little white chairs under a Cinzano umbrella, looking across the A9 to Dunbeath castle and the cliffs, downing lots of long alcoholic drinks and relaxing.

Ollie quickly found the key of Richard's tongue, and he told all. Our highlights and lowlights, our communication problems, our adventures. Ollie's green roller pen squiggled incomprehensibly over pages of paper. Then it was all over.

'It'll be in the Express this Sunday, July 30th.'

'Please remember it is a charity walk,' I said pressing one of our cards into his hand.

We headed off up the A9, and looked back to see him still scribbling, his coffee cup untouched.

We finally shook the dust of the A9 off at Brora Beach and celebrated with a swim, followed by the luxury of a siesta. Brora had no campsite, but a kind gentleman in the Tourist Office was helpful.

'Try George MacBeth. His place is a mile down the road on the left.'

George MacBeth was living on the family croft. The original homestead was now an outbuilding beside a smart new house. He still owned the ten acres of raised beach that his grandparents had been given to subsist on. George was a tall fit-looking man of sixty, with blue eyes and a kind smile.

'Aye. Ye're welcome to camp heer. There's a wee tap on the outhouse. The beach belongs to me so do go down and enjoy the seals.'

We pitched our tent among the grazing sheep, before wandering down the sandy slope to the beach.

'Strange shaped rocks,' I said puzzling over the U-shaped forms.

'There's a seal on each one,' Richard said, gazing through the binoculars.

'It's definitely a yoga class.' Seals, like giant slugs, had taken possession of each rock, however small. They were basking, heads and tails skywards, fore-flippers reverently touching, rear flippers neatly forked. As we approached they began a mournful wailing, and the nearest inshore, slipped grudgingly off their rocks disturbed by our presence. They then tried to dislodge their neighbours in order to continue their meditations. The wailing reached a crescendo; I retreated.

'Sorry chaps. I didn't mean to disturb your snooze time.'

Once more we were the intruders.

That night we were lulled to sleep by these sirens of the deep.

George came to see us before we left. We learned that both he and his father had been gardeners at Dunrobin Castle. George had just left in disgust after twenty four years service.

'The new gardener appointed last year 'was a Sassenach who could na' grow a daisy in a winda borks!'

Richard pointed to the large monument crowning a hill to the south.

'Could you tell us what that is?'

George frowned and said with some passion,

'Och weil, that's the Mannie. We don't talk about heem.'

The Mannie, as it is disaffectionetly known, is a colossus of Lord Stafford the 1st Duke of Sutherland who was responsible for many of the inhumane Highland Clearances of the early 19th century. Known as 'The Leviathan of Wealth' the Duke evicted some 15,000 tenants and grassed their fields for sheep. The irony is, that the vast monument on the mountain of Beinn a'Bhragaidh, was erected and paid for by his 'grateful tenants.' Its glowering presence followed us for many miles.

We took the Green Road, a pleasant coastal path to Dunrobin Castle, taylor-made for the infamous Dukes of Sutherland. Golden beaches, grassy swards, mature woods and gently rising hills made this a perfect setting for Lord Stafford's Ruritanian extravaganza. It was here we met our first backpacker on the east coast. He was a good-looking cheerful Dutchman called Hans, who was on a charity walk from Land's End to John O'Groats.

'I was seventy yes old laast burthday, and I haf to walk on the roads because I haf a pacemaker,' he told us proudly. 'I wear this medi-alert too, but inside I put some paper with the vords 'I like whisky!'

It was a mutual admiration society and we shook hands warmly. We should have offered him a wee dram if out supply hadn't run out.

Supplies were replenished in Golspie, a symmetrical town like Helmsdale and Brora, built for Sutherland's evicted tenants.

Here the A9 threads its way along the narrow coastal strip in the shadow of Beinn a'Bhragaidh. We paused at the head of Loch Fleet, to watch the wild salmon collecting in a pool near some sluice gates, waiting for the tide to turn when they would be able to travel up the river to spawn. Every few seconds a huge fish would leap out of the water, force itself forward through the air, or describe a powerful circle, before splashing noisily back again. Standing in a car park beside a major road was the last place we expected to see such an Olympian display.

A handful of cattle chewed the cud on a sand spit by the River Fleet, and further down, a pair of ospreys perched in the branches of a dead tree. A golden eagle flew softly past Lord Stafford's monument, watching and waiting.

We approached Dornoch across the golf course, past elegant hotels where nattily-dressed golfers practised their swings. The click of balls vied with the ascending skylarks. For a moment we had lost our wild Highlands and touched down on the tourist track. Our path now vanished into meadows purple and blue with thistles and harebells. We took off our boots to ford a river, a real pleasure in the heat, before reaching the deserted mud flats of the Dornoch Firth and crossing the Meikel Bridge, into Tain.

It was Sunday, July 30th and we dived into the first newsagent to see what Ollie had said about us in his Sunday Express article.

We thumbed our way through the scanty news and views, special offers on planters and house coats, and the features section.

'It's not in any of this lot. D'you think he was just wasting our time?' Richard was remembering the Evening Standard at Burry Port.

'Well, it's certainly not in the colour supplement. That's choc-o-block with the Queen Mum.'

We binned the paper and got on with the walk.

That evening Jo rang. 'A friend's just rung me up to say she doesn't think your marriage will last very long. The Sunday Express article's called *Walking back to happiness* and it's all about you rowing and Daddy walking miles ahead. He said you looked quite a sight and never mentioned your charities once.' She sounded cross and upset. 'The graphics are good and Granny liked it anyway,' she added more calmly.

We had to wait to reach Nairn before we had a chance to read it for ourselves. Richard was annoyed because there was no mention of our charities.

'That's the only reason we agreed to let them do it,' he said angrily.

I felt very betrayed. The article had just mentioned the negative things. There was so much that was positive about our walk, the people, the places, the way we responded to the challenge, the charity money . . . I fumed for many miles.

The Mediterranean weather persisted into August. The smallest car ferry in Europe took our feet from Nigg to The Black Isle across the mouth of the Cromarty Firth. Here the massive rocky sutors reminded me of the Heads at the mouth of Sydney harbour. Whales and porpoises are often trapped in this natural basin of water, but there was no sign of them. On the banks of the Firth, the unspoiled eighteenth century sandstone cottages and tollbooth of the little town of Cromarty rose above the grey shingle, softened by green trees from a protecting hill. A strange hot silence hung over the water, where late twentieth century giant oil rigs shimmered like extra-terrestrial robots

The Black Isle, a fertile peninsula, lies between the Cromarty and Moray Firths. Inland, it was very English, undulating and wooded, with fields golden with harvest and roadside verges smothered in harebells. The warm sandstone cliffs, red sands and deep blue sea, gave the coast a Mediterranean richness. The walking was easy, but sweaty and tiring in the heat. We bought drinks wherever we could to keep our fluids up and prevent dehydration.

It was August 1st. The temperature now reached 87 degrees. We had been nomadic for seven months. We knew London was sweltering in the nineties, but we had never expected anything like this north of the border. It bought its share of small problems. Richard had now discarded his T-shirt, and preferred to walk bare chested. His weight loss meant that his lumbar spines now protruded like knuckle dusters, and rubbed by his heavy pack, produced sores. My pack, already padded, was giving me sores on my prominent hip bones. We had to dress these every morning, padding them with animal wool, obligingly left on fields and fences for us by the local sheep.

At Culloden Moor we decided to visit the infamous battlefield, reconstructed by the Scottish National Trust. We were thankful to shed our packs and put our sticky bodies onto plastic chairs infront of the Audio-Visual. Transported back to 1746 we watched the 'rose-ringed' legend of Bonnie Prince Charlie and the 'black butcher' Cumberland unfold effortlessly before our eyes. The auditorium was full, with most of the visitors wearing headphones.

'I think we're the only English,' I whispered, shifting myself onto a cooler bit of plastic seat.

Outside, along the battle lines, an authentic National Trust Highlander, in plaid and round leather shield, explained the finer details of the battle to some Germans in a genuine Scottish accent. Beside the refurbished eighteenth century farmhouse, a Scottish lassie in highland gear, was draping an authentic highland plaid around the small frame of a Japanese tourist. He nearly disappeared behind the great round shield, but managed a drowning smile for his girlfriend's camera.

The Battle of Culloden Moor on April 16th, 1746, was the last battle fought on British soil. It marked the end of the clan system and the beginning of the end for the Highland Clansman; it also marked the beginning of a romantic legend, which flourished in the wake of Clans and Crofters, and endures today.

We marched along the road to Nairn, foot soldiers in sweltering heat, imagining Cumberland's men marching the other way, a well-trained and disciplined army, more than a match for the hungry and bewildered Highlanders.

'D'you see that great fort on the side of the Moray Firth?' Richard pointed out Fort George, described as 'one of the finest artillery fortresses in Europe'. It was distant brick edifice like a child's toy.

'It wasn't built till after the defeat of the 1745 Uprising which goes to show how paranoid the Hanovarians were about the Jacobites.'

The little village of Ardersier gave us a rather different experience. In a gift shop selling silk scarves, hand-made jewellery and polished stones, Patty, the owner, was intrigued with our walk.

'You must ache all over,' she said, sympathetically. I nodded gratefully.

'Right,' she said. 'I'd like to give you something.'

With this, she picked up two polished quartz stones from a pile in a basket, and began to describe a variety of lines and circles on my unsuspecting back, explaining in plausible mumbo-jumbo why quartz had healing properties.

'You must try it on each other,' she said firmly when she'd finished. 'It'll help the aches and pains.'

'Wonderful,' I mumbled unconvinced. 'I'll have two stones to take with us.'

Ten minutes after leaving the shop I felt a warm glow down my back and an indescribable sensation of well-being. I had visions of setting up a quartz clinic in Tunbridge Wells and making a fortune.

'Terrific! My achilles tendons don't hurt at all now,' Richard said sarcastically, after I'd drawn on his back with the stones during a lunch break beside the River Findhorn. Richard's heels always seized up after a lengthy rest, and it took a few minutes before he could walk without a limp. Patty must have had healing hands, but I never quite gave up on the stones. After a long hard day, when aches and pains got the upper hand, I would ask Richard to perform the quartz 'cure'. There was always a temporary placebo effect, which would probably have been just as effective without the quartz.

The seven mile scoop of bay, from Findhorn to Burghead, was a joy to walk on; firm golden sands, seabirds and solitude. Gentle sea breezes kept the temperature down. Burghead's rocky promintory grew slowly larger. The little port was a deserted stage-set, lit by a brilliant sun. The sheltered harbour was now empty of boats. The many warehouses, once filled with grain, lay pristine and silent. Two youngsters shouted obscenities into the hot air. Warm blue waves slurped the long stone jetty. We ate our sandwiches by the harbour, and crept quietly away.

Bracken and heather-covered sandstone cliffs made pleasant walking. The blue hills of the Black Isle accompanied us as far as

Lossiemouth. The heat wave continued. At our campsite at Lossiemouth, I asked how far we had to go the next day.

'Findochty's a good eighteen miles,' Richard replied from the depths of John Prebble's book on Culloden.

'Let's make an early start,' I suggested. 'I'm finding it hard to complete the days walk in this heat. The early morning's are cooler, and you've often said yourself it's good for morale if we arrive early.'

'Uh huh,' came the grunt from Cumberland's army.

I was up and ready by 8 a.m. Richard was still munching, plate in one hand, Culloden in the other. The Jacobites were ready to charge. I took down the tent by myself and waited impatiently. By the time Mr. Prebble had been reluctantly stowed away, washing up done and the key returned to reception, it was 9 a.m. Richard then decided he had to fix the strap on his pack. This took time. My temper rose. By the time we reached the beach I charged a volley of abuse that the Highlanders would have been proud of, and stormed off towards Lossiemouth as if Cumberland was after me.

When Richard caught up it was his turn for verbal assault. When this was over he made a suggestion.

'You know where Findochty is on the map. I suggest you find your own way.'

'Right, I'll do just that. I think I must have left the camera back at the campsite. I'll walk back and collect it and make my own way. I'll hitch a lift or catch a bus if I have to.'

We parted at Lossiemouth harbour.

I tried to hitch a lift back to campsite, but after a few cars had sailed past, gave up. No-one in their right mind would want to give a lift to a toothless fifty-two-year-old scarecrow. It was a good mile back along the beach, but there was no sign of the camera. Back again into Lossiemouth and I finally had the sense to think which shops I had been into. The camera was in safe custody of the Post Office.

'I cud see it was a gud one,' the postmistress beamed. 'You layfd it on the ledge outside. Lucky some folk are honest.'

I cursed myself, and then had a look at the map on the wall of the Tourist Office to get my bearings. It was a straightforward walk, but I needed to divert inland to cross the River Spey.

One look at the melting tarmac on the road to Elgin and public transport, sent me off along the sandy beach where there was a tiny breeze. I glanced at my watch. It was 11 a.m. and I felt in better spirits and ready for the challenge.

Once I had left Lossiemouth behind, I seemed to be the only person in the world. The golden sand soon turned to shingle which banked steeply on my right, obliterating any view of the hinterland. On my left the tide was coming in fast, and rapidly covering any trace of firm sand. It was strange but rather exciting to be alone on this small strip of narrowing beach. Branches of dead trees were all I could see along the shingle bank. It was lunch time, but I thought I had better not stop. At last one or two people swam into focus on the horizon. An elderly man with grey beard and a kind face was walking his dog.

'It's a hot day for a lass to be carryin' all that weight, and on your own too.'

Feeling foolishly proud of myself, I tried to look cool.

'Is there a bridge near here across the Spey,' I asked casually, sweat trickling wilfully from my brow.

'Aye. If you come off the beach in about a mile you'll see Kingston just down the road, and the bridge is no' far.'

I thanked him and continued. Now small rivers of sand threaded their way between the shingle and I found some footprints where the owner's soles were so worn on the outside edge that they were instantly recognisable. I followed them for half a mile and then they disappeared. At this stage I went over the shingle bar and along a dusty path beside the golf links. The footsteps reappeared until I reached the road. Here a convenient seat was too tempting to pass, and I had a bite to eat and a drink, watched by a couple of old boys in their garden.

'And wheer are ye going lassie with all that on yer back?' Asked the larger man, leaning heavily on his garden fork.

I told him briefly, and he grinned.

'D'ye hear that Jock? She's walking round Britain and she's lost her wee man!'

His friend peered at me over the gate.

'Och weil now. Wait till I tell ole Beachcomber. Even he's never seen a round Britain walker.'

His dentures wobbled unsteadily as he grinned.

Feeling like the last Great Auk, I checked my route.

'Buckie's over theer across Spey Bay. Follow this road til ye come to th' bridge and then turn layfd back to the bay.'

I thanked them and followed their instructions. Buckie hadn't looked far across the bay, but by the time I had crossed the river and regained the beach near Port Gordon, it seemed as far away as

Eastbourne. I looked down and saw the same worn-down footprints.

Portgordon was like a Spanish town at siesta time. The symmetrical streets were silent and deserted. It was now 3 p.m. and very hot. My feet were complaining lustily, and the rest of my body a chorus of creaks and groans. Suddenly two dogs, owner in tow, charged across the road towards me barking furiously. The smaller one was intent on drawing blood. I froze like a frightened rabbit and felt the canines sink into my bare calf.

'Come back heer at once,' came a furious bellow. The jaws withdrew snarling malevolently. The dog got a kick from his owner, and retreated reluctantly.

I was relieved to see that, apart from the imprints of two sets of teeth, my calf was intact. My legs felt like underset jelly as I plodded on towards Buckie, and, somewhere in the outback, a place called Findochty.

'Hey laddie, stop a moment will ye?'

The shouts came from behind me. I ignored them, feeling that if I stopped I should never start again. I heard the sound of hurried feet and turned reluctantly, to see a summer version of Father Christmas, panting towards me.

'Och deer,' he panted apologetically. 'I see your a lassie.'

It was becoming more and more like Alice in Wonderland.

'Er yes. I was this morning I'm sure. Can I help you?'

The old boy was lonely and curious. He'd seen my back and big rucksack from his front room, and wanted to know all about me.

'Will ye come home and have a cup of tae?' He asked anxiously.

'Thanks but I must get on. My husband will be waiting at the campsite and wondering where I am.'

I trudged on. Buckie still had a harbour full of fishing boats and a sign in a fish shop window read 'FRESH HERRINGS FOR SALE!' Now these 'silver darlings' which had once bought so much prosperity to the coast were a rarity.

It was now 6.45 p.m. and I knew there were two campsites, but wasn't sure which one he would use. A bus drew alongside and I took a ride to the campsite between Buckie and Findochty. It was so late, I knew Richard would be concerned. The receptionist was on the phone as I walked in. Cupping it in her hand she asked me if I was Mrs Hunt.

'Your husband's very anxious about you,' she said reprovingly. 'I'm on the phone now to the warden at Findochty.'

'How far is that?' I asked.

'Only a mile and a half' she said, staring curiously at me.

'Thanks. I'll be on my way.'

Now that Richard knew I was coming, I felt able to have a rest. I found a seat on a footpath, and sank down with feet and bum in reverse order. Two ladies approached. I shut my eyes and played dead.

'If it's yer feet that hert, try putting them in the sea,' said one.

'Salt'll do them a power of gud,' added the other.

I grunted and wished they'd just leave me in peace. I was feeling tired and suddenly rather sorry for myself. When I came to get up, I realised stopping had been a mistake. The next mile was the longest of the entire trip so far. My feet and legs were made of lead. When I finally shuffled into the campsite there was no sign of Richard. I found the empty tent and tried to brew a cup of tea. A kind neighbour had her eye on me.

'I'll get you a cup while you go back to reception. Your husband still doesn't know where you are, and they're about to call the police.'

Just as I arrived, Richard and the warden drew up in a car. They had been out looking for me. Richard was searching for me when I rang an hour or so before. Recriminations followed.

'You must have walked twenty two miles. Why didn't you get a lift or catch a bus. I've been expecting you since four o'clock. I think we'd better pack this whole thing in and go home.'

'What a welcome,' I said miserably. 'I found the camera, I got here without a map. If I'm late it's because there were no buses till I got to Buckie and it's a bloody long way. I'm too old to hitch-hike.' Two tears rolled down my cheeks. 'Anyway, you told me to find my way alone, remember? I've had a great time on my own thanks.'

As I retreated into the womb of my sleeping bag I recalled Ollie's parting shot in his Sunday Express article, 'It's a long long road to Tunbridge Wells'.

Chapter Nineteen

Light walks the sky, leaving no print
And there is always day, the shining of some sun,
In those high globes I cannot count,
And some shine for a second and are gone,
Leaving no print.
Dylan Thomas

If my lone walk had exhausted me physically, it had been a good morale booster. I had proved both to Richard and myself that I could find my own way without even holding a map upside down.

At Banff we met John, a recently retired salmon fisherman, who, like many in his trade, had given up the unequal struggle to earn a living from the sea. He walked with us from MacDuff along the cliffs, until the 'path' disappeard among the undergrowth. Wading blindly through knee-high vegetation, on an eroded path pock marked with rabbit holes, was dangerous and tiring. We retreated to the road, where John gave us his thoughts on the demise of the salmon fishing industry.

'It's the grey seals d'you ken. Their numbers have increased from 30,000 to 300,000 in a decade and that number eat a lot of fish.'

The falling price of fish, due to cheap imports from the Shetlands and salmon farms, was, he thought, another cause of the demise of the small fisherman.

'You'll no' make a living when your only offered £1 a pound d'you ken.'

Nor was he impressed with the new trends in the fishing industry. The multi-million pound boats dredged the seas dry and only employed a handful of men. They had to gross £30-50,000 per week just to make a living. Most off this would be needed to furnish their loan on the boat. When I asked whether they had the same skills as the traditional fishermen he said scornfully,

'Skills? Och no. They can' even tie a knot d'you ken. I'm glad to be out of it.'

As if to prove the point Gardenstown's cluster of old houses falling down the hill, lay basking in the warm afternoon sun with only a few open boats sitting in the protected harbour. In the last century it boasted a hundred fishermen and sixty boats. An old boy was shuffling along the front spitting onto a finger which he waved in front of us.

'Winds on the change. Mark my words, see.' We didn't.

'I think the heat has gone to his head. He must be quite lost without a strong east wind.'

Crovie, to the East of Gamrie Bay, consists of a single line of cottages, their red and grey roofs at right angles to the sea, or 'shoulders to the wind'. These are tucked snugly under the cliff and are now mainly holiday homes. Washing flapped jauntily across the little concrete path, the only access to these cottages. Cars had to be parked at the end, and everything carried to the doors in little wooden hand-carts. 'Everything', these days, consisted mainly of polythene bags bulging with supermarket shopping being disgorged from Volvo estates.

Our packs had been taken for us that day, making the walk much more enjoyable. Our host promised she would bring them over to our campsite at Rosehearty at 5 p.m. The municipal site was just a large square of mown grass by the sea, behind the bus shelter and children's playground. The facilities were spotlessly clean and very inexpensive. It was August 7th, the weather was excellent, yet the place was deserted. We sat at a municipal picnic table and had a drink. I looked at my watch. It was now 5.30 p.m. and there was no sign of our friend or our packs. Panic began to stir somewhere inside us. We felt desolate and vulnerable. Our packs were our survival kit, only at moments like this did we realize what they meant to us. We paced up and down. Another half hour crawled past. When they finally arrived, our relief was palpable.

It was a special evening for we had just clocked up 3,000 miles. We set off, after supper, to celebrate in the usual way. Rosehearty was a dreary little town with long bare streets of granite terraced houses and a bald silent square. The pub was frequented by men only. I wrote in my diary,

Typical Scottish pub. Sparsely furnished. Only one table and six chairs. The serious drinkers perched on bar stools and the others round the pool table. Two fruit machines lit the dim corners and a huge T.V. screen filled a quarter of the room. The Glenmorrangie was great.

For much of our walk down this east coast of Scotland, we were on long beaches, alone with the sea birds. Every place we skirted, however small, had its own golf links, now brown and parched under the blistering sun. Only the greens got a drink, vivid oases in a desert. The ruins of ancient castles perched on cliffs and promontories were reminders of harsher times.

Like Burghead, most fishing ports along this coast were still and silent, so it was a relief to find Fraserburgh humming with life and vitality. A few high-tech monster boats were sitting in the harbour. Men in oilskins were sorting nets on the quay (John's stories were beginning to lose credibility), and great crates of fish waited to be processed into anonymity. Contemporary ice machines differ from the old subterranean bunkers we had noticed in places like Findhorn and Spey Bay. Now they shot skywards from a jetty, corrugated iron gantries with a bright plastic elephantine tubes to deliver the ice. There was a rich smell of fish and diesel fumes; the noise of engines from trucks, factories and boats were signs that this port was alive and well.

The beach to Rattray Head was memorably long. We planned to camp on the headland where we knew there would be no water. A hotel at St. Combs, called The Tufted Duck, looked like a cross between a barracks and a prison, but quenched our thirst and provided us with all the water we could carry. I began to empathise with women in the Third World, and thought how much easier it would be to carry it with a pot on my head.

Rattray lighthouse, perched on black rocks above the lethal skerries, lured us on along an endless stretch of beach. Black-backed gulls, kittiwakes and ringed plovers were our only companions. It was getting late when we finally reached the headland.

Next we had to find somewhere to pitch our tent in this inhospitable wilderness. Richard struck off across the huge soft-scooped dunes, which swallowed our feet and took away our breath. Ten minutes later we were looking down onto a strange circle of spongy vegetation, liberally sprinkled with thistles, ragwort and rabbit droppings. It made a perfect campsite; soft, dry and sheltered. Our only lack, was water, so we had to trek back to the beach and use the sea for all our ablutions. By this time it was getting dark.

Out on the great beach the sun was setting. A few hundred yards to the north, the powerful beam of the lighthouse swept the booming surf at regular intervals. To the south the blurred orange lights of Peterhead hung silently in a distant sky. Behind acres of rolling sand, a myriad fairy lights from the gas terminal glowed like red and green stars. The insistent roar of burning gas filled the approaching darkness. A full moon silvered a path across the sea, casting dark shadows on the monochrome sandunes. I shuffled back across the cold soft sand to our camp, where, spread-eagled on the spongy ground, the tent looked like an alien from outer space.

We were still in a fantasy world as we passed the gaunt ruined tower of Old Slains castle. It was destroyed by James V1 in 1594 because the owner, Earl Erroll was involved in a plot to land Spanish troops on the Aberdeenshire coast. Undaunted, the 9th Earl built another castle just five miles along the coast, which was added to and improved on, by subsequent earls. It was admired by Johnson and Boswell on their travels in 1773, and reached its zenith in Edwardian times. In 1895 Bam Stoker used the castle as inspiration for Dracula's castle of the vampire while staying in Whinnyfold near Cruden Bay.

Cruden Bay, our destination for the night, narrowly missed becoming the Brighton of Aberdeenshire at the end of the last century. It was developed as a luxury resort by the railway company who built a golf course and luxury hotel. The little place was too isolated for the venture to succeed, and now lies quietly back from its two mile long sandy beach and empty fishing harbour.

There was certainly no luxury hotel for us. Our fisherman friend had told us to use the fishing bothy there. As we came off the cliff path, I asked a young lad where Berty Brewster's bothy was. He looked at me as if I had spoken in Russian. I repeated the question. His face finally cleared.

'Oh Bairt Bruuster's place,' I nodded encouragement. 'Aye it's just o'er the road past the fishing naytes.'

The fine stone bothy was locked and deserted. We pitched our tent under the orange curtain of nets hung out to dry. That night, through the hazy drapes, we had a view of the moon rising over the beach, illuminating a church spire on the cliffs beyond. Only the rustling waves broke the silence. With Slain's castle only a mile behind us, I wouldn't have been surprised to hear a wolf baying. I crept back into my green cocoon. The only sound inside the tent was Richard snoring.

The fulmar's slow-growing chicks were beginning to get their feathers in readiness for their maiden flights across the sheer cliffs and stacks of the Bullars of Buchan. At Forvie, we left the cliffs for sandy beaches, turning inland across high shifting sand dunes which have swallowed Iron Age and Medieval settlements. The last remnants of an ancient kirk still stands, and the area is covered in heather, lichens and marram grass.

Once across the River Ythan, we were back on the beach with a few keen fishermen and rafts of eider duck. The long shingly sands ran straight down to Aberdeen and were punctuated with drunken pill boxes and salmon nets. These squared-off 'goal posts' were intended to trap fish at high tide. A stray fisherman was inspecting his nets and I asked him how many fish he caught in them.

'The wind's wrong this yeer. We need a west wind for a gud catch.' He sounded grumpy.

'We catch four to six salmon on a gud day, sometimes none.' He finished tweaking the net, jumped into his landrover and drove off in a slough of sand.

As the tide came up we had to walk on soft sand. It was hard going with our boots sinking in at every step. As we neared Aberdeen, two runners passed us effortlessly. Having made an early start, for once we had time to spare. Flinging ourselves down on the sand beside a cock-eyed pill box, we crashed out like a couple of flat fish, and dozed for an hour before tackling Aberdeen; the first city we had walked through since leaving Liverpool.

It was a bewildering experience. Great granite buildings frowned down on us, streets surged with people, traffic roared and hooted, lights flashed, sirens blared in an organised urban bedlam. We inhaled the unfamiliar smell of exhaust, felt bemused by the many shopping centres and nearly got run over. We had to collect maps and have photographs developed, but felt like visitors from another planet. It was a relief to be picked up and taken to the quiet suburbs for the night, where letters from family and friends awaited us and a jiffy bag contained my 'smile' in the shape of a little 'spoon' denture.

'Good old Mike,' I said, pushing it in and grinning at Richard. 'I can face the world now, as long as it's not a big city.'

'It'll take a bit of getting used to' was the unenthusiastic reply.

I panicked about supper, but fortunately it was fish pie. I was unusually quiet, but my new tooth remained in situ. Lunch next day was a different story. I bit hungrily into my sandwich which abruptly filled with plastic. Marge stuck to the denture like glue and after several more attempts I gave up. Richard was looking at me with the hint of a smirk on his face.

'It's impossible,' I said.

'Keep it in place with your tongue. You'll get used to it eventually.' No sympathy from this dentist.

'Just as well we've got nine days before we reach Edinburgh. I'm going to need lots of practice.'

Such minor problems were soon forgotten as we walked on under the blazing sun. A straighter coast made for easier walking, with cliffs, castles and fishing villages to take the mind off fatigue. We were spell-bound by St. Cyrus Kirkyard, tucked under the cliffs near Montrose. The church had fallen into a miserable ruin, but an assortment of decorated tombstones, crooked and weathered with age, had a fascinating story to tell. Pictorial descriptions of the occupations of the deceased was usual in the seventeenth century, and here, gathered together in stony silence, were a whole congregation of teachers, bakers, fishermen, farmers, ministers, innkeepers, quarriers, foresters and midwives. The tailor's trade emblem was scissors and goose, the wright had a square and dividers, the farmer a plough and wheat sheaf. Skulls and crossbones, winged souls and hourglasses were much in evidence. A certain bone-setter, called Alexander Webster, was depicted setting a patient's arm-bone, watched by a group of admirers. Dated 1759, the inscription ran simply:

As runs the glass
Man's life doth pass. Momento mori.

In 1891, the tragic poet George Beattie, a lawyer of Montrose, fell in love with a beautiful heiress. When she jilted him in favour of a more worthy suitor, he was so broken hearted he shot himself on this very spot. 'The memorial,' we read, 'was erected by his friends.'

'Who,' I said, shedding a mock tear, 'were saved the cost of porterage.'

Richard was busy reading another 19th century epitaph which sounds strange in our secular society:

When I first drew the breath of life
I nothing knew at all.
Yet long before my death I knew
That I with Adam fell.
My body lies near to this stone,
Waiting the morning call.
When Christ will take me by the hand
He is my all and all.

'I hope he's patient. I wonder whether anyone will understand the significance of that in another hundred years?' I muttered.

Just as we left, I noticed a contemporary memorial stone to *'Neil Hunter, a word smith'*, complete with quill pen and inkstand:

> *Goodnight sweet prince,*
> *And flights of angels*
> *Sing thee to thy rest.*

The tradition, it seems, continues.

It was now August, yet these east coast beaches were frequented only by seabirds. Sandwich terns diving like rockets, rafts of eider duck, hundreds of gooseanders, ringed plovers, knots and two red-crested humans with brown legs and hunch backs. Our bare feet made their impression among the delicate patterns of web and claw. The space, light and solitude was intoxicating. The groups of seabirds, mainly gulls and terns, screeched as we approached. Reluctantly they rose, hovering lightly over dark shadows, before settled back, a few hundred yards further on. The sea broke rhythmically, frothing round our feet, and retreated leaving a mirror of wet sky. Near the cliffs, the water was covered in a thick film of guano and feathers, which meant intrepid swimmers had to keep both mouth and nostrils shut. I gave my feet some sea water therapy, and left the rest of me to get on with it.

Beyond the sand, miles of golf links lay brown and parched. Hoses played on the vivid greens. The heat was intense; inland, flying insects were out in force. Hover flies, horse flies and flying beetles were having the summer of their lives and attacking any flesh they could find. Ripened corn rattled on tinder-dry stalks, dead yarrow crackled loudly in the hedgerows, and broom pods exploded like shot guns. On a short stretch inland, the farm track was so dusty we could have been in Africa. Carrying enough liquid became a problem, and several times I had to knock on doors and beg for water.

Having tasted an Arbroath 'smokie' we thought we should find out a little more about its history; the Signal House Museum in Arbroath told all.

The cliff-top village of Auchmithie, three miles north of Arbroath, was the true home of the Arbroath Smokie. The fisher women were a special breed. Amazonian ladies who thought nothing of hitching up their skirts (*kilt their coats*) and wading out to the fishing boats with their men on their backs so they should reach the boats with dry feet. Not only did these women launch the boats and haul them up onto the beach, (there was no harbour until 1890), but prepared and baited the lines, cleaned mussels, cooked, knitted, fetched water and last but not least prepared and sold the smokies.

No wonder *'a fisherman without a wife was like a ship without a sail'* and he chose his wife and his boat with equal care. She certainly needed to be as physically strong and tireless as a workhorse; from the photographs she looked as though she thrived on it. It was a culture apart even within the town of Arbroath. The street where the fisher 'fowk' lived was called the 'Fit O' the Toon'. They carried skulls, wore bluecoats, redded lines, smoked cutties, ate matties and slept in a bun breest.

Richard's last C.C.F. Camp had been spent at Budden Ness near Carnoustie. Budden Army Camp was memory lane for him. With the tide up to the rocks at Budden Head, we couldn't avoid walking through the army ranges, which a local informed us would be quite safe. It was our hottest day so far, and the little path through the sand dunes was like a sauna bath. Richard explained the intricacies of snap shooting to me as we passed the targets. A tarmac road, straight across the camp to the lighthouse, was the quickest and coolest way of arriving back at the beach again. I ducked under a barrier and Richard reluctantly followed. I couldn't see anyone playing soldiers, but Richard was sure he spotted some camouflaged helmets among the sand dunes. Back on the beach, we threw off our boots and paddled like a couple of kids out of school. At this moment, a soldier in full battledress, rifle held across his chest, ran towards us shouting in a very English accent.

'You shouldn't have been walking through the camp. There's a very big exercise on. Please explain yourselves.'

Richard stiffened to attention, ankle deep in the water and explained with military precision.

The soldier, sweating profusely, continued his polite cross-questioning. Finally he shook us warmly by the hand and wished us well.

We celebrated our escape with a blow-out from Monifeith's Tesco, and several wee drams.

Walking across the mile-long Tay Bride we felt like two pawns on a vast chess board. Square paving slabs in different tones of brown stretched as far as the eye could see in perfect perspective.

After the long dreary walk through the industrial zone of Dundee, it was good to be passing golden fields of stubble, dotted with great reels of straw and bordered with wildflowers. Our next bridge would be across the Firth of Forth to Edinburgh, where we were meeting friends and family. The English border was not so very far away.

In East Neuk we came across our first haa. This is a regional sea mist which descends like a gauze curtain turning the beach into a damp and muted underworld of looming shapes, disembodied voices, and unseen cries. The haa clears as abruptly as it descends. In well-preserved fishing villages like East and West Anstruther, Pittenween, St Monace and Elie, the mellow sandstone houses had crow-stepped gables, warm pantile roofs, and roses round their eighteenth century doorways. The little harbours were filled with colourful fishing boats and the streets full of colourful tourists.

It was in Pittenween that we met friends from Tunbridge Wells. Although we kept in touch with our close family by phone once a week, we had really forgotten about our other life. The commitment of each day took most of our physical and mental energies. Our thoughts were usually on making sure we had somewhere to camp, enough to eat and drink and our route. Anything over was necessary to absorb the changing world around us. We were both very excited about meeting Jo and Tim in Edinburgh, and having a few days of 'time out'. I was surprised, therefore, how emotional I felt when greeted warmly by old friends from home.

During a relaxed meal that evening the stories came tumbling out.

'OK.' said Paddy, 'Which tooth is it?'

'Not telling. I've only had it a week and I'm just beginning to get it sussed.'

I still felt self-conscious about my newly filled gap.

The next day we were able to leave our packs, while Paddy took us on the Chain Walk. It sounded like a route march for convicts, but turned out to be an exhilarating scramble around the cliffs hanging onto ropes and chains for several miles. Purple medusa jelly fish floated on the deep sea-water pools and ravines below us. The conglomerate and basalt cliffs were sculptured into disjointed organ pipes and bizarre cancellations.

Janet, a physio friend, had come equipped with her ultrasound machine and treated Richard's achilles tendons and my troublesome left foot.

'It's wonderful. I'm ache-free today,' I said gratefully, wondering whether it was the ultrasound, seeing friends or the exciting scenery. I decided it was a mixture of all three.

'Hang on tight for this one.'

Richard had to stretch his long legs over a wide crack in the rocks.

'Smile you two!' Click. Paddy had a picture of us both clinging to the sheer cliffs like a couple of monkeys.

Edinburgh was in carnival mood. The Festival was in full swing and everybody who could do anything, was on the streets dressed up and doing it. Jugglers, stilt walkers, buskers, vendors, Fringe players, mummers and musicians, watched by crowds who thronged the streets, spilled out of cafes and pubs and sprawled across the parks. The hot streets vibrated with sounds, singing, shouting, bagpipes, bugle and drum. The smell of beer, coffee, bodies and perfume wafted across the swarming throngs. Edinburgh was open house and it was one hell of a party.

We hung up our boots for three days and entered into the carnival spirit with Jo and Tim, eyes bulging, camera clicking. We sweltered during a Fringe monologue, ate haggis, neaps and tatties, admired Thomas Faed's *The Last of the Clan,* and several paintings by the Glasgow Boys, in the Scottish National Gallery. Our last evening we listened to Andras Schiff playing Schubert sonatas in the Usher Hall. The liquid notes of those perfectly constructed melodies fell on starved ears. It was a strange and memorable interlude.

The Bass Rock, lay basking in the blue waters of the Firth of Forth. The monstrous head of this whale-like rock, rises 350 feet out of the water. This volcanic plug glistens white with tightly packed colonies of seabirds, their guano coating the sides like icing sugar. Most of the birds are gannets, and we watched their precise high velocity dives with awe. They pierce air and water like a rapier, surfacing with a fish every time. The great rock slowly receeded as we walked along smooth beaches and slippery rocks where sandstone stacks were wind-whipped into strange heraldic beasts, totem poles and giant primeval faces.

In spite of this exciting scenery, my diary entry the day after we left Edinburgh read as follows:

North Berwick attractive, English-looking and touristy. In spite of
three days rest, my left foot and right thigh give me lots of cramp. What
a week. The pack also seems very heavy.

It was at Dunbar that I got hooked on teashops. We had four miles
further to walk to reach our campsite at East Barnes, and that felt
four miles too far. However, having decided that I could only get
there on a fix of tea, we found a scruffy cafe and sat down heavily.
Surreptitiously I loosened my laces, and then slid my boots off
under the table. My toes wriggled with relief, and I hoped somebody
was having welsh rabbit. A pot of tea and a large slice of cake later,
my progress, if not velocity-driven, was at least respectable.

The weather had been unsettled since we left Edinburgh, and
hard showers were almost a relief after the intense heat of the past
few weeks. Richard, trying to avoid more walking than necessary
on the A1, opted to stay on the beach just south of Torness Power
Station. The beach soon disappeared, leaving us picking our way
through slippery rocks and pools amongst giant sandstone columns
and natural arches.

'Look. Just ahead. There's a Great Auk.' Richard was pointing
to a large grey seabird which was trying desperately to fly.

'I thought the last Great Auk was shot in Papa Westray,' I said,
my camera at the ready to film this renascent bird.

As we neared it, Richard changed his mind.

'It's an immature gannet. They can't fly once they're grounded.
I'm afraid that one's doomed.'

There was nothing we could do. A little further on we spotted
another casualty, this time a oil-covered guillemot.

'I think this one's in with a chance of survival.' The bird was
cleaning himself and looked reasonably perky.

We were still walking over very slippery seaweed-coated rocks,
stepping over pools and, without mentioning it to each other,
concerned for our own survival. The tide was coming in on one
side, and sheer sandstone cliffs loomed up on the other. Had we
turned an ankle at this point, we should have been in a lot of trouble.
St. David seemed to have lent us his guardian angel, for we reached
the path onto the A1 safely, leaving natural hazards for technical
ones.

A few miles of walking inside the thin strip between life and
death would bring us back into England. Overhead, the sky was
full of thick black clouds, while brightness still lit the cliffs and

sea. The dramatic cliffs of St. Abb's Head, bright with golden stubble, were visible to the North, and we could just make out Holy Island to the South. The great trunk road stretched across the rolling landscape like a broad grey ribbon; cars and lorries roared past us in a whirlwind of exhaust. Up a slight incline and under the iron band of a motor way bridge; there, below us, lay a simple stone plaque with ENGLAND written on it. No river, no hills, no natural boundary, just fields and a few granite sets.

We felt a strange mixture of emotions. Glad to be back in our own country, but sad to leave Bonnie Scotland which had given us so much for the past three and a half months. We shared our last juice drink sitting quietly on the low wall, immersed in our own thoughts. At that moment, two large lads leapt out of a very small car, rushed up to the border stone and proceeded to leap about in the air like a couple of frogs in a fit, whooping with joy. After this little display, they returned to their car and drove off hooting in a northerly direction.

'I always though that's just what I would do here' I said, noisily draining the last drops from the juice carton. 'There's only another thousand miles. My body's pleased, but I'm not sure I am.'

Richard was gazing into the middle distance, and I guessed he felt the same.

'Come on,' he said looking at his watch. 'It's time to go. There's still plenty to see. It's not over yet.'

Hand in hand we crossed the border into England. It was one hundred and seven days since we crossed the River Sark at Gretna Green.

Chapter Twenty

To see a World in a Grain of Sand,
And a Heaven in a Wild Flower,
Hold infinity in the palm of your hand,
And Eternity in an hour.
William Blake - *Auguries of Innocence*

The north east corner of England welcomed us with historic and well-preserved towns like Berwick-Upon-Tweed and Warkworth. Every age in history seemed to have left a legacy: an homogenous collection of vernacular castles and ramparts, ancient bridges and mellow stoned houses. Soft Scottish accents were replaced with robust Geordie tones. These regional accents gave local flavour each area, and were as varied as the scenery we walked through.

The coast of Northumberland seemed all sea, sky and sand. Our campsite called Beachcombers, two miles from Holy Island, was one of the most isolated we had used. The beaches are so vast, that at low tide, the sea is no more than booming surf on the horizon under an overarching sky.

In this world of sand and sky, Holy Island shimmered on the horizon like a mirage. At this point Richard consulted his map and turned inland behind two mountainous sand dunes I followed, only feet behind. Suddenly there was a shout ahead,

'Look out! Quicksands.' I watched as Richard's right leg disappeared into the sand, fortunately reappearing with equal rapidity. Two careful steps further on, my foot did a repeat performance. We could now see the dangerous soft sand, and made sure we put our feet on firmer areas. It was only after this that I began to see warning notices.

Once our tent was pitched, we brewed up as usual, but the little cooker was as thirsty as we were. If we wanted any supper, we had no choice but to walk a seven mile round trip to a petrol station on the A1. Our return journey round Beal Point was a disgusting squelch through an undergrowth of detritus brought in on the high tides; scum, dead birds, jelly fish, seaweed, disposable nappies and condoms. Back 'home' we fed well, then adjourned to the luxury of chairs and a fire, in the campsite pub. The weather was grey and overcast and I noted in my diary that the evenings were drawing in.

Foot-slogging it over the causeway to Holy Island was an interesting experience. The island is cut off by the tide for ten hours in every twenty four, which means the inhabitants would have to chose their time carefully to have acute appendicitis or a premature birth. Half way along the causeway, a small box on stilts has been thoughtfully provided for any pedestrian who might be caught by the rising tide. The thought of being cooped up in it for five hours like a battery hen, didn't appeal, but if being drowned was the only alternative, any port in a storm.

Cars poured over the causeway with us. While they roared past, we were able to watch many of the birds for which these mud flats are famous. Dunlins, redshanks, curlews and godwits, stalked beside the watery patterns, carved in the wide mud flats under a monochrome sky.

Lindesfarne caters for its tidal tourists. Cafes, card shops, museums, car parks, coach parks, ice cream vans; St. Aiden would probably turn in his grave. The little town is gawped at and wandered round for a few low-tide hours every day. Then the tourists depart, leaving their litter and their money, and the inhabitants can relax until the next wave comes.

For all our superior views about cow-towing to tourists, we were as glad of a cafe for elevenses as all the other visitors. A large po-faced man, served us two hot chocolates and two sticky buns, incredibly slowly. The queue lengthened.

Friar Tuck, complete with balding pate and Franciscan robes, was sitting at an adjoining table, trying to impress the middle-aged deaconess opposite him. His booming public school voice would have needed no amplification in a cathedral.

'Now take a man like Earl Grey. Wealth, breeding, an intellectual of the highest order. Literary, an ornithologist, excellent fisherman.' Here he put the tips of the fingers of each hand together in a Giotto pose. 'No money worries. The quintessential cultural liberal. Now there's a man I admire.' His companion nodded politely, gathered up a large unfashionable handbag, and rose to leave. We processed out after them.

Skirting the priory, museum, and anywhere anyone was queuing and paying, we walked down to the peaceful isle, where St. Aiden had his own little chapel in the seventh century. This wild spot feels so right for prayer and meditation. It is ironic that the tides of tourists threaten the very peace and tranquillity they seek in this cradle of Christianity. It looks towards the bare Northumbrian coast and the watchful silhouette of Bamburgh castle. Like the Orkneys there is a feeling here of space and light under the huge sky. We walked past the warm sandstone ruins of the old priory, to the little harbour where Lutyens' renovated castle looks down from its cone-shaped knoll to the upturned herring boats, lying among the lobster pots and ropes. They had little doors in them and looked so like Peggotty's house I felt as enchanted as David Copperfield.

The north side of the island was empty and deserted. Gaps in the grassy dunes gave views of the wide white beach, and beyond Berwick, the cliffs of St. Abbs Head. Between us and them just the pounding surf and a carpet of parnassus grass in flower. We rejoined the road to the causeway, and scurried across like sandpipers running from the waves.

We sank down in a teashop in Seahouses in order to get me the last two miles to a campsite in Beadnell. The dingy little room heaved with humanity; screaming children, moody teenagers, tetchy parents, exhausted grannies, all playing happy families. Gradually the tables emptied and calm was restored. Enter three elderly ladies clasping day sacks, handbags and telescopic walking sticks. Colourful bandannas and head scarves adorned their thinning white heads. Stiffly, they removed their packs and bags, shrank their sticks, and placed their large bottoms clad in baggy shorts on the wooden wheel backs. A chorus of 'Let me help you dear, mind where you put your bag Joan!' rose to a crescendo as they struggled out of their low-tech anoraks and squeezed their knarled legs and high-tech trainers under the table. I poured myself a third cup of tea, and promised myself not to wear shorts, should I become an eccentric geriatric pedestrian.

Wide beaches and small villages, where a few graceful fishing cobles bobbed gently on the waves, soon gave way to the flat greyness of the industrial North East.

Richard was back at school, hatching in the great Northumberland/Durham coal fields.

'It feels strange to be walking on one of those hatchings forty years on.'

'If we have any grandchildren, they won't be doing that,' I said, thinking of all the recent pit closures.

As we walked over a rusty railway crossing, we passed a mounted pit tub sporting a few smutty salvias.

'Erected in 1984 to mark the site of West Leekburn Bedlington E. colliery,' Richard read. 'Sunk in 1860 it employed 970 men at peak, producing up to 292,000 tons of coal annually. The colliery closed in 1962.'

The only feature in this flatscape was a forest of chimneys, the rectangular bulk of a coal fired power station and a giant octopus with metal tentacles which turned out to be an aluminium smelting plant. The beaches were black and a few people were busy filling bags with pieces of coal. Scruffy-looking piebald horses were cobbled in the black-grassed fields.

'Gypsies collect the coal round here and sell it,' Richard told me.

Sadly there wasn't a gypsy in sight.

Industrial death and decay was all around; a necrotic landscape which is gradually being purged of its scabs. The Woodham Colliery, stark and silent among the weeds, is now a museum.

North Blyth typified the end of an era. The coal staithes (wooden chutes which funnelled the coal into the ship's hold) were being dismantled. Rows of terraced brick houses had been razed to the ground, leaving only the pub; a lone monument to a vanished community. The Russian klondykes (factory fishing ships) had moved into Blyth, their great rusty hulks filling the harbour like so many vultures.

As we plodded through the empty dreariness of North Blyth, a cheery voice called out

'Ya can't get through that way. It's a dead end.'

'The whole place is a dead end,' I muttered.

We turned round and there, outside a hairdresser's shop on the corner, were two middle aged women in pink nylon tabards.

We explained that we were to cross to South Blyth on the ferry. The ladies disappeared.

'I'm ready for elevenses. Let's stop here.' I indicated a convenient seat.

Richard was gazing round at the tarmac emptiness. 'We'd better hurry up before they move this too.'

''Wud yer like a cup o' tea? We've plenty 'ere,' insisted the same cheery voice from across the street.

We were soon ensconced in the ladies' hairdresser's (a novel experience for Richard) chatting to very friendly staff, while their white haired clients had to wait patiently for their perms.

Tea and coffee flowed with the questions. Everyone talked at once. We felt like celebrities.

I mentioned the demise of the coal industry.

'Ma granddad was in coal and ma dad was killed at 56 down the shaft. Ma son went into it, but now he's go' anuther job,' one of the pink tabards told us.

'They seem to have pulled down all the houses round here,' Richard said, scrunching up his chocolate paper.

'O yer. They've pooled down seven rows o' houses down the road. It's aw gone now. But we get by.'

We asked what people did with their time.

'O it's a gud communidy,' the stouter one said, grinning.

'We've go' the bowling club, whist drives, an the men's clubs. Then o' course there's the hairdressers.'

She reluctantly picked up a curler and began rolling a white strand round it.

'That corner shop's real bad,' volunteered a customer with cotton wool in her ears, who was waiting for her well-crimped hair to be combed out. 'We use the supermarket in Blyth, but they've naw time for yer.'

The boss was looking hard at my matted locks.

'Wud yer like a hairdo?'

I declined politely, but felt she was dropping a hint. Instead I asked to use their loo.

'Out the back in the yard to yer left,' she told me. The original thunder box was now a water closet, but only just.

Walking along the de luxe promenade at South Shields, set off with fairy lights, fun fairs and toy parks, we saw a huge cruise liner a mile or so off shore. It was, we learned, the QE2 which was on a rare voyage up the east coast, probably because the skipper was a Yorkshire man. The shining boat loomed out of the mist, shadowed by a klondyke, in an ironic juxtaposition of anachronistic capitalism, and rusty communism.

Having crossed the Tyne and the Weir, we felt we were well on our way south. Sunderland, recently dismantled, was being given cosmetic surgery. In place of wharves and warehouses, machinery was being used to landscape the scarred riverside, and a university was being built. We stopped to eat our sarnies by the Weirmouth bridge, a mini-version of the one in Sydney Harbour. Here a plaque informed us, that what had once been the commercial centre of downtown Sunderland, was now 'transformed into an appealing place for other users'.

Our coasts were in a state of transition.

'We'll have to do the walk again in ten years time and see it all transformed,' I said sarcastically, eating as slowly as I could hoping my feet could stay off the ground a little longer.

Richard was already shouldering his pack. 'We'd better get on, there's a dinner party in Seaham tonight.'

We had psyched ourselves up for this industrial belt, telling ourselves it would be interesting. Even the dullest landscape had something to commend it, if observed with a positive enough attitude, we told ourselves. However, my body refused to have a positive attitude when walking through soulless streets for miles on end. Seaham might have been the other side of the world, the effort to get there was so great. As time ticked by, Richard changed gear and the pace increased, (or perhaps I changed into a lower gear). The gap between us lengthened until he disappeared. I decided to give in. There were some trees beside the road and I collapsed onto a convenient seat by some traffic lights. Across the wide road, I thought I saw the nets twitch. A few minutes later, Richard appeared from the undergrowth some way ahead. He didn't see me, and I bawled something rude up the street. Richard turned and waited while I limped nearer, too tired to say more than:

'Remember I don't know where we're going. It would look odd if you arrived on your own.' Together we made the last mile to our Rotary hosts in New Seaham. We were late.

The door opened and we were ushered in. A reporter was sitting comfortably in an armchair sipping tea.

'I tried to catch you on the road earlier,' she said, watching us remove our boots. Any unpleasant smells were drowned in her perfume.

'If you could spare me a few minutes. A photographer's on his way. I've been here an hour waiting for you.'

We sank down, clutching china tea cups and answered as many questions as we could manage between gulps. The doorbell rang.

Betty answered it.

'It's the photographer,' she said, 'he wants you outside in your walking gear with packs please.'

She looked apologetic, and glanced at the clock.

'Our guests will be here in a minute too.'

We disappeared up to our room for our packs and anoraks. As we reached the hall, the doorbell rang again. It was the guests. Controlled pandemonium followed.

'Hello. Yes, er, we're just off. Goodbye. Er, see you soon.' We squeezed ourselves and our packs past smart suits and well-dressed ladies and were swallowed up into the photographers's car. He took us down the road, where we eased our stiff limbs out of the back seat, and posed up an incline, backed by fields and woods, just off the pavement.

'Smile - you're enjoying this,' the photographer reassured us. Click, click and it was almost over. Another photo on the doorstep with the chains of office. Tired and dishevelled we changed clothes, (no time for a shower), and descended for dinner. In our haste we upset our petrol-driven cooker and joined the assembled company smelling as though we had come off an oil rig.

'Ah ha,' said an elderly but sprightly guest, 'I've seen you two already this evening.'

I remembered the twitching nets . . .

The Tees, the last great river of this decaying industrial belt, was memorable. It was major roads all day from Hartlepool to Middlesbrough. Rain tipped ceaselessly down from a grey sky onto grey tarmac. It was too much for my light kagool and I was soaked to the skin. I stood unashamedly by a roundabout and changed all my top clothes in order to keep warm. White cars streamed blindly past. The last miles towards the transporter bridge had no pavement. It was the rush hour. Cars and lorries threw waves of black spray onto us from below, while grey rain soaked us from above. It was possibly the most dangerous moment of the entire walk.

* * *

It was misty and damp as we climbed the 660 feet high cliffs above Skinningrove on the Cleveland Way. The sea, cliffs and wide open spaces were a welcome antidote to traffic and exhaust fumes. Physically and mentally we were on a high. Bald heaps of alum spoil lay piled on the cliff tops as though a giant had poured blue-grey dust there. My happy trail guide was back on duty.

'Those heaps are the remnants of Britain's first chemical industry. Alum was used in dying wool, tanning leather and sizing paper. They operated the mines from 1600 to 1870.'

Richard looked wistfully to the farm track on our right.

'We could go and see them, but I don't think we've got time.'

The elevenses gong was making noises in my inside, and with perfect timing, we stumbled across The Walkers Halt at Boulby. A note in the window read -

WALKERS WITH MUDDY BOOTS WELCOME. YOU MAY EAT YOUR OWN SANDWICHES.

We opened the door and found ourselves inside a cosy threadbare sitting room. A large pine table and wooden pew looked inviting, and we ordered coffee and a cake from the elderly couple who had been refreshing walkers since they retired. We chatted to the wife, while her husband in blue-striped pinny, stayed firmly in the kitchen. They had served several marathon walkers, including John Merrill.

'He was kind enough to mention us in his guide,' she said, proudly showing us her visitors book.

Our high spirits must have lifted the clouds; in Staithes, we crossed the border between Cleveland and North Yorkshire in sunshine. This old fishing port tucks itself deep inside the cupped hands of the shale cliffs. From above, the slate and pantiled roofs jamb together; and the fishing cobles in the little harbour look like stranded fish at low tide. We were in James Cook country, and felt he might well have recognised the town where he spent some months as an apprentice to a haberdasher in 1744.

We threaded our way through the 'squeezy-belly' alleys, and up onto the cliffs where we spotted one man and his dog coming towards us.

'Hallo you two! I've got some days off. Alison's got a bad back so I thought I'd check on my itinerant patient.'

'Mike! What a friend!' We were both overjoyed to see him.

'D'you approve of my smile?' I asked grinning. 'Eating with your new tooth has been a steep learning curve but it's terrific to flash white plastic instead of a gap.'

We adjourned into the nearest pub where I discovered that my Kilmarnock boots leaked badly. They had walked 1,000 miles without rain, and with the advent of damp weather were less than waterproof. As I squeezed black water out of my socks for the third day running, I knew I should have to buy another pair of boots.

Several hours, and two pairs of rather weaker legs later, we left Mike and fell down the coast to Whitby, where I spent an agonising half hour choosing my final pair of boots.

Good and bad days seemed to alternate, and the nineteen miles from Whitby to Scarborough was bad. We had a late start, and with the evenings drawing in, we felt pressurised from the start. My new boots had the usual fight with my feet; the boots won, and I had to stop frequently to tape sheep's wool onto my heels to prevent blisters. It was the wrong time of the month, I had a headache and stomach cramps. The weather was in tune with my mood. The charms of Robin Hood's Bay, official end of Wainwright's Coast to Coast Path, escaped me.

As we climbed the steep cliffs at Ravenscar, I stopped yet again to doctor my heels. Richard looked anxiously at his watch and back to me.

'I don't think we'll make it. We'll have to camp rough.'

'No, we shan't,' I snapped. 'It doesn't help just to be negative. It's encouragement I need.'

I swallowed a couple of paracetamol and we continued in single file silence. As the afternoon wore on, our exertions made us thirsty. We had very little water, and there was no sign of habitation of any kind. If we were going to camp rough, we needed water, and apart from the sea beating below us there were no rivers or streams.

'Look,' I said spotting a lone farm. 'I'll get some water there and then we'll be OK if I can't make it.'

I was rather hoping Richard would volunteer, but he'd rather die of thirst than ask for water, so I hobbled across several fields and eventually reached the farm which now vibrated to the barking of several furious Jack Russell's. All the doors were firmly shut, and there was no-one to be seen anywhere. I searched for a tap, but all I could find was a water butt with some rather stagnant looking liquid covered in a rheumy film. I filled a bottle with this, thinking we could boil the bugs out of it, and returned to where Richard was sitting.

We took a couple of slurps of clean water from our dwindling supply and we shared a Mars bar. My mood didn't improve, when my new tooth disappeared into the toffee like a foot into quicksand.

'What the hell are we doing this for. I've had enough,' I wailed as soon as I could speak.

'And all you can do is to laugh and sit there admiring the view while I take my blisters the extra mile to get water. It's worse than being a woman in the Third World.'

I put my pack on again, determined to get to the campsite at all costs.

'We'll take the road at Hayburn Wyke and make it a bit easier,' was Richard's reply.

My pace slowed to a crawl and Richard continued to worry about my inability to reach our destination before dark.

'Go on your own,' I said, sinking down onto a seat by the road. 'I'll get there at my own pace, and that'll be a lot easier without you fretting all the time.'

Reluctantly Richard agreed.

'It's only a mile and a half. You can't miss the campsite. I'll get the tent up and see you later.'

I felt relieved as I watched his rapidly retreating form.

I trudged on, stopping when I felt like it, counting my steps in order to keep one foot going after the other, reaching what I thought was the campsite at 7.30 p.m. The site was a mass of static caravans, and there was no sign of our tent. As I approached the house to enquire, a middle aged couple in the front room were looking at me with shock horror on their faces. They flailed their arms in the air like a couple of windmills and pointed down the road. It reminded me of Coldingham, where a gentleman on a similar campsite had opened his van door and shouted at us 'Nae tents heer!' and then slammed the door in our faces. The trouble was I still had no idea how much further down the road I had to go. My feet had just decided that the supine position was all they would tolerate. Fortunately it was only two hundred yards. Our little green tent was up and ready for me to crash out in.

'Well done,' said my partner as I limped home.

The long, straight, shingle-and-sand beaches, dying resorts and crumbling cliffs of the next two weeks were a struggle. Scarborough was, however, an exception. With two wide clean bays, two harbours and elegant buildings, it isn't surprising that Scarborough was probably Britain's first seaside resort. A mediaeval castle sits on the cliff top along with a Roman signal station. In the seventeenth century the town became a spa. In addition to drinking the foul-tasting water, a certain Dr Wittie advocated seabathing. This set a trend for 'nuddy' bathing, which seems to have taken four hundred years to be recycled.

The sky was blue, the sun shone, the funfair buzzed with life, the doughnuts were delicious. Scarborough, we decided, had everything. The harbour had real fishing boats, the sand had real donkeys on it, the Romany Palmist was busy in her booth. The Grand Hotel was the grandest, built in 1867 with 365 rooms, 52 chimneys, 12 floors and 4 turrets representing the days, weeks, months and seasons of the year.

'Monte Carlo's got nothing on this,' I said, shedding my boots and wriggling my warped toes in the sand.

'A couple of days in there,' I nodded to The Grand, 'would put me back on the map.'

'In case you've forgotten, you are on the map,' Richard said, and treated me to a hot chocolate.

At Filey we were sad to reach the end of the Cleveland Way, but Bempton's chalk cliffs were as grand as any we had seen, and were still housing sea birds on some of the ledges. We were now able to view the huge gannets at very close quarters, last guests of the season in their Grand Hotel. These are the largest sea birds in Britain with an adult wingspan of six feet, fierce well-defined beaks and peach-blush heads. Having watched them plummet out of the sky in a rapier dive for fish, we now watched them regurgitating their food and feeding their young with infinite tenderness.

Flamborough Head's weighty cliffs plummeted seawards, as surely as the hungry gannets; a high-rise scenic finale, before we settled into the testing flatness of Holderness and Lincolnshire.

Chapter Twenty-one

From Hull's sunset ridge
Humber is melting eastward, my south skyline.
A loaded single vein, it drains
The effort of the inert north.
Ted Hughes

From Bridlington, the coasts swoops south in an uninterrupted line as far as Spurn Head, a littoral tail at the mouth of the Humber. It looked so easy on a map, yet I was finding it harder and harder to complete a day of more than sixteen miles.

'Nineteen today,' Richard said cheerfully. 'There's no campsite and nowhere to stay until we get to Aldbrough.' He pointed to the map. From there we'll go to Kilnsea, that's near Spurn Head, and then it'll be a B & B in Patrington before we reach Hull.'

'Piece of cake. Let's go.' I didn't feel as positive as I sounded, but it was no good being negative when I was still fresh and the sun was shining.

The dark boulder-clay cliffs crumbled into a hungry, gravy-coloured sea. Walking across miles of shingly sand in their shadow, our good spirits eroded and we fell into a hurtful argument about mileages. My Irish blood is ever prone to hyperbole, while Richard is master of the understatement. I usually reckoned we averaged about three miles and hour, and was often surprised by the accuracy of my guesstimates. However, I would err on the high side on a bad day, to boost my own morale.

'We don't average three miles an hour. You're wrong. I did not underestimate yesterday's mileage. The trouble is you're slow in the afternoons and I'm always having to cut corners out and take buses to keep on schedule.'

The truth of these words hurt unbearably. I was struggling and I knew it. I moved away from Richard nearer the dank cliffs and talked to my alter ego.

'Come on. You're doing fine. Don't worry you can make it,' came the comforting words from the cyberspace. I kicked a dead stick away angrily, and wished I could go through just one day without feeling exhausted at the end of it.

Witherensea was an appropriate name for this relic of a resort. It had the seedy run-down look of a junky. Its tacky remnants are in danger of being washed into the sea. Heavy machinery was renewing sea defences at the eleventh hour. We sat on a concrete seat, set in a concrete path around a square of tired grass. Surrounded by concrete tubs filled with litter instead of flowers, it suited the mood. The silence was broken only by the monotonous jingle from an amusement arcade. The sun shone hotly down. As we left the dull promenade we passed an elderly Yorkshire man who looked admiringly at our packs.

'Oose is t' 'eaviest?' he asked, leering at me.

'Hers of course,' said Richard, striding on ahead.

'O aye, looks like it an all. She's nearer te ground.'

'Laggin' be'ind, are we?' commented his friend.

'I know my place,' I answered, silently cursing them all.

Up on the cliff tops, we wondered whether our left legs would suddenly disappear beachwards. The dry earth was full of gaping cracks and the ground here was eroding at one point seven meters per year. Near Hornsea, fragmented tarmac stopped abruptly at the cliff edge, tiny islands of smooth-topped boulder-clay jigsaw pieces, waited their turn to plunge seawards. Our path took us through a farm with a very short life expectancy. The stubble from this year's harvest had already moved several meters seawards. Where the path disappeared, we often found ourselves in deep fissures like first world war trenches. It was hard going and we were glad to regain the minor road.

Richard could see I wasn't going to make it to Kilnsea.

'We can go inland and camp at Easington.' He said, showing me the map. It's not so far.'

'Thanks. It looks far enough but I'll be OK as long as I take it slowly.'

Damn. I thought. He's doing it again. Making allowances for me. I wallowed in depression which made the last mile past the great gas terminal even harder. I told Richard to go on ahead and by the time I reached the tent I needed my wee dram badly.

That night I couldn't sleep. I wanted to complete the walk so much, yet my body wasn't co-operating. I decided that the next day I would separate from Richard and walk the seven miles into Patrington by myself, while he explored Spurn Head. I'd find a

B & B and meet him at the church at 5 p.m. I was sure I would feel better after an easy day. For the second time since we left home, I doubted my ability to finish. I felt quite sorry for my body struggling to get through each afternoon. My mind and my body were two separate phenomena.

As I set off next day, I used my recorder as a confessional and felt better for it. It was good to be on my own, and I was sure Richard would enjoy a day going his own pace. It was a misty autumn morning, with a heavy dew. Delicate spider's webs glistened amongst the teasals and dead grasses, the hedgerows were scarlet with hips and hawthorn berries; the air smelt rich and damp.

I had forgotten to put a pad on my foot and it was letting me know. Feeling uneasy about exposing my anomalous feet to all and sundry in Easington village square, I sought refuge in the church porch. The bells intoned a jaunty rhythm as I busied myself with surgical felt, micropore and scissors. The bells ceased.

'Good morning.'

The vicar's face beamed a welcome. Sock in one hand and scissors in the other, I beamed back, hoping to distract him from my naked foot, swathed in plasters, felt and micropore. Even my bunion was blushing.

I thought of saying something facetious about church porches and paupers, but decided against it.

'I'm, er, just re-arranging my foot. I thought the church porch would be a quiet spot for a little chiropody.' I said rapidly pulling on my sock.

The vicar looked at me hard.

'I've seen you before. I passed you on my bike yesterday near the gas terminal. I'd have stopped if it hadn't been uphill.'

I remembered his tweed jacket and bald pate wobbling up the hill with a bible balanced on the handle bars.

'Sorry about the bells. I do them on my own and it's a bit tricky. I'm holding a service in a minute. Would you like to join us?'

At this moment the first aged member of the congregation swayed slowly up the path. I crept away, just as the second member arrived on her sit-up-and-beg-bike complete with wicker basket. His congregation had just doubled.

Patrington church spire was unambiguously an outward and visible sign of Christianity, towering gracefully heavenwards and visible for miles. Inside it boasts to be 'England's finest parish church', and enjoys the status of being Queen of Holderness, while

St. Augustine's at Hedon is the King. John Betjeman described this queen as sailing '*in honey-coloured limestone like a ship over the flat estuary land at the mouth of the Humber*'.

I found a peaceful seat among the roses and dog shit of the queen's garden. I was relaxing in the warm sunshine when an overweight elderly man with his overweight elderly dog disturbed the peace.

'Ee, you can't sit there. Them seats for 65 year-olds!'

'I feel like a 65 year old,' I said, trying to prevent his overfed labrador from eating my lunch.

My elderly companion had a host of stories about the miseries of new boots, blisters, and walkers who don't wait for you to rest when you've caught them up. We empathised.

'Annoyin' in't it,' he said while his dog panted so hard I thought he might expire.

He really got going when I mentioned Hospice.

'Me bruther was in 'ospice. 'E died of cancer of the liver. Me daughter had myloid leukaemia. The wife's got artheritis in both knees, she don't walk much now.'

Before he got on to his own ailments, I asked if there was anywhere to stay in Patrington.

'Try 'Ildyard Arms. They might 'elp ya.'

I vacated my seat for the bona fide pensioner, and headed off in search of a bed for the night.

We had half a rest day in Hull. A city neither of us knew, and one which seems to have weathered the demise of its important fishing industry. Hotels, marinas and shopping centres have replaced fishing boats and warehouses. Every old building in Hull has been restored to former glory and even the flowers in Queen's gardens were bright with civic pride. The Victorian loos were magnificently restored with mahogany wooden thrones, brass fittings and blocks of shiny new tiles decorated with an abundance of assorted fruits.

Richard bought his third and last pair of walking boots. No longer down-at-heel we marched cheerfully over the Humber bridge, the largest single span suspension bridge in the world, feeling ready to face whatever Lincolnshire had in store for us.

Barton-Upon-Humber was not of this century. Described by Daniel Defoe as '*a struggling mean town noted for nothing but an ill-favoured ferry*' it tucks itself under the new bridge, sleeping like Rip Van Winkle. It was a thriving port and trading town in the middle ages and there are still one hundred and seventy seven buildings listed as being of architectural or historical interest.

Ever observant, Richard remarked,

'D'you see how the eighteenth century barns and cowsheds are still here. Some are falling down or used for other purposes, but it's a feature we don't get in south east.'

Barton was into brewing beer and making bricks and clay tiles in the last century. We counted at least seven pubs and felt obliged to sample the local brew before I cooked a five star supper of kedgeree (fresh fish from Hull) fresh veg. and plums, gathered from the trees above our tent in an orchard.

'From now on we shall be walking mainly on sea walls and it'll be flat as a pancake. We'll give Grimsby a miss and take the train from Thornton Abbey to Cleethorpes where we can camp.'

Richard helped himself to another plum.

I looked at him suspiciously. 'Are you sure this train business isn't just for my benefit?'

'Nope. I had planned that all along.'

'Honest injun?'

He nodded.

After several grey days, a September sun lit the graceful suspension bridge and the estuary, giving vitality to this flat grey landscape. Old and new working boats sat easily on the glistening mud waiting for the tide. In one of these creeks, a Swedish cargo boat was unloading timber in the traditional way, sitting there at low tide while cranes swung the planks from ship to shore. There was just one house, a few fishing boats and wooden landing stage. I took a picture feeling that scenes like this would soon be assigned to the history books.

Cleethorpes was the first tacky taste of a Lincolnshire seaside resort. Alive with amusement arcades, lettered rock and fish and chips, it did provide a welcome cuppa. We then progressed along the prom, past the stubby pier, past the fun fair, past the landscaped lake with landscaped trees and landscaped ducks, to a caravan site that graciously took tents.

Reception was a quarter of a mile from the road, past hundreds of static vans. A security guard, who looked as though he had just sprung from Wormwood Scrubs, gave us a key to the toilet block.

'You can put yer tent on grass near car park.' He didn't waste words.

Weaving our way past more vans, we reached the sea wall, and camped on a windy fag-end filled patch of grass near the car park and locked public loos. A couple of streetwise youngsters watched us carefully; two alsations from a nearby caravan growled a welcome.

For the first time we felt unable to leave the tent unattended.

'You go first,' Richard said, handing me the key of the toilet block.

It was a long walk. The key didn't fit. A kind lady let me in. The showers had been vandalised and were out of order, cold water trickled from a leaky brass tap at a dirty washbasin, and the loo floor was covered in water - at least I hoped it was water.

Back at reception they were apologetic.

'Yer toilet block's gone. Someone's just took it away. We've only just learned about it.'

We had a problem lighting our cooker: it didn't like the wind. Our security guard came round in his van to check out our missing toilet block.

'Wind must be bad here in the winter,' Richard said by way of conversation.

'A bit bracing,' was the reply. A few words into his walky-talky and he was gone.

It was surreal. I wondered whether we would still be there in the morning.

'I'm going over the top,' Richard announced after supper.

From the top of our sea wall miles of watery sand stretched out to a distant sea. Two forts sat offshore like great destroyers, guarding the regiments of fixed caravans and chalets. A few people were out exercising their dogs, Lowrie-like figures in the distance. The bracing wind howled and we soon retreated 'home' where Richard concentrated on the maps.

'Well done. Nineteen miles today. Using your method of calculating the number of miles, we only have 550 to Eastbourne.'

'No problem,' I said confidently from the supine position.

The rocking tent lulled us into an uneasy repose.

The Lincolnshire coast seemed unending. Grey sky, grey mud, grey-green marshlands, grey sea somewhere out in the grey space. Everything was horizontal or perpendicular. The sluice gates, the drains, the sea walls, the poplars, the brassicas; even the rivers had been drawn with a ruler.

Shiny regiments of static caravans lined miles of the coast. Chapel St. Leonards was a quintessential example of pure tack. Leisure park after leisure park stretched shiny metal in all directions. We tried the first of these called Robin Hood, complete with artificial castle with 'reception' written on it. Inside the castellated brick walls, acres of carpetted drawbridge led to a smart reception desk smothered in artificial flowers. An artificial lady looked down her powdered nose at us.

'No tents here. Try Happy Lands just down the road on the left.'

Unhappily, they were no help either.

'Try The Golden Anchor.'

Our aching feet trudged on past amusements, plastic looking pubs and more vans until we were nearly out of the town.

The Golden Anchor had no-one at reception so we found ourselves a piece of unappetising grass by a ploughed field, and pitched the tent with difficulty due to a 'bracing' wind. Fortunately the toilet blocks had not been removed and did not need a key.

'I don't think anyone's been near them for months,' Richard said on his return. 'At least they've got running water.'

After my ablutions all I could say was,

'Give me a Scottish burn any day.'

Lincolnshire, was not all bad. Mablethorpe's golden sands, where a little train chugs visitors up and down, was bright, clean and cheerful. We sat among the sand dunes, feeding the inner man, and watching a couple of riders galloping across the beach.

'Did you know Tennyson sat right here with his brother declaiming verses to the empty sands,' I said showing off my newly acquired knowledge.

Richard's eyes were shut but he murmured,

'Mmm. Just don't start declaiming your doggerel.'

Donna Nook's desolate shore was decorated in red flags and enormous white eggs upended in the sand. Distant target boats for the RAF bombing range sat in a sandscape where even marram grass and sea lavender looked as though they had been bombed.

Sand and sea defences fell straight down to Skegness which welcomed us with flashing lights, popcorn, robotic voices, burger bars and ten-pin bowling. We were not feeling well disposed towards this resort on a wet and windy day. My recording echoes my prejudices.

'Now we've got some gardens with red toadstool lights. A little plastic train with little plastic puffs of smoke, plastic flowers and plastic cats. This place even has a pier, and a Romany Palmist, which is shut. Scales to jump on and weigh yourself after your candy floss and popcorn. Lots of lost children and first aid, charabancs of pensioners, mainly women, car lots and clock towers, Adventure Centres and Treasure Island, bowling greens and lots of rain. You name it, it's in Skegness.'

Gibralter Point Nature Reserve gave temporary relief. Here the silver-leafed buckthorn bushes were a mass of orange berries, and although it was not the season for seeing many waders, there were lots of unplastic small birds to be spotted. Richard was doing well listing redstarts, black caps, wheatears, and flycatcher.

'Look behind,' I said. 'They used to be a rare species, but now they're on the increase; known to arrive suddenly in large flocks, all hung about with large lenses and tripods. I believe they're even threatening smaller species.'

A young man, in green barbour and wellies, was pointing a very large lens at a row of bushes and stalking closer. We moved off quietly and left him twitching in peace.

At Wainfleet All Saints, we met my father in his van. He spent the next three days shadowing us and at Sutton Bridge took our camping gear away with him. It seemed an eternity since our first camp at Ulverston in Cumbria, on May 1st. We were sad to lose our independence, but with shorter days and lots of dew, camping was becoming more difficult. Walking was much easier with less weight to carry. It was at this point that our own emaciated bodies began to fill out slightly.

The warden at our campsite near Wainfleet was an interesting local man in his early seventies. He extolled the virtues of Lincolnshire and told us something of his life.

'I love it meself. Wide skies, fens, kingfishers darting across the drains. It's God's own country. I woudn' live anywhere else.'

I thought what a good thing it was that we are all differerent.

'When I came out of RAF, I went down mines at Barnsely Colliary and worked me way up to management level. Eight hundred feet down at coal face it were once th' surface of th'earth. I used to think - I'm going where no-one has ever trod before. I couldn't understand why th'others didn't think like me. I'm a religious man, but I don't go to church.'

Before I had time for the inquisition, he added darkly,

'Too many things 'appen in church that shouldna be 'appenin.'

If God's own country was flat and featureless, it certainly was fertile. The air vibrated with the whirring of tractors and every kind of lethal machinery for harvesting every type of crop. The brassicas looked so large, succulent and perfect it was hard to believe I wasn't looking at the front of a seed packet. Time is money up here and there is plenty of the latter. We saw one vast field with six tractors harvesting a hundred or so acres in one day. We were not surprised to learn that 75% of UK vegetables are grown in Lincolnshire.

Johnson's seeds were busy growing under glass in Boston. This bustling market town and busy port must take first prize for the inverted snobbery for which the north east is renowned. They call their canals drains and their elegant church tower a stump.

The canal, lined with warm brick houses, pantiles roofs and windmills, had a Dutch look. The wide market square was filled with unsophisticated Georgian houses; the River Haven caters for business and pleasure. Cargo ships lined the docks, loading and unloading, while silt was being dredged to keep the river navigable. Silos and steel terminals, transformers and pylons showed Boston's industrial systems were in good health.

Above this hive of activity, the two hundred and seventy two foot Boston Stump reared its famous octagonal lantern tower, to lure the weary traveller from afar. On a clear day it is possible to see Lincoln cathedral thirty miles away. We had the visibility but not the time to check this out and just managed a quick peek inside the beautiful church.

'Look at this plaque' Richard whispered. 'George Bass, Joseph Bankes, Matthew Flinders and John Franklin all came from here'

'Wow. Where would Australia be without them? They've certainly found secular immortality over there.'

As if that wasn't enough, in 1607 the earliest Pilgrim Fathers made an abortive attempt to set sail from Scotia Creek. Undaunted, in 1620 a further groups sailed from Southampton in the *Mayflower* and yet more Boston citizens founded the city of Boston Massachusetts in 1630. Boston, Lincolnshire, had much to be proud of.

Richard hated my recorder and spoke into it as little as possible. However, after a pint of Bateman's beer (or was it two?) at The Ship Inn at Fosdyke Bridge, he agreed.

'Shally has asked me to - squeeze those two, and watch that little hole - so here goes. Looking carefully at the map round the Wash, I could find only two small contour lines. When I examined them closely, I discovered that they were zero contour lines. That means the rest of the map must be below sea level. Thank you!' He released 'those two' and stopped watching the 'little hole'.

Bateman's must be a very alcoholic beveridge because a young customer perched on a bar stool saw our charity badge on the rucksack and said,

'Ave yer only walked 43 miles for yer charities? I don't call that much.'

When we saw a coaster unloading fertilizer on the River Welland, Richard expressed astonishment,

'We're miles from the sea, and the river here is narrow and fast flowing.'

'Perhaps we're seeing things,' I suggested, feeling too sober on just one cup of tea.

On September 23rd we gave up our tent and continued the last five weeks with lighter loads and heavier feet. Our first sighting of the Hunstanton cliffs on the Norfolk coast was cheering.

'Hooray! A natural feature that's more than two feet high.' I shouted to the indifferent cows.

'I've had enough of plodding on endless sea walls, enough of drains, poplars, pylons and slimy silt, wide skies and wind'

The nearest cow farted loudly.

Chapter Twenty-two

At the same times the same dull views to see,
The bounding marsh-bank and the blighted tree;
The water only, when the tides were high,
When low, the mud, half-covered and half-dry.
George Crabbe

Like the Welland and the Nene, the River Ouse is grey and straight; a steely band with a jewel on it. King's Lynn's prosperous past is set in brick and stone. It goes back a long way. King John granted it a charter in 1204 and it grew and prospered to a final flowering in the eighteenth century. We only had time to oh and ah at the Georgian facades, before being swept inland to a small village called Gayton.

Norfolk was definately different. Geographically on the edge of the British bulge, it has been a blue-bloodied backwater which is only reluctantly being swept along in the current of contemporary society. We stayed with a fifth generation master baker and his wife, who had retired to Norfolk from Buckinghamshire. Here we began to learn about the Norfolk 'fowk'.

'They don't like incomers, they don't travel, they really are provincial,' David explained.

I was tempted to ask why he moved to Norfolk, but resisted.

'It goes back a long way. Centuries ago, the marshes between Norfolk and Suffolk were so difficult to negotiate that the area was divided into North Folk and South Folk.' David filled his pipe with slow deliberation.

'They're resistant to change. Take Gayton, for example. There can't be many villages left that stop the traffic in the high street twice a day to let the cows through.'

A cloud of smoke rose gently above his head.

'You won't catch any Norfolk folk with new cars either.'

A disembodied voice from the kitchen called,

'Nor new clothes. They keep them till they fall off their bodies.'

Later David told us that his family came from Skye and had been sent packing in the Highland Clearances. His forebears emigrated to Australia.

Hunstanton had its own individuality. The striking cliffs we had seen from the Wash, were formed a hundred million years ago, and are made of carr stone and red and white chalk. The effect was of a cake topped with a thin layer of jam and a good dollop of cream. Connoisseurs though we were, we hadn't seen anything like them before.

'Look at the sun,' Richard said turning round. 'We can see it setting. Hunstanton is the only resort on the east coast to face due west.' True enough, the large red orb was colouring the greyness of the Wash.

Our host's daughter that night was herself born in Hunstanton, but she made no bones about those over 75 who could call themselves 'born and bred' Norfolk.

'They're very insular. If you go into a pub as a stranger, they look at you as if you came from outer space. They're a strange breed.'

Her father was a fifth generation show man. Impeccably dressed in pinstripe suit and co-ordinating shirt and tie, he owned and ran all the amusement arcades in the area, and was not ashamed of his wealth or his business.

'I get holiday makers here with fistfuls of notes. If they go home and haven't spent their brass, they feel the holiday's been a failure.'

'Are you from Norfolk?' I asked.

'As much as anywhere,' he answered. 'After I left Uppingham, I spent three years on the road with fairgrounds, and a year in the Marines. Then I started up this business.'

Mike was also a pillar of the community, and had chaired nearly every organisation in the district. His manners were as impeccable as his clothes.

As we passed Sandringham, we realised how the Royals had become an integral part of the local culture. Until recently they had been accepted, admired and deferred to, at least by the born and bred folk. However, even in this Royalist stronghold, things were changing; with the exception of Princess Ann, they had little time for the younger members.

Autumn was on its way. Dead leaves floated under the horse chestnut trees, a few green cases had fallen and split, exposing shiny brown conkers on their soft white beds. The hedgerows dripped with autumn fruits. We grazed blackberries as we walked.

Norfolk villages seemed unchanged by time. The mellow brick houses had old pantile roofs and were attractively decorated with carr stones, dressed and undressed flints. Hollyhocks gave colour outside their original Georgian doorways, and there was always a good pub and an ancient flintstone church. There were seldom any ugly suburbs, just an old heart that refuses to stop ticking.

We were back on the dinner party circuit. At Wells, we were entertained by an indefatigable raconteur, who could change his middle class accent for Norfolk dialect on request, or even not on request.

'In Norfolk,' he said, 'we play bowels, not bowls.' Turning to me he enquired politely, 'How's the bias on yer bowels? Go to Bootses for yer subscriptions,' he advised me, earnestly.

Leaning back in his chair, he warmed to his theme,

'When a group of men get together in a pub they'll have a good mardle. They'll be on about their courvettes and whether they've been tricolating their second hand cars.'

He was unstoppable, and his resonant voice notched up a few decibels.

'I knew a gamekeeper once. He got some beaters together before a shoot and shouted:

'Cor blast, you lot! Spread you out together will 'e.'

The rest of the table were now listening, except his wife who was pretending not to.

Looking at the assembled company, this Rotary Sergeant at Arms addressed the audience in rich dialect,

'Cor blast you lot. Take no regard of me. I'm talkin' a lot of old squit!'

* * *

The samphire grass glowed deep red among the water and reeds of the coastal marshes. Handfuls of clinker built boats and dinghies sat purposefully in the rivers and creeks. The only sounds were the cries of curlew and redshank. Hopeful fisherman with large umbrellas, mushroomed on the long banks of shingle, where a few yellow-horned poppies still flowered.

I was dawdling along happily. Tomorrow was our last rest day and I relished the prospect. Richard waited patiently.

'OK?' He could see I was.

'Drawin' along nicely, thank 'ee,' I said, in my best Norfowk accent. 'You can see from that expression that they are boating people about these parts.'

We walked side by side for a while.

'By the way Mr Dictionary, what are 'Stewkey Blues'? I didn't know this part of the world was much into jazz.'

'Mmm . . . delicious,' was not quite the reply I expected.

'They're very special mussels which are found in Stiffkey. If you say that with a Norfolk accent you're there.'

Our rest day was in a cottage at Langham near Cley, (pronounced Cli by the cognoscenti). The owner, an energetic retired dentist, was there to welcome us. He grasped Richard warmly by the hand and beamed.

'I'm so pleased to see a dentist actually doing something!'

It was the thought of 'actually doing nothing' which appealed to me. My diary entry for September 28th reads:

Rest day. Only nine miles. Lie in till 8.30.

Perfect weather drove us out to catch a boat to Blakeney Point, a place Richard had always wanted to visit since he read Malcome Saville's story *Redshanks Warning* as a child. Had we walked, the round trip would have been seventeen miles.

Down at the coast, a group of weather-beaten Norfowk fisherman, with bright oilskins and busy tongues, mardled, while the lengthening queue of tourists waited patiently for the tide to come in. We were packed tightly into two graceful clinker built boats, and motored gently over to Blakeney Point which sits across the harbour like a goulish hand on the end of a long bony wrist. Watching the seals from an overcrowded boat did not give us the thrill it had at Brora, but it felt right to view the land here from the water. Sand spits, shingle banks, and pristine working boats, bobbed up and down as we slurped through the water. Inland, windmills turned lazy sails, while distant churches drew their village round them like a mother hen draws her chicks.

Bacton was dismal. Unrelieved eroding cliffs, sea defences, shingle beaches with groynes that we had clamber over. A huge gas terminal glowed up on the cliffs and an unpleasant smell of gas escaped from the pipes running under the sand.

I was feeling a little worried about our accommodation for the night. A long-standing friend of my parents were putting us up. John had been a Master of Foxhounds, and I hadn't seen him since I went to their rather grand house for a Hunt Ball when I was still a student. I remember feeling rather intimidated by the ancestors peering down from the walls, and the black patch that John wore over one eye. I also remember being given my first Bloody Mary, after which I didn't remember much else.

Sitting in the back of an old Norfolk car, I got the impression that the crab sandwich I'd had for lunch, was in mortal combat with my stomach. There were no doors in the back, and I was trying to make polite conversation to John's son Charles, who seemed to be showing us most of the county. Back at The Old Rectory, John, black patch still in situ, was waiting for us in the hall.

After the briefest of greetings, John enquired jovially.

'Now which Hunt Ball was that?'

My stomach had lost the battle, and I ran upstairs to what I hoped was a bathroom. As I hugged the Twyford, the old Norfolk mahogany seat crashed down onto my nose. For one terrible moment I thought I was vomiting fresh blood.

'It's all over,' I thought, until I examined my battered nose in the mirror.

I rejoined the company downstairs and toyed with a whisky and soda while Charles gave us the menu.

'I've made a very simple supper, just nursery cottage pie and our own raspberries. For starters we thought you'd like some dressed crab.'

As we left next day, Charles shook us warmly by the hand and said simply,

'When you get home, don't let things be the same.'

We have not forgotten his wise words.

* * *

From Lowestoft to Aldeburgh the coast drops down like a plumb line. The beaches, promenades and sea defences disappear to a pinprick on the horizon. It was almost a relief to walk up the River Blyth at Walberswick, past the landing stages where working and pleasure boats were moored, and across the windy reed-filled marshes alight with with samphire grass. A good wide track led us to Sizewell Nuclear Power Station. An eerie light glowed from a solitary aperture of this white-domed temple of power. Behind the new gas-cooled reactor, the monolithic block of Sizewell B, stood four-square to the winds, a latter-day Ozymandias:

> *My name is Ozymandias, King of Kings:*
> *Look on my works, ye mighty, and despair!*
> *Nothing beside remains. Round the decay*
> *Of that colossal wreck, boundless and bare*
> *The lone and level sands stretch far away.*

Aldburgh in Suffolk looked like a set from a Benjamen Britten opera. Traditional fishing boats were drawn up on the shingle, which was littered with coloured floats and lobster pots. The sixteenth century moot hall stood out among the Victorian houses. A clock struck six. The low sun, polished pebbles on the beach. A splinter of rainbow might have been the soul of Peter Grimes.

In the pub, a party of young professional musicians gathered round a table, their middle class accents reminding us that we were not far from home. At Snape, a Thames barge with furled rust-coloured sails was moored near the Maltings. As we walked past the open windows of the concert hall, a rich baritone voice was singing an aria from Britten's Curlew River. Among the rustling reeds and silted creeks this music seemed to encapsulate the atmosphere a haunting landscape.

It was not just the accents that were changing at this point. Large rivers now infiltrated the marshy landscape. The Deben, Orwell, Stour, Colne, Blackwater and Roach all had to be crossed. The Felixstowe to Harwich ferry wasn't running, which meant we had to walk for twenty miles a day for three days to get us round the Orwell and the Stour. Psychologically this was hard going. There was nothing for it but to walk up the Orwell to Ipswich, then down to Manningtree and along the Stour to Dovercourt. The weather was good, and there were plenty of working boats and waders to enjoy up the innumerable creeks.

We snaked along sea walls that endlessly wove like Celtish knots, seemingly taking you away from your destination. Weary travellers needed faith that these tortuous walls would lead them home. I was beginning to feel constantly nauseated and was sleeping badly. Every afternoon was more of an effort.

Our spirits rose when we crossed the Orwell and met Katie at Ipswich station. We gossiped the dull miles away as we plodded companionably across the marshes, through Georgian villages, passed disused breweries, behind the flapping blue trousers. An old milestone informed us that we were now only sixty three miles from London, and we could almost smell the fumes. We crossed the River Stour, entered Essex and saw Katie and her newly formed blisters back on a train to the metropolis. She gave us big hugs as we parted and said brightly

'Only another 344 miles Mum! You'll be back in three weeks.'

Quintessentially genteel, Frinton is class conscious. Hierarchical streets like Upper Third and Upper Forth, vie with First and Second Avenues. Less grand are the streets of Oxford and Cambridge, Winchester and Eton. Large houses with large garages and large gardens hide behind mature trees, only walking distance away from the tennis, golf and cricket clubs.

'The High Street here used to be known as The Bond Street of Essex,' our host told us proudly as he gave us a chauffer-driven tour of the resort.

'Now it's just a shadow of its former self, and some of the smart stores have been replaced with charity shops.' His voice betrayed his disappointment as he pulled the car up near the smart golf course.

'Of course it's still the only seaside resort without a single pub.' He grinned, shook us warmly by the hand, and wished us a good journey.

Summer returned. We sat on the promenade in Clacton stuffing our faces with doughnuts, chips and hot chocolate, reading the Independent and feeling in holiday mood.

'Did you know,' Richard said, raising his eyes from the paper, to stuff in a few more chips, 'the shopping centre is 600 metres, the loos 800, and the next café 230.'

The metric system had finally arrived.

'Goodbye to the Empire, the Imperial gallon and the inch,' I said through sugary lips, raising a mock toast with my hot chocolate. I wonder how long we can hang on to the mile? Mind you, we must have walked an aweful lot of kilometres.' I licked the jam off my fingers and we metred our way on towards the River Colne.

Brightlingsea was bursting with indignation about live animal exports. Every house had a poster in the window - BAN LIVE EXPORTS - TO DO NOTHING IS TO CONSENT. As we walked along the road, several trucks of sheep passed us escorted by the entire Essex constabulary, on motor bikes, buses and police cars. Bringing up the rear were two ambulances. I felt sorry for the sheep, as no doubt their departure would be delayed by the demonstrations, making an unwelcome stay of execution.

The white weather-boarded mill beside the blue reservoir at Thorrington, reminded us that we were in Constable country. Mature trees, fertile fields, reeds, creeks and rivers made pleasant walking. We sat on a bench overlooking the River Colne, watching a boat loading up with gravel from some pits on the opposite bank. Swans and ducks swam beside the unspoiled village of Wivanhoe, where steep narrow streets threaded their way between 18th century cottages, bright with shiny brass and geraniums. The church clock boomed twelve times, barely audible above the sound of firing shells from the Fingringhoe MOD ranges on the opposite bank.

We approached Malden from the Heybridge Basin, where the graceful hulls of graceful tall-masted yachts, were mirrored in the glassy water. Fisherman were busy under large umbrellas, expensive rods bristled over the waters of the canal, empty nets waited patiently. Maldon quay was alive with boats, spritsail barges, gaffers, cobles and fishing boats sat on the rich mud under the shadow of the ancient town. A Mecca for boat lovers. Richard could hardly drag himself away.

I was limping by the time we reached the High Street and our hotel. The owner, Ray, and his wife, Marion, were on the lookout for us.

'You're limping. Are you alright?'

'Fine. Just the end of the day.'

I was longing for a bath, meal and bed in quick succession. Our room was very comfortable and in no time I was flat on my back. There was a knock on the door.

'We've got a Rotary meeting at 7.30. Could you both come and perhaps give us a little talk about your walk?' Ray asked politely, propping open the door.

Autumn mists wrapped the marshes and sea walls in a thick wet blanket. We were heading for one of the most isolated spots on the Essex coast, Bradwell-on-Sea on the Dengie marshes. We were to stay at the Othona Community, a non-denominational retreat for all those seeking peace and a prayerful atmosphere. The mist thickened as we passed through the little village of Bradwell. Tall poplars bordered the road; their diminishing leaves rustled and dripped, accentuating the silence. Soon the mist was so thick we had no idea what lay ahead. Through the white shroud Vwe eventually spotted a sign to Othona. This directed us up a very long track. We felt like pilgrims, travelling hopefully into the unseen. A simple modern building loomed out of the mist.

We knocked on the door.

'Hello. Come in. We're expecting you'.

The warden showed us our sparsely furnished room.

'Supper's at 6.30.'

There were only five of us round the communal table. The community was run by a core staff and there were no other visitors that day. A young man with a long black pigtail and kind brown eyes produced lashings of shepherds pie and apple crumble. We all helped with the chores and fell into bed. I slept well for the first time for weeks.

The mists had lifted a little by morning, and we walked the few hundred yards to the ancient chapel of St. Peter's-on-the-wall which has served as a place of Christian worship for longer than anywhere else in Britain. It was one of the simplest and holiest places I have ever visited. Outside, the stone and brick chapel looked like an old barn. It had been built in the seventh century by a Celtish saint called St. Cedd, on the site of the Roman Fort of Othona. As a lapsed Christian I was surprised to find myself overcome with an indescribable sense of release and tranquility. I offered myself and my thanks to those four stone walls and emerged stronger in spirit.

The Essex marshes stretched flatly around us. A grey-green watery interface between a sightless sea and a distant hinterland of small villages, farms and minor roads. Nothing except drainage ditches, sea walls, flat fields and absolute quiet. A skein of Brent geese flew overhead. Foulness point loomed through the clearing mist. At the mouth of the River Crouch we saw long strands of mud alive with waders, knot, godwit and turnstones all facing the wind, like a vast fleet of tiny planes waiting for take off. As the little islands submerged, a squadron of stripes beat the air in unison, wheeled and disappeared. Samphire grass and michaelmass daisies spread patches of colour along the drains. The heavy grey sky rose and thinned as the sun struggled through, lighting the chestnut backs of two kestrals.

Our sea wall turned west, and we were no longer alone. Three catamarans passed us on the wide straight waterway. Fishing boats chugged gently about their business and several marine carcasses rotted quietly beside the water. As we neared Burnham, the horizon became a forest of masts from several smart yacht clubs. Slowly, boatyards and chandlers gave way to mellow red-brick Georgian houses along the quay.

My birthday, spent with Rotarians in Burnham-on-Crouch, was very special. I arrived to a large pile of cards, phone calls flooded in, and our host busied himself chilling champagne.

'We've got company tonight. Our son and his girlfriend are coming to supper and I think he's going to pop the question to her this weekend. We've got your birthday and their engagement to celebrate so why don't we do it in style?'

Two bottles were tucked into the fridge.

At the end of a good meal, our hostess produced a beautiful cake with one large candle and 'Happy Birthday Shally' written round a green map of Great Britain. A small pair of brown walking boots looked good enough to eat. I was so overcome I had trouble blowing the candle out, which gave everyone a laugh.

We were put up in Chelmsford. As our hostess was away to work early, we walked into the town to catch a bus to Woodham Ferrers. We meandered through the streets and precincts like sleep-walkers, passed Woolworth and Marks and Spencer, Nat. West banks and pizza houses. Everything in the shops looked tacky, commerce seemed irrelevant, goods and chattles unnecessary. Sitting on the bus, I felt sick. Sick of walking, sick of aching, sick with the crazy world we had left behind. I nearly fainted in a supermarket queue in Woodham Ferrers, and realised that months of pushing myself were having an effect on my mind if not my body. I told all to my recorder as we plodded on the never-ending sea walls of the Essex marshes.

My low flat voice echoed my thoughts.

I feel it's time to talk about us, or at least about me and how I feel. Constant nausea makes me low and depressed. I'm sure a lot of this is because the end is in sight. I suppose I've been pushing myself for so long, that now I know it's nearly the end I'm beginning to unwind. I've got to get over this somehow just to get through the next few weeks.

Richard was encouraging. 'We've done just on 4,000 miles. We'll soon be at The Thames and back in Kent. You'll do it.'

Southend pier was built in 1889 and is the longest in the world. The only snag is that careless boats run into the superstructure from time to time. Fortunes have been spent on rebuilding it, only for it to catch fire in 1993. Now the end is a twisted metal sculpture that the Tate Gallery would be proud of.

As we sat eating greasy doughnuts and ices the colour of highlighter pens, Richard reminisced.

'I came here for the Rugby Festival when I was a student at King's. After the match, a dance was laid on in that building.' He pointed to a grand Victorian edifice called The Palace Hotel.

'I have vague recollections of lurching out onto the beach with a couple of drunk medical students. One of them undid a painter and watched the boat float away. I believe he's a consultant now.'

That evening we learned that the Palace Hotel is under D.H.S.S. control and does bed and breakfasts for the homeless.

Home and a change of lifestyle was looming. The respectability of Leigh-on-sea forced us to purchase underpants and deodorant. We stuffed a plastic card into the wall with rather depressing results. A phone call followed to make sure the house would still be let. The new tenants wanted it until December 27th which meant we wouldn't be home for Christmas. Richard was philosophical.

'Never mind. We've got no choice. Anyway Christmas seems a long way off.'

As we sat watching geese on the mud flats below Hadleigh Castle, I asked Richard how he felt about getting back.

'I don't know,' he replied from behind the binoculars. 'It'll be good to see family and friends again, but I don't want it to end.'

I was staring at the industrial landscape of the Thames Estuary.

'Katie says there'll be a big reception at Eastbourne, two mayors and television. It all sounds a bit daunting.'

'It'll be OK as long as they don't expect us to do a lap of honour.'

Essex reaches its lowest ebb at Canvey Island. Reclaimed from the sea by the Dutch in the sixteenth century, it lies below sea level. The island is a prisoner to the sea. Sixty three lives were lost in the disastrous floods of 1953, and now a massive sea wall defends the island.

Our hosts were third generation islanders.

'My grandparents moved here in 1900,' Norman told us proudly. 'The buildings were then mainly caravans, shacks and old railway carriages used as holiday homes by East Enders.'

'Is oil and gas still stored here?' Richard asked as we sat in the kitchen drinking tea.

'Oil is still stored, but the refinery's at Shell Haven. Gas was stored in underground caverns here in the 1960's. We were the first to use natural gas. Now that's all gone.'

'Didn't you every feel you were living on a time bomb?' I asked.

'We're more worried about the American ammo ship, Montgomery which sank off Sheerness Harbour. Now that could be very explosive.'

As we walked round the 'prison' wall, passed the deserted oil storage tanks, and looked across Hole Haven Creek to the pill boxes and chimneys of Coryton I remembered an ambiguous paragraph written about Canvey Island between the wars:

'Canvey may boast of an unique combination of attractions, as possibly no other district is favoured with, which endows it with every feature of a desirable residential locality.'

Having circumnavigated the entire island, we passed a mountainous waste tip. A few lorries crawled over it like colourful dung beetles. I had to admit that the attractions of Canvey Island were indeed unique.

Our hosts at Stanford-le-Hope were not born and bred Essex, but having lived there for forty years wouldn't have a word said against it. Ian was a retired G.P. and model steam train enthusiast. He opened the door of his surgery, and instead of a patient on the table, there was a gleaming brass steam train. A zero gauge track in the crazy paving circumnavigated the marigolds in the garden. Richard's eyes took on a glazed look.

'The patterns for those trains were in The Eagle Comics,' he told me later as we walked towards the container port at Tilbury docks. 'I would have loved to have done them if I'd had the tools. Nowadays lots of people make models but all you need to do is to push out plastic parts, use a little glue and patience, colour it and hey presto! The Eagle print-outs were proper engineering plans to make rolling stock and even engines. It required a lot of expertise to cut the metals and bore holes with precision.'

His voice trailed off.

'Well all I remember about The Girl comic is Lettuce Leaf, the greenest girl in the school.'

'That figures,' Richard grinned as we turned off the dreary road onto a footpath.

Up on a slight rise, through a forest of pylons, chimneys, oil refineries and coal-fired power stations, we could see Old Father Thames with the gently rising hills of Kent looking rural and inviting on the far side. Piebald horses grazed the few fields that were not a mass of metal and steel. We imagined they belonged to gypsies, more likely to be tolerated on this less desirable land.

At Stanford-le-Hope I found a poem called *Progress* written by a fifteen year old boy. To me it summed the area up perfectly.

The progress bomb has exploded;
Industry rules here with a rod of iron,
And the countryside cowers before it, defeated.
The footpath is a well-worn and beaten track,
Twisting and winding its way to nowhere in particular.
There are enormous white pill boxes all around,
Pipes that hiss and steam, chimneys that belch smoke.
Two anglers scowl in the special way that all anglers
Are taught to do.
Gulls hover and dive for some creature in the murky water below.
All around is the silent truth. Pollution rules OK?

Chapter Twenty-three

We shall not cease from exploration
And the end of all our exploring
Will be to arrive where we started
And know the place for the first time.
T.S. Eliot.

We sank down in the World's End pub at Tilbury, awaiting our last ferry to Gravesend and home. The best thing about Tilbury was its fort, built by the xenophobic Charles II in 1682 to keep the Dutch and French at bay. The only casualties in its history were three dead and one wounded in a Kent v Essex cricket match in 1820!

Gravesend was a lot better than it sounds. The buildings are all being restored to their original facades. It is recorded that Samuel Pepys 'Kissed a good handsome wench at Gravesend in 1660', which gives the town a certain historical perspective. The statue of Princess Pocahontas looked very pleased with herself, for a Walt Disney film of her life story had just been released, and the Princess had been given a new set of lights. There was an interesting assortment of traffic on the Thames, tugs pulled lighters laden with wooden crates, the ferry plied to and fro, and the occasional container ship made stately progress. Palmerston, as xenophobic as Charles II, built forts on both sides of this stretch of river, which guard it like a couple of bull dogs.

The marshes of Dicken's *Great Expectations* looked benign in an Indian Summer, although I quite expected to see Pip peering out from a tombstone in the quiet little churchyard at Coolham. We now hugged the coast, following a Viking helmet with two horns, on the Saxon Shore Way.

Rochester, or 'Dullborough' as Dicken's called it, looked reassuringly familiar. We knew we should have Rotary hospitality here, but no details had been given. We were met near the cathedral as arranged, and then followed my leader to an old blue door in an even older wall. He rang a bell. The door opened into a large airy pine-and-glass kitchen at the back of the Bishop's Palace. Our hostess showed us to our room at the top of this extraordinary old house, which was bursting with cosmopolitan visitors.

'Please don't smoke, and be careful the steam from the bath doesn't set the alarm off,' our hostess instructed politely.

'I once had an African visitor who smoked like a chimney. I told him upstairs was a No Smoking area. Then the smoke alarm went off. I came up to hear terrific shouting. My guest, wrapped in small bath towel and large amounts of steam, was very agitated crying "No smoke! No smoke! Missus."'

We had an hour or so to get ready, before we were due to meet the local Rotary Club at the pub. Our room at the top, looked out on one side to the floodlit Norman castle, and on the other to the floodlit cathedral. There was a radio in the room and Richard lost no time in finding Radio Three. Benjamin Britten's *Les Illuminations* floated out into the ether. Transmuted, we lay on the comfortable beds letting the music wash through us. Suddenly a loud bleeping drowned the music. Wisps of steam entered the room. We had forgotten the bath water.

The meal that night was in a local pub.

'Much frequented by the Bishop's household in days gone by. It's so near, inebriated members could be wheeled home in a barrow,' our host told us.

A good number of the Rotary Club and their wives were there to meet us. We all squeezed round a large table and were given a good meal. I was on the inside, sitting opposite the chains of office. Suddenly the room swam and my stomach heaved. I couldn't get out, and felt unable to eat. A mixture of exhaustion, heat, and culture shock hit me at a bad moment. I hoped our kind hosts didn't notice my glazed eyes and long pauses. I got through the evening, but wished I could have been carted back in a barrow.

Richard's cousin welcomed us to the Isle of Sheppey. Its island status was reinforced when the Kingsferry bridge over the Swayle closed, even to pedestrians. The central section of road acts like an elevator. The approaching coaster hoots loudly, the elevator section rises up four tall concrete pillars, until there is sufficient head room to allow the boat to pass through. Watching this mighty chunk of road rise skywards was surreal.

'It makes a marvellous excuse for being late. When I go to Canterbury I just tell them I had a spot of road lag,' Robin told us.

This tall ebullient man was vicar of Queenborough and took us up the fourteenth century tower of his church to show us 'the best panoramic view in Kent'. It was all laid out in front of us, the tangled cranes of Sheerness Docks, Leigh-on-Sea, Shell Haven oil refinery, the Isle of Grain's deserted power station, Gillingham's gasometer, Medway towns, North Downs and the massive pillars of the Swayle bridge.

'If you look over there,' Robin pointed North East, 'you can see the masts of the Liberty Ship, Richard Montgomery. It was wrecked on a sand bank out there in 1944 with a hold full of ammunitions that have never been defused. Shipping has to give it a wide birth.'

Over supper Robin was a hive of information.

'We've all heard of hamburgers, but there aren't many places can boast of a Seaxburga,' he said walloping spaghetti onto our plates. 'She ruled East Anglia after her husband the king died in 640. She must have made a good job of it because she was canonised in 709.'

I didn't get a chance to ask how many children she'd produced.

After supper, Robin told us a David and Goliath story.

'The Pilkington Plate Glass factory here closed many years ago, leaving a desolate little avenue of decrepit houses where redundant workers languished. Vociferous complaints, sent to the management, fell on deaf ears. The houses continued to disintegrate.'

Robin leaned back, his huge frame tipping the chair. His eyes turned to Heaven.

'Prayers were then answered. My hot line suggested I should become a shareholder and complain at Pilkington's A.G.M. So, with my dog collar on, and £50 worth of shares under my belt, I travelled north in some trepidation. I composed my statement-cum-sermon and a press release, and then counted all the churches I saw out of the train window, by way of supporters.'

Robin's big laugh was infectious.

'I was racked with nerves,' he grinned. 'But there was no going back. I stood at the door of Pilkington's imposing Head Office, and handed out my statement to the Great and the Good. The huge Board Room was like The Old Bailey, with the V.I.P.'s on special seats in the woodwork.'

Robin took a gulp of coffee as he relived the moment.

'Sir Alistair Pilkington was in the chair and it was his swan song. Pleasant speeches were made, resolutions were passed. There was an air of mutual admiration and smug satisfaction. Then someone asked if there were any more questions?

'I took a gulp of air, rose to my feet, and launched my diatribe about Pilkington's shameful neglect of their little community in Queenborough. Once on my feet, nerves disappeared; I left nothing unsaid. Sir Alistair made fluent excuses. Shortly afterwards we adjourned for the bun fight.

'As I left the room I was congratulated by a steely business man in a shiny suit.

'"Mr Murch," he said in a broad Lancastrian accent, "you've made things 'appen in this Boardroom as 'aven't 'appened for years. Well dun!"'

We were all laughing in shared relief. Robin continued.

'At the tea I thought I'd better apologise to Sir Alistair. My tea cup and scone rattled as I threaded my way towards the mighty man. He was graciousness itself.

'"You've got big responsibilities," he said generously.

'And I've got bigger ones.' Robin threw his head back and laughed again.

'A limousine was ordered to take me to the station. Back on the train I had the pleasure of the company of a motherly Methodist. She was a good listener. With the help of a few drinks, I debriefed into her sympathetic ear.

'"Praise the Lord! The Kingdom's coming!" she intoned at regular intervals.

'Back home miracles soon happened. Measly Mr. Green, who had taken no notice of our complaints, was suddenly grovelling on my doorstep. I told him that the media might give him a bad time.'

Robin's laugh rocked the table.

'I was winding him up, of course. Half the media wouldn't even be able to find the Isle of Sheppey!'

Later Robin proudly showed us the modern bungalows which now replaced the decaying terraces. It was called Hillside Avenue.

'Robin's Row to the cognoscenti!'

In spite of industry, the marshes were rich in bird life. We were constantly disturbing great flocks of waders, flying low across the water, flashing their striped wings in unison. On the seawalls the only sounds were the distant roar of traffic and the haunting cry of curlews and redshank. Geese and lapwings grazed the fields, and starlings gathered in their thousands on telegraph poles, filling the air with high pitched cacophony. The straight bare river was filled with boats, alive and dead. Spritsail barges with their russet coloured sails, moved quietly along the Swayle with the pleasure dinghies.

The skeletons of old hulks lay on the mud, rotting like decaying mouths, and occasionally we would spot wartime relics like the wooden carcasses of motor torpedo boats, marine kamikazes.

'I'm going to miss the birds, the sea, the boats and just being outside all the time,' I said as we looked across to Oare Creek with its forests of masts from working boats, drawn up neatly on the mud. The furled sails of the Thames barges made a nineteenth century water colour.

'These flat marsh lands are an acquired taste, but they're growing on me.'

'Just remember we haven't seen them in really bad weather.' As usual Richard bought me down to earth.

As we approached Whitstable, seawalls, rivers and marshes were exchanged for chalk cliffs, sand, concrete, buildings and tarmac. Since the advent of the train, the resorts of the south east have given working class Londoners a chance to enjoy sand and sea air. As we walked round the 'tail' of England, we rejoined the piers, promenades and poopscoops. London was only an arm's length away. Here there were more cars, more people, more dogs and more candyfloss than we had seen since leaving Poole. We were back on home ground.

Whitstable boasts the largest oyster hatchery in Europe, advertised by the delicious smell of cooking shellfish, emanating from the bars and restaurants along the shingle beach. I had promised myself an oyster here, but the incident of the Cromer crabs was still fresh in my memory. If we didn't feed the stomach, we fed the mind.

A genuine Whitstable oyster yawl was on display near the tall weather-boarded fishermen's huts. This attractive two-masted fishing boat would drift sideways when dredging for oysters, so more than one dredge could be used at the same time. Drifting in this manner was called 'yawing'.

'Now you know what we did across the Pentland Firth,' said Richard at my elbow.

'Ah but did you know St. James of Compostello was the patron saint of oysters and dredgemen. His feast day was on the 25th July and it was a tradition in Whitstable for children to celebrate by making grottoes out of oyster shells, putting a candle inside, and asking passers-by for a penny for the grotto?'

'Makes a change from penny for the guy.'

Herne Bay was bathed in evening sunshine and had the quirkiest pier in Britain, just two ends and no middle. Damaged in a storm

in 1978, the distal end floats out at sea like a vast crate, a sad fate for
the second longest pier in Britain. At Westgate we saw the first
chalk cliffs since Flamborough Head. Low and smoothly
sculptured, they made a natural fortress against the elements and
the submerged chalk rocks gave the water gave a clear
Mediterranean look. Turnstones, perfectly camouflaged against the
brown and white shingle, were busy feeding at the tide line.

Our last week was a surprise. If we had thought about it at all,
we had imagined ourselves battling against equinoctial gales along
a dreary coastline, counting the steps to Eastbourne. Yet here we
were in T-shirts and shorts, wishing the days would not disappear
so fast.

'It's ironic,' I announced. 'On January 3rd at Littlehampton, I
tried to forget that we still had 4,240 miles to go. Now, with less
than a hundred miles to Eastbourne, I want to forget that we've
done 4,200 and pretend it's not all over.'

We were sitting on the beach, watching the low sun light the
round white cliffs. Two small children played on the beach, and a
man was collecting lug worms.

Richard was watching the turnstones.

'Time to go. We don't want to keep anyone waiting.'

I recalled the strange clock behind the bar of The Anchor Inn,
Seatown. Now we were no longer behind the clock, time was the
same but we were different.

Margate was on half term. The beaches were full of buckets and
spades, children, grannies and a rare parent. The pier, known as
the jetty, was swept away in the same storm that had wrecked
Herne Bay's pride and joy, and is now just twisted metal sticking
out of the water like joints of spare ribs.

'When my Dad was a boy he used to come here on high days
and holidays, on a paddle steamer with a cargo of East Enders from
London.'

Richard stopped talking to do some sums.

'Must have been eighty five years ago. The steamers were called
'Margate Hoys' and would land passengers on the pier there.' He
pointed to the jetty.

'It was a Mecca for East Enders. I think most of them have
settled here now, so they don't come and spend their money as
trippers anymore. Many of these large Victorian houses are run by
the DHSS for the homeless.

Richard was back in Margate before the first World War.

'The landladies here were a formidable breed. Armed with a large basket, they would meet steamers and London trains, and do a hard sell to the passengers. Once they had secured their guests, they would ask them what they wanted to eat for supper.'

'Sounds like pretty good service.'

'You have to remember there were no fridges then, and no-one, least of all the Margate landlady could afford to waste food.'

We were both feeling in high spirits. At Foreness Point I thought we were rounding the bottom right-hand corner and into the home straight. Richard told me we were only beginning to turn round, and I had to wait a few more miles until we reached North Foreland.

'Turning by degrees like this makes me feel like a large tanker,' I said.

Richard looked at my skinny frame. 'More like Margate pier.'

Turning right at the bottom of Britain meant that we had nearly closed the circle. For the first time during the walk I had no doubts about finishing. Just at this momentous point, we met a fit-looking man walking along our coast path in the opposite direction. On his back was a very big rucksack with a bed roll. He was clutching a map in a Marks and Spencer's case. We thought he might be doing the same thing the other way round. He was one of the very few backpackers we had seen round the coasts in ten months. It was 4.30 p.m. and at that moment the sun sank over low hills to the west. Someone told us it had been the hottest October since records began three hundred years ago.

Ramsgate marina and harbour were a forest of masts under a cloudless sky. Car ferries, coasters, fishing boats and yachts, all jostled for space beneath the solid Victorian architecture. The old fish cellars were now chandlers and boat stores. Houses and shops were brightly painted and cafés spilled out onto the pavements. It could have been Monte Carlo. Friends met us here and we walked to Sandwich with them. We were heading inexorably back to reality.

Our feeling of achievement was tempered with concern. With only a few days left, our itinerary bristled with deadlines, phone calls, meeting family and friends, the press, dinner parties . . . We had been our own free agents for so long that all this was a little intimidating. Walking with friends had always presented minor problems. Whatever you felt like, you had to be sociable. They would often think we were super-fast walkers, and speed off at a great rate, while it was all I could do in the afternoon to keep up. Then there was a problem with comfort stops. We were so used to being able to relieve ourselves at any time, that our bladders became unaccustomed to holding on.

'Hello there!' The reporter from the Sunday Express grasped us firmly by the hand. We sat outside a pub, just off the beach, drinking coffee, while Peter rolled his green pen rather briefly across a shorthand pad.

'Just back from Sumatra,' he informed us. 'We were carrying heavy packs in very humid conditions. Pythons and orang-utans were quite a problem in the jungle. We were looking for the 'wild man of Borneo'.'

I wondered whether I should have had the pad and pen.

'What charities? How much have you raised? Good, good.' He stood up. Something about him reminded me of a slimmer version of Robin Day with a tanned leathery face.

'Well I must get back to town. We'll send a photographer to Camber Sands, but I've brought a camera. Mind if I take a few shots?'

We obliged while Peter fumbled with the camera. Either it wasn't his, or he wasn't used to taking pictures.

The heavens opened in a short sharp shower. Peter jumped into his smart car, waved a hand and disappeared. We were not surprised when there was no photographer at Camber Sands, no article in the Sunday Express to say that we had finished, and how much we had raised for our charities.

A rare morning of rain and sea mist made walking down the steep cliff path into Folkstone difficult and eerie. Three Martello towers loomed out of the white shroud. Out of an original one-hundred-and-three, built for defence purposes in the South-East at the beginning of the nineteenth century, forty three are left, all of which we must have seen. Suddenly a figure loomed ahead. A young man sitting quietly, hands clasped round his knees, gazing out to sea. He was wearing a flying helmet. It took us a moment to realise that it was a memorial to the young fighter pilots killed in the Battle of Britain. Churchill's words *'Never in the field of human conflict, was so much owed by so many to so few',* had a special poignancy at that moment.

Dover's sheer chalk cliffs dropped steeply into a choppy sea. Car ferries and container ships ploughed serenely through the grey waves, entering and leaving the harbour. The coast of France was clearly visible. A stormy sun glittered on the ventilation shafts of the Channel Tunnel. We walked quietly westwards, lost in our own thoughts.

Fishing boats, draped in nets and plastic balls, rode high on the shingle at Greatstone, their bare hulls exposed to the air. Gulls circled and squabbled round stinking left-over fish. A wall of pebbles separated us from the brightly painted Victorian houses along the front. We were on a deserted beach threading its way between an invisible town on our right, and the sea on our left. Dark clouds gathered behind us in a freshening wind. There was a distant rumble of thunder. We were at that moment between sleep and waking, when reality is still only an awareness. We needed to remember the dream. A young couple were walking the other way.

'Please could you take a photo of us?' I pleaded.

A few drops of rain fell. Reluctantly we left the beach and joined the road. We walked past people with shopping bags and bowed heads, past limp shrimping nets and tired straw hats, past stoney banks and building societies, past peeling beach huts and see-through waste-paper bins.

Reaching the familiar territory of Dungerness felt very strange. We both liked this rather bleak headland which is still littered with traditional shacks and fishing boats. The little Hythe and Dymchurch Railway still steams along the shingle, dropping passengers. Our hostess from Canvey Island spoke fondly of family holidays at Dungerness.

'We had a shack on the shingle called *The Mascott*. When I was a little girl in the 1930's we used to go there with brothers, sisters, aunties, cousins, grannies. I don't know how we all squeezed in.' There was a faraway look in her eyes.

'We'd get off the little train and leave our cases at The Pilot pub. Then we'd put herring boxes on our feet to walk across the shingle to the cottage. There was an outside privy, and I remember hearing my Dad scrunch across the shingle and empty the pail into the sea every morning.'

Derek Jarman's black shack, with its bright yellow door and windows, is a monument to a very courageous man. His shingle garden is filled with natural and man-made debris from the beach, pieces of groyne, rusty iron pipes, dead tree trunks, all stand vertically in front of the telegraph poles, pylons and nuclear power station, which hum with energy. Among these lifeless sculptures, he has grown the natural plants that thrive so well on the shingle:

sea cabbages, yellow-horned poppy and yucca. T.S. Eliot's *Wasteland* came to mind. *'With these fragments I shore up my life . . .'*

Camber Sands treated us to a rare sunset. A great sweep of dark, dappled sand led to the cliffs of Fairlight on the far side of the bay. The last orange glow in the sky was mirrored in the watery channels. Richard was walking off into the sunset. I wondered if he would overshoot Eastbourne and keep going, and I felt a mixture of emotions as we walked along the dusky sea wall into Rye. The old village spills down a hill, and the rooves and church tower were black silhouettes against the dying glow of the sun. I recorded the following words as we walked along by the river:

Walking along by the river in the last glow of the sunset feels very fitting. The sun is setting on our walk. It's just as well there is a sunset or it would quite dark. We have walked eighteen miles today and it is getting late. There are lots and lots of geese on these marshes. Two herons have just flown softly by and a few bats. It's almost dark now. We are very nearly at the road.

Sunday, October 29th dawned. We shouldered our packs for the last time and were alone on deserted beaches for two short hours. Then it was over. Friends who had come to meet us while we were still far off, had now come to take us gently home. Along the swathes of tarmac through Eastbourne's Business Park, I trailed in a double wake. Richard and Fred were on the horizon. My cerebral friend told me that it was the very last time I should have to keep Richard's back in view. My body rejoiced, but my heart was heavy.

As the shimmering pier grew larger, cars stopped and hooted, people stared at us, cameras clicked. Beachy Head basked in sunshine as it had done ten months ago. There was a lump in my throat. I thought of the marathon runner's words to us on our first day. 4,298 miles later, life had indeed been good to us. We had swallowed such a draught of elixir, how could things ever be the same?

Unreal. We had completed our three hundred and two day walk. Foot by foot and hand in hand, we strode up the promenade towards the pier and a crowd of people. I squeezed Richard's palm as we passed a pub called THE BITTER END. Swept away on a tide of emotion, long before we reached the pier, I was ready to hug anyone who approached, whether I knew them or not. The Meridian camera man looked a little surprised. Katie had bought us caps to wear; mine read: WE MUM and Richard's DID IT DAD. The words Mum and Dad were lined up on the peaks when we were side by side. I had blown up a yellow and blue balloon that morning, depicting Rotary colours. It was perhaps significant that one of them was running out of air. Richard's Union Jack and windmill were, however, looking good.

A huge crowd had gathered round the pier and I was vaguely aware of a banner with the words WELCOME HOME - CONGRATULATIONS! on it. A red tape swam into view, held by Katie and Jo. Then my eyes focused on a bottle of champagne, held by Spud, who had done the same walk two years before. Just as we were riding the crest of the wave, we both froze. Barring our way, like a battleship in full sail, was Richard's proud mother, camera at the ready, putting us in the picture. Seconds seemed like hours. The next moment we slid down the wave into the arms of family and friends, drenched in sticky sweet bubbles and hugging more people than I can ever remember.

* * *

It feels strange having the sea on our right. The path winds its way steeply between rocky outcrops as it traverses the cliff between Cape Cornwall and Land's End. We barely notice the inclines, only the feeling of familiarity. Pausing, I look back to Cape Cornwall, a little green hill crowned by a tall chimney, perched on sheer cliffs which have been scooped out into a series of little coves. Far below us, smooth round boulders, like speckled dinosaur eggs, pile up behind the darker granite rocks, wet from the pounding surf. Less than a mile off shore, the two Brison rocks loom blackly out of the water, like the back and head of a half submerged monster. We round a corner, and scrambling over a gouged and sculptured rocky outcrop, now see the broad sweep of Whitesands Bay.

The long line of sand is deserted except for a group of black-backed gulls bordering the tideline. Sennen sits quietly at the far end of the bay. Beyond, the group of white buildings marking Land's End, crouch on the high cliffs, looking west. Out to sea, rising above the line of black rocks, the Longships Lighthouse gleams. The low winter sun softens and warms the granite cliffs. On the horizon the Scilly Isles are visible to the naked eye, a row of saucepan lids.

It feels as though a cork has been removed from a bottle of champagne somewhere inside me. As we reach the soft sand, I unlace my walking boots. I want to dance, and shout and scream with elation. I do all these things and then grab Richard by the hand.

He is keeping his champagne cool. I race towards the long smooth rollers, checked only by the icy water. 'We've done it! We've walked the whole way round!' I attempt an unsteady cartwheel, and regret it. When the world stops turning, I focus on a stick of driftwood, grab it and write in bold letters in the wet sand - *Richard and Shally walked 4,300 miles round the coasts of Britain in 1995*. As I completed the five, an urgent rush of foam fills the letters and drains away leaving a blur. Another powerful wave pushes eagerly forward, swirls with triumph, and falls back, leaving nothing but wet sand and small line of crackling bubbles.